MOUNTAIN GUNNER

Major Anthony Fowle, M.C., R.A.

MOUNTAIN GUNNER

The Wartime Adventures of Tony Fowle M.C. 1939 - 1951

RUPERT WILLOUGHBY

Chiselbury

Published by Chiselbury Publishing, a division of Woodstock Leasor Limited, 14 Devonia Road, London N1 8JH, United Kingdom

www.chiselbury.com

ISBN: 978-1-917837-12-5 (hardback)
ISBN: 978-1-917837-13-2 (ebook)

A CIP catalogue record for this book is available from the British Library

www.rupertwilloughby.co.uk

Designed by the author

Cover design: Indra Murugiah

CONTENTS

LIST OF MAPS

The illustrations at pages 2, 83 - 86, 171 - 174, 229 - 232, 261 - 264 and 323 are from Tony Fowle's personal collection. Any unacknowledged copyright should be notified to the publisher, who will be pleased to correct it.

FOREWORD

by Tony Fowle's children - Charles, Katharine, Diana and Michael

When our father died in September 2016 we discovered an old file amongst his papers. In it were the 232 letters he had written to his parents while he was a young officer during the Second World War, afterwards in India/ Pakistan and then in the Korean War. We had always known about these letters, but our father was a deeply private man and had never actually showed them to us. Finally reading them came as a revelation as we discovered a completely different side to him.

In later life our father had seemed a rather conventional figure, slightly old-fashioned in his tweed jacket with his pipe in one hand, and perhaps a tiny bit boring. At school we longed for a 'Cool Dad', someone more exciting and glamorous, and these letters revealed that our father was exactly that, but that middle age and an office job had masked those aspects of his character. Reading the letters was like meeting another person – we recognised the same spirit of public service, deep love of the natural world and family and gentle sense of humour – but also found that exciting and glamorous figure we had always secretly hoped for as a father. Someone fired by a young man's love of adventure and zest for life, an occasional rule-breaker who relished the excitement of the unknown and above all a courageous soldier who enthusiastically embraced all that the world had to offer – a fascinating, charming character we wish we had known better.

We are very grateful to Rupert Willoughby for weaving these letters together into a single narrative which has enabled us 'to meet' the younger version of our father and better understand his military career, and to Stuart Leasor for publishing it. We believe our father was typical of his generation in his willingness to serve his King and Country, but we think his wartime experiences in what was then Persia and later in India and Korea are less typical and we hope that the reader will find them interesting and enjoy 'meeting' our father in the same way we have.

As children we had always known that our father was 'in the war' and occasionally he would be persuaded to tell some of his war stories. He never told us about how he won his Military Cross; instead he would regale us with funny tales about fishing in far-off places and persuading the seemingly dangerous local population to tell him where were the best places to find the largest trout. Reading this book has been an opportunity to find out what happened when he was not fishing, the bits that did not make the after-dinner stories but which were about real soldiering in difficult times and frightening places. It makes us proud to be his children, and grateful that he, like so many of his contemporaries, was prepared to give up his youth doing what he saw as his duty, fighting to protect his country so that we were able to have a safe, happy childhood.

INTRODUCTION

The Evolution of a Mountain Gunner

In October 1939, while Hitler was rounding up Jews in Poland and a complacent, ill-prepared British Expeditionary Force was entrenching itself in northern France, Tony Fowle was an eighteen-year-old boarder at Cranleigh School. He was determined to make a career as a soldier and, with the headmaster's 'grudging permission', took a day off school to enlist. Almost a dozen years later, he was a regular officer in the Royal Artillery, serving in war-ravaged Korea, and had just been decorated with the Military Cross.

While waiting for his call-up (in those early years of the war one needed to be above the age of 20), Tony had eventually abandoned Cranleigh altogether and had enrolled on a six-month forestry course in Argyllshire. This, and his (not undistinguished) service in the local Home Guard, had prepared him well for the military life. He underwent his basic training in Yorkshire in the harsh winter of 1940-1, and received his first exposure to severe conditions in the field.

Tony was a natural leader of men, a lover of the outdoors and of physical challenges, and he relished every moment of his new life. He was steered towards the Royal Artillery, to which he was admirably suited, and posted to East Kent. There, he encountered senior officers of irresistible allure, men like Major Richard de Carteret Yeo, who preserved the pre-war mounted tradition of the regiment. Unhorsed now, these men were still elegantly attired in their gunner-pattern breeches and highly-polished field boots. Tony discovered that mounted batteries existed still, in the Indian Army, for deployment in mountainous, frontier regions that were unsuitable for vehicles. That was to be Tony's goal thereafter and, characterised by a marked streak of single-mindedness, he was to be relentless in his pursuit of it.

On 11 February 1942, Tony embarked in the S.S. *Mooltan* at Liverpool and set sail for a destination unknown. He changed ships in South Africa and was eventually landed from the *Île de France* in Egypt. After a few more weeks of uncertainty, he was posted to the elite 2nd Royal Horse Artillery, though his 'horse' was an armoured car. In June he participated in the ferocious Battle of Knightsbridge in the Western Desert, but mercifully was away from the regiment when, a week later, it was almost annihilated at Mersa Matruh.

It was in July 1942 that, thanks to his friends in the R.H.A., Tony was finally attached to the Indian Army, which he joined at its depot in Egypt. The regiment to which he had been assigned, the 2nd Indian Field, was, unfortunately, fully mechanised. Even more unfortunately, the regiment shipped out of Egypt while Tony was recovering from a bout of sandfly fever. Astonishingly, and to Tony's intense frustration, for he hated being idle, he lost track of it altogether for several weeks. After an adventurous train journey through Palestine and in a 'Nairn bus' through the intervening desert, he pursued it into the scorching furnace of Iraq.

Once more obliged to wait 'while they find out where the regiment is', Tony was given a temporary job with the 1st Indian Anti-Tank Regiment. By mid-September 1942, he found himself in command of over a hundred martial Indians on a remote hillside near Kirkuk, and under fire from tribesmen. The habitual tent-dwelling, with the added chance of a 'scrap', was, as Tony put it, 'just the sort of life I like', and set a pattern for the coming years. The tent would typically measure six feet by eight and ideally it would be dug into a hole in the ground. Its sparse furnishings would include the little, flat-woven, blue rug or 'Dhurri' that was issued to all Indian troops. Tony was always ready to move at a moment's notice. 'I certainly have no objection,' he wrote, 'as I love travelling about.'

During his service in the Middle East, Tony inured himself to the very harshest conditions, from intense 'sticky' heat in the summer to frost and snow in the winter, to raging winds that would blow away an entire encampment and rainstorms that would reduce it to a sea of mud, not to mention the endemic 'bush sores'. Tony believed that 'an officer ought to go out into the wilds', to explore and accustom himself to rough terrain, and to do so was his own greatest pleasure. He loved to fish, shoot and hunt with hounds, and had a marked taste for solitude and for remote, mountainous places. He had all the necessary skills to live off the land and the resilience to survive the odd night in a snow-filled dug-out, without even the benefit of a tent, as in Kashmir in 1948. By the time he arrived in Korea in 1950, he claimed not to 'mind the cold' at all, though the winters there were positively Arctic, and when required to spend several wintry nights on a mountainside without proper clothing or even a blanket, he did so with equanimity.

In late September 1942, the 2nd Indian Field were at last able to reclaim him. Tony was now to embark on one of the most exhilarating periods of his life. An 'extended Cook's tour' took him through regions of Kurdistan ('the grandest country I have ever seen') and especially the Kifri Valley ('a Paradise on Earth'). His battery commander, James Hepper, sharing his passion for mountains, horses and artillery, became his firmest friend and ally. In May 1944, when Hepper took command of the 29th Indian Mountain Regiment, he offered Tony the adjutancy. The regiment was still fully mounted, so it seemed that his dream would at last come true.

Yet life often seemed too good for Tony. The parson's son felt himself to be a 'fraud' and was wracked with guilt for being absent from the main theatres of the war; he yearned above all for 'an active command in battle'. To his lasting regret, while Hepper's regiment were holding back the Japanese in Burma, even fighting them off with their bayonets and the butts of their rifles, Tony was detained in Syria in an intelligence role, in circumstances so pleasant that it seemed 'like a holiday'. When at last he was able to join them, on 21 December 1944, it was at their headquarters in Peshawar, India, and the prospects of seeing active service in Burma were fast receding.

Garrison life in Peshawar was not without its compensations. Tony was quartered in a 'palatial' bungalow with a large garden, four live-in domestics and a stable that contained his personal charger. Best of all were the opportunities to ride out with the regiment 'in column', an extraordinarily dignified and picturesque procession of mounted men and pack-mules laden with the disassembled guns, all of which harked straight back to the nineteenth century and the pages of Kipling.

Tony was a committed linguist, taking his first faltering steps in Hindustani while on the *Mooltan.* He picked up Arabic in Egypt, fluent Urdu from his years in the Indian Army and good-enough Pashtu to converse with a camel-driver in the *souk.* He was thus ideally placed for post-Independence attachment to the Royal Pakistan Army, where he re-visited his old stamping grounds, and for consequent embroilment in the secretive war against the Indians in Kashmir. That involvement was ultimately unsustainable and Tony was recalled to England in 1950, only to be thrown almost immediately into the Korean War, where his years of preparing for battle were gloriously vindicated at last.

Home-Letters

Throughout these years, Tony had been an assiduous letter-writer. Always a most dutiful son, he had communicated regularly and at length with his parents at home, which, of course, was not unusual at the time. During the war, the morale-boosting postal service, run by men in uniform, was so efficient that letters from even the most remote outposts only very rarely failed to arrive. It was different in independent Pakistan, where the collapse of the postal service became a national embarrassment. No fewer than 230 of Tony's home-letters have survived nonetheless and they are an extraordinary record of his service, owing to the quality of the writing and to their descriptions of both well-known and obscure events, often in the most far-away places. In particular, his first-hand accounts of the Kashmir and Korean wars are of considerable historical importance.

If not, by Goethe's exacting standard, a belletrist, Tony was an extremely fluent and competent writer. He must have brought the same directness and clarity to his regimental and intelligence reports. His matter-of-fact style conceals nothing. When he describes his achievements to his parents there is no hint either of false modesty or of boastfulness; he knows that they would want to be told, for example, that he had achieved a 'distinction' in this or that exam, but that they would not for a moment be impressed by any sort of bragging. For fear of upsetting or embarrassing them he is reticent about his romantic life; and he claims on one of his ocean voyages to have been absorbed in bridge rather than poker, which must surely qualify as a 'white lie'. In his own transcriptions of the letters, to which Tony applied himself in later life, he interpolates the odd annotation that clarifies matters. His accounts of being in action are also, to some extent, toned down. On the whole, the hallmark of the letters is their frankness and honesty.[1]

Inevitably, they are strewn with military acronyms and foreign words (a glossary is provided here) and refer to events and individuals that might have been well-known at the time, but would mean nothing to a modern reader: hence this attempt to boil down the content of the letters into a coherent narrative which places them fully in context.

Pick up any letter at random and the first difficulty is to establish whence they came. Where, for example, are 'BDRA', 'PAIF' and 'BAPO', all of which appear as addresses? The wartime letters were rigorously censored, and Tony was the soul of discretion, especially about his work as an intelligence officer.

---

[1] Tony arranged the letters chronologically but was muddled on a couple of occasions. For the purposes of citation, the present writer has numbered them in strict date order. A key to the letters is appended.

It seems only to have been some unflattering remarks about the R.A.F. that ever drew the censor's pen. So one is often left to guess where he is or has recently been; place-names are simply not mentioned. In most instances Tony has left sufficient clues (such as his visiting 'the house of an ancient oculist' in an unspecified city, evidently that of the sage Yuhanna Ibn Masawaih in Damascus, or his reference to the colour of the soil which places him in a particular desert) to enable one, with a little detective work, and with an atlas and encyclopaedia to hand, to trace his movements. But few casual readers would have the knowledge that Tony assumes of contemporary events. For example, his reference on 23 November 1943 to that 'grim little incident with the negro' is entirely unexplained; it would be all too easy to miss the significance of the remark and the fascinating story behind it.

Students of the letters will come to know Tony very well and will find him an admirable and very likeable young man. One is invited to be his privileged companion on a great adventure. The boy who has never been anywhere more exotic than Bridlington suddenly has whole continents opened up to him. When he first arrives at Freetown (the contrast to Bridlington could hardly have been greater), he is touchingly excited. A remarkably sharp-eyed observer, extremely knowledgeable about flora and fauna, he devours the local colour with wide-eyed curiosity. He is fascinated by ancient civilisations and the variety of races that he meets along the way. His encounter with a tribe of troglodytes in Kashmir, who mistake his jeep for a fire-breathing monster, is especially memorable. It compares in outlandishness with the discovery by Alexander the Great's admiral Nearchos of the 'fish-eaters' of Baluchistan, twenty-two centuries before.

Tony is at his best when describing nature and landscape. There are neat descriptions of such cities as Cairo, Baghdad and Peshawar; the walled city of Kirkuk is a distant mirage, but seems to capture the essence of the Orient. His description of the coast of Ceylon (a 'forest of palm trees right down to the very blue sea where huge rollers cast up mountains of spray') is admirably succinct and evocative. When he travels along a perilous mountain road, as he does on at least three occasions ('In several places the track is built out on tree trunks set into the rock face … there are "S" bends where even a Jeep has to "tack" to get round'), the reader cannot fail to share the sheer gut-wrenching terror of the experience. His description of the severe earthquake of 4 March 1949 (it measured 7.5 on the Richter scale) in Nowshera, Pakistan, tells us everything we need to know about such an event (when two trees were brought down outside the 'electric light cable snapped between two poles like a piece of cotton but with a report like a gun'). Witnessing a sunrise through the mists over the Khyber Pass, Tony is profoundly moved, for the snow-clad peaks 'seemed to be floating about a hand's breath above the horizon; a sea of gold and scarlet completely detached from the earth'. On such occasions, Tony has always been left to speak for himself.

While the awesomeness of nature never fails to stir his emotions, Tony is not obviously interested in his fellow man. If the letters have a fault, it is the marked lack of a human element. Few of the bit-players in the story are dignified with a name and if they are it might only be 'John' or 'Derek'. Character sketches are sadly lacking. Even good friends like James Hepper flit through the letters like mere shadows. Tony was the most self-contained of men and a natural solitary, able to draw on his own abundant resources. Adventures are often shared with a single companion, but that is in situations where it would be imprudent to travel alone.

There are some striking instances of these pairings. Charged on his Officer's Training course with the reconnaissance of an 'enemy' position, Tony enlists the only 'intelligent' cadet in the unit. Together, they crawl 'for ages over ice, snow and mud', but he is careful to send the fellow back before launching an 'attack'. Determined to explore the ruined city of Ranigat, Tony cadges a lift from a fellow-officer, but has to wriggle into its dark interior on his own.

He seems to have preferred it when his companion was an 'other rank' and therefore under orders: the Punjabi soldier with whom he shares a long drive through Palestine; the fearless *shikari* (variously described as a 'thug' and 'an escaped desperado') who guides him through the Kala Chitta hills in pursuit of urial and panther (Tony has to fish him out of the ravine into which he carelessly falls); above all, his British wireless-operator in Korea, with whom he shares a series of dangers and privations, including three nights in the open without a blanket, when they take turns to lie on top of each other for warmth, and are sustained by Tony's supply of Horlick's tablets. Tony does not dwell on the close bond that must have been formed with each of these men, and none of them is named. Perhaps Tony thought his parents would not be interested; perhaps he was not much interested himself.[2]

A Victorian Upbringing

The future Lieutenant-Colonel Anthony Peter Hedley Bruce Fowle, M.C., Royal Artillery, 'Tony' to everyone except his parents, was born in his father's Rectory at Hardenhuish, on the edge of Chippenham, on 17 August 1921. Appropriately, Hardenhuish Rectory had been the birthplace in 1840 of another committed self-chronicler, the Rev. Francis Kilvert. The celebrated diarist was the son of a previous incumbent, from whom John Sydney Fowle was the seventh in succession. Tony's mother, Noel Artiax Gwen, was the daughter of Highett Philip Westbury, an Edinburgh-trained physician in practice in Amesbury, and sometime Surgeon of the 2nd (Volunteer) Battalion, The Duke of Cornwall's Light Infantry.

2 In fairness to both men, Tony never forgot the wireless-operator and identifies him nearly 25 years later as the redoubtable Gunner Lawrie. See Appendix.

While the Westburys came from Burbage, in the Vale of Pewsey, the Fowles, who emerge as prosperous yeomen in the sixteenth century, were settled for many generations at Stanton St Bernard, at the other end of the Vale, so Tony had proud Wiltshire lineage on both sides of the family.[3]

By the mid-seventeenth century, the senior branch of the Fowles had risen to great prominence in the county and included the goldsmith and banker Sir Thomas Fowle, sometime Alderman and Sheriff of the City of London, whose premises in Fleet Street had miraculously survived the Great Fire in 1666.[4] There was also William Fowle, who in the year of Trafalgar had acquired, on the proceeds of 'slave-property' in Jamaica, a Wiltshire estate of nearly a thousand acres. This was centred on Chute Lodge, an attractive red-brick 'nabob's' house of *c.*1768. Situated in the middle of a forest, it had 24 bed- and dressing-rooms, and was the seat of William's family until 1906.[5] There are occasional allusions to the 'Chute Fowles' in Tony's letters.

Another Thomas, baptised at Pewsey in 1726, progressed from Oxford into Holy Orders and married into the family of the Earl of Craven, thereby acquiring the Vicarage of Kintbury, just over the border in Berkshire. The Kintbury Fowles were intimately and intricately associated with the family of Jane Austen, whom Thomas's eldest son, Fulwar Craven Fowle, recalled as a pretty, doll-like creature. Despite owning first editions of the novels (one of which, inscribed with his name, was recently put up for auction at Sotheby's), Fulwar does not seem to have been an admirer of her work. Indeed, it was reported to Jane that he 'did not bother to read anything of *Emma* except the first and last chapters, because he had heard it was not interesting'. Jane's sister Cassandra was briefly engaged to Fulwar's younger brother Tom Fowle, and her

---

3 Typescript Fowle Pedigree in the possession of Charles Fowle.

4 D.M. Mitchell, 'Sir Thomas Fowle' in *Oxford Dictionary of National Biography.*

5 *A History of the County of Wiltshire,* Vol.16 (London, 1999), pp.120-6.

brother James Austen married Fulwar's sister-in-law, Mary Lloyd.[6] A third connection was Tony Fowle's own marriage in 1958 to Evelyn Impey, a direct descendant of James and Mary.

Belonging to a junior branch of the family, Tony was aware of his wider kindred, some of whom were still in the service, and, in idle moments, liked to trace their careers in the *Army List.* 'Is Brigadier John le Clerk Fowle in India anything to do with our little lot?' he asks on one occasion. There was indeed a strong military tradition in Fulwar's line and a connection with India dating from 1842. Colonel Trenchard Fowle, who entered the Royal Artillery in 1874 and served at the Siege of Ladysmith, ultimately became the Inspector-General of Ordnance in India. His son Lieutenant-Colonel Sir Trenchard Fowle (1884 - 1940), an inveterate Orientalist, traveller and collector, had served in the 3rd Royal Munster Fusiliers (a militia battalion) and for 24 years as a Political Resident in the Gulf. It is unlikely that these connections were at the back of Tony's mind when he himself joined the Royal Artillery and embarked on his own years of service in the Middle East and India. Indeed, he never knew them; but they were men after his own heart.

Tony's father, the Rev. John Sydney Fowle, had also served in uniform, as a padre during the Great War, and has left a fascinating account of his experiences. A photograph dated 1916 shows him wearing the impressive Sam Browne belt that he later passed on to Tony, along with his boots. By all accounts, Tony wore them more naturally. John Sydney seems like a classically benign parson as well as a very loving and kindly father, though he clearly had a streak of toughness to match his son's and was to surpass him in longevity. Born in 1867, he died in 1969, shortly before his 102nd birthday. Tony was 54 years his junior.

In 1929, when Tony was still a child, the family moved to the East Riding of Yorkshire, to a bleak coastal district originally settled by the Viking Bjorn. The Rectory that they occupied at

[6] Deirdre Le Faye ed., *Jane Austen's Letters* (Oxford, 1996), pp.524-6.

Barmston, dating from about 1700, was enormous and stately, but to the day they left it in 1941 (with some relief, for the smaller and more convenient Rectory at Ogbourne St George), there was no electrical power in the house. It was lit instead by candles and gas-lamps. There were open fires to warm the rooms, and hot water was supplied, intermittently, by the kitchen range. In this cold, isolated place of flickering shadows, presided over by his ageing father, Tony can truly be said to have had a 'Victorian' upbringing. The spartan environment at Barmston, no doubt replicated at his two boarding schools, was to equip him well for the rigours of his future life, including exposure to some very extreme weather. It would also have accustomed him to solitude.

There is no doubt that he also acquired 'a very old-school outlook on life'. Father and son were both men of strict principle and firm religious conviction. Tony's Christianity is an ever-present theme of the letters, and his faith is never stronger than in Korea, when he is faced with the shattering loss of large numbers of his comrades. (He also very movingly describes the turning to God of his fellow soldiers, which is well-known to be a common reaction in such situations.) Tony believes in hierarchy, discipline and not suffering fools gladly. It is characteristic of him that, in later life, he should proudly point to the blood stains on his old Indian carpet on which Don, his ferocious bull mastiff, had brought down a *dacoit,* or burglar. It is also revealing that, while his contemporaries were all puffing on cigarettes, Tony was a pipe-smoker from the age of 18. Wearing his 'vintage' Sam Browne belt and brandishing his pipe, he would have seemed visibly out of his time. He often expresses his intolerance of callow youth, preferring to consort with and emulate older men.

Life Line

One evening in May 1951, during a lull in the fighting after the Battle of the Imjin, Tony submitted to having his palm read. Open-minded about the 'mysteries of the East', he refers to some intriguing, apparently inexplicable occurrences during his time there. The palmist was not an Indian, but an officer in the tough, near-piratical Corps de Volontaires pour la Corée, the Belgian battalion that Tony's mortar battery had supported in the battle. 'He was remarkably accurate,' writes Tony; 'he told me that my father was a priest and that my mother had a doctor in her family. Evidently I am a pretty low type: he called me a "corsair" and branded me as a dangerous man who found it as easy to go against the law as with it.'[7] The appeal of those wild, empty places to which he was constantly drawn was precisely the absence of regulation, their remoteness from all the pettiness and irritations of modern life. It was only there that he could feel utterly liberated.

Tony's maverick, unconventional and sometimes artless approach usually worked out well for him. For example, he would brook no obstacle in the way of his fishing. In October 1946, when holed up in the fort at Thal, he decided that he would go down to the Kurram river to fish. A regulation was then in force, requiring officers to be escorted on all occasions by at least twelve riflemen. Tony ventured out nonetheless, alone and unarmed. The Afridi warriors were not maniacs, and he was sure that they would not molest him for no reason. It was only when weapons were waved in front of them that they would feel honour-bound to try and steal them. As expected, he soon attracted attention; but the tribesmen were friendly, offering tips about where to fish and, in due course, inviting him back to their homes for tea.

---

[7] Letter 226.

There was a similar incident in Korea when, alone and armed with nothing but a rod, Tony was caught midstream by a Chinese patrol. The situation could have ended very badly. Aware that they must be starving, Tony handed over his catch without a word, turned his back on them and resumed his fishing. There is something disarming about the nonchalance of fishermen - when the Palais des Tuileries was set on fire by a drunken mob in May 1871, a dozen keen anglers settled down on the bank of the Seine below, taking advantage of the chaos overhead to fish at a prohibited time - and, as Tony's experience suggests, there seems to be some universal code that they are sacrosanct.[8]

Tony was essentially a very serious young man, who expressed a love of 'calibration' and whose idea of light reading was Bertrand Russell's *Introduction to Mathematical Philosophy.* He was made for an active, practical sort of life, not one of inner reflection. Declining a staff job, he told his commanding officer 'that in civil life I would rather be a farm worker than a bank clerk and the same went for the army'. According to family legend, his future wife Evelyn was very impressed by the initials 'R.A.' after his name, assuming them to mean 'Royal Academician'. She did not, at that time, know him very well. Years later, when poised to leave the army, Tony took a 'career aptitude test'. Candidates were assessed on their suitability for work in various fields, and the results were marked from A to E. Tony scored 'A plus' for careers involving science, but for anything that required an artistic temperament, the result was an emphatic 'E minus'.

Though notoriously set in his ways, cantankerous and bloody-minded, Tony was possessed of an understated, very English sense of humour, which is preserved both in the letters and in the memories of those who knew him. Describing a boxing match at Catterick, where he was pitted against an ex-miner, he refers to his opponent's 'thick ears, eyebrows that meet in the middle and a

[8] For Tony's full account of the incident, see Appendix.

chest that looked like a barrel bound with steel hoops. I tried out a little bluff by swinging on the ropes to warm up and in an attempt to look professional.' That same week, he and a friend are invited to dine with the Archbishop of York ('Ebor') at Bishopsthorpe Palace. Much to their surprise, soup is followed by roast turkey which is 'placed on the sideboard for Ebor to carve'. An unexpected gourmand, he tucks into it with as much relish as the boys and between them they 'devoured quite half the bird'. Likewise, 'a first class boiled pudding … soon completely vanished.' Tony's own appetite at the time is insatiable and his obsession with food is a running theme of the early letters.

Tony was also a notable raconteur and one of his best stories (not in the letters) concerned a cobra in India. The disgruntled reptile emerged from the bathroom drain as the bath-water was being emptied into it. Much to Tony's annoyance, his terrified batman held the bathroom door firmly shut, confining the betowelled Tony in a small, wet space and expecting him to deal with it alone. Tony would doubtless have rebuked him with some apposite phrases in Urdu.

After the period of this book, Tony had a more conventional army career, with postings in Germany, Australia and England, but nothing compared with those years in the Middle East and in India. Forever afterwards, he would nostalgically smother his food with chilli sauce, as if re-capturing the savour of that heady time. Promoted to Major in 1955 and to Lieutenant-Colonel in 1964, he retired from the army on 7 September 1974. As Honorary Secretary of the Royal Society for Asian Affairs, he was then able to lead tours to some of his youthful haunts, and to re-connect with old friends, including former pupils who were now generals in the Pakistan Army. In 1981, for example, he accompanied 28 members of the Society to the Khyber Pass, to Swat, where they were entertained by its colourful ruler, the Wali; and to his beloved Kaghan Valley, where they camped beside the river and negotiated the perilous mountain road in jeeps. 'The flight to Gilgit from Rawalpindi was tense,' wrote a participant.

'After a delay caused by bad weather, the plane was about level with Nanga Parbat mountain when the pilot announced he was turning back due to cloud. "No, no," shouted our Colonel Tony Fowle, "Go on." The pilot was so startled he did go on! But as we neared our destination he announced dramatically, "We are now approaching Gilgit, *Inshallah.* Goodbye."'[9]

Tony does not mention the Belgian palmist's reading of his life line, which is one of the five main lines in palmistry; but his firm belief in providence had been confirmed by a series of extremely close shaves. Curving down from the edge of the palm above the thumb towards the wrist, Tony's life line was assuredly long and vigorous. He died at home in Hampshire on 27 September 2016, aged 95.

[9] Hugh Leach, with Susan Maria Farrington, *Strolling About on the Roof of the World: The First Hundred Years of the Royal Society for Asian Affairs* (London, 2003), p.163.

CHAPTER 1

'IF I CANNOT GET ON TO BARMSTON BY BREAKFAST TIME I AM NO LONGER AN ENGLISHMAN'

Cranleigh

From St Michael's, his preparatory school at Otford, near Sevenoaks, Tony went in 1935 to Cranleigh School, on the Surrey-Sussex border.

Then in its seventieth anniversary year, Cranleigh was the classic Victorian public school, with imposing red-brick buildings, including an enormous chapel, and 280 acres of land, on which organised games were pursued like a rival religion. The Cranleigh motto, neatly encapsulating the ethos of the school, was *Ex Cultu Robur* ('From Culture Comes Strength'), which, to quote an eminent old boy, Andrew Roberts, 'must have seemed almost axiomatic to people brought up in the power and might of the British Empire in the twentieth century'.[1]

Cranleigh had nevertheless been intended for the sons of local farmers, few of whom became Empire-builders. Though it had soon attracted the sons of gentlemen from further afield, its most distinguished old boys have been either actors or cricketers. Fred Emney and Laurence Naismith are two notable thespians who had been and gone; and Michael Redgrave had taught there, though he had left the previous year. This was not quite Tony's *milieu.* He was in the First teams for 'rugger', shooting and boxing, achieved the rank of sergeant in the Officer Training Corps, passed his School Certificate at Grade 'A'[2] and ended up as captain of his house, '1 North'; but he never felt entirely at home at Cranleigh.

---

1 Andrew Roberts, 'The Meaning of Ex Cultu Robur', https://www.cranleigh.org/culture/issue-1/meaning-ex-cultu-robur/.

2 Letter 7.

Indeed, he gave the impression to his children that he had disliked it.[3]

Embarking on his final year in September 1939, Tony was consoled to have at last been given a study 'with a bit of a view', as 'on a clear day I can easily see across to the South Downs'. However, he seems to have had little ambition to achieve the Higher Certificate (equivalent to the current 'A' Levels) and, with war declared and expected to be over by Christmas, he was itching to get away.[4]

The three masters who ran the O.T.C. had already been recalled to the colours. It had always been Tony's intention to apply for a place at Sandhurst, but new entries by competitive examination had been suspended for the duration. The only route was 'through an officer-producing unit'.

Tony identified the Honourable Artillery Company, the London territorial regiment that was well-known for its 'gentleman-rankers', as such a unit. He had a connection with its C.O. and, without consulting either his parents or his Headmaster, applied for an interview. An invitation to present himself at Armoury House, Finsbury, at 2 p.m. on 11 October, arrived by return of post.

With the 'grudging permission' of the Headmaster, Tony duly attended on the appointed day, was received by a 'most engaging and obliging officer', passed his 'medical' and was sworn in. It was explained to him, however, that men under twenty were not currently being called up. Though he was now registered as a 'potential officer', there would be a hiatus of at least six months, probably more, and Tony was advised to see out his time at school. At very short notice, the enlistee forwarded a 'consent' form to his parents, asking them to sign and return it (no stamp required), and resigned himself to a long wait.[5]

---

[3] Charles Fowle, funeral eulogy.

[4] Letters 1 and 2.

[5] Letter 2.

Tony endured Cranleigh until the end of the Lent term. Still with no prospect of being called up, he then came up with a more congenial alternative. In 1924, the heir to the Younger brewing family had donated his estate in Argyllshire to the nation. Benmore, overlooking Holy Loch, was famous for its rich walled gardens and other exotic features, including a Redwood Avenue of Giant Sequoias, a fernery, waterfalls and ponds and formal woodland trails. There was also an enormous glasshouse.

The property had appropriately been handed over to the Forestry Commission, which in 1930 had opened it as one of its Forester Training Schools. Tony had somehow got hold of the prospectus: *'The schools are open to young men who in the opinion of the Forestry Commissioners are suitable for training as working foresters. Selected applicants must be able and willing to perform the full duties of a woodman ... The course of training which extends over three years is given free. No charge is made for tools, books and stationery used by the apprentices.'*[6]

Resourceful, determined and confident, Tony had no difficulty in convincing the distinguished knight who interviewed him of his suitability. In March 1940 he left Cranleigh and immediately travelled to Scotland to embark on his new life as a forester.[7]

Benmore

Benmore was, in retrospect, the perfect preparation for Tony's impending military career. It provided the most gentle introduction to a disciplined, outdoor life, as well as an opportunity to mix, on equal terms, with men from other backgrounds, who included members of 'the working class'. The lifestyle was healthy and wholesome. Tony soon put on weight and became extremely fit.

---

[6] Henry Smith and Geoff Waygood eds., *The Forester Training Schools, 1904 - 1971: Recollections from Ex-Students* (2004).

[7] Letters 3 and 11 (referring to 'Sir John').

The mansion-house, in which the students were accommodated and had their formal lessons, looked like a reduced version of Balmoral. It was mostly Victorian Scots-baronial, with a riot of pinnacles and turrets, but was attached to an eighteenth-century tower-house, once the seat of the Campbells of Ballochyle. Immediately surrounding the house were neat gardens and lawns including some exceptionally tall conifers, and beyond them, an endless wilderness of mountains, forests and rivers.

It is clear from his letters that, even then, Tony had not only a keen eye for the landscape, but also superior powers of observation. He relished the increasingly snow-covered countryside on his journey up, occupying 'an excellent corner seat' in the train 'next to a very large window'. The train took him as far as it could. From Gourock, he was conveyed by ferry to the farther end of Holy Loch, disembarking at Kilmun. 'We passed twenty destroyers,' he wrote, 'two aircraft carriers, three large battleships and countless merchant vessels. The Captain told me that the "Queen Mary" was lying further up the river embarking troops for Norway.' Needless to say, in those innocent months before Dunkirk, it had yet to be inculcated into the public that such 'careless talk' might actually cost lives.

Mounted on his 'ancient' but well-maintained bicycle, Tony was escorted the four miles to Benmore by the 'two very nice boys' who had been sent down to meet him, and was introduced to his room. It was in the original tower of the lairds, and romantically accessed by a spiral staircase. He was to share this room with 'a boy from the Isle of Skye', one of a number of Gaelic-speakers in the school, many of them kilted; there was even a piper among them, who could be heard practising from his room on an upper floor.[8]

The décor was decidedly spartan - civil service chic, down to the light bulbs stamped with the royal cipher. Tony's first impulse was to cheer the place up. He applied to his indulgent parents, and

[8] Letters 3, 6 and 7.

duly received, a large cloth for his desk, specifying that it should be 'on the gay side'.[9] The trainees were all men - it was inconceivable that there should be women among them - but the adjective was not then loaded with meaning as it is today.

Tony was shown the common-room, where the students relaxed over games of table tennis or chess, or simply gathered 'round a massive log fire'. They seemed mostly to be Scotsmen and 'working class chaps'. There were also what he called 'varsity men', who were already equipped with university degrees from Cambridge, Glasgow or Edinburgh, and therefore 'expected to know all about it'. These eleven men were being fast-tracked for service in Forestry at home or in the Colonies.[10]

In spite of their disparate backgrounds, Tony was to discover that the students 'mix very well'. There were no distinctions of dress, treatment or accommodation. Tony was particularly struck by the warmth and good humour of the Scots, who 'seem able to turn anything into a joke and love having their legs pulled, in fact almost as much as they love pulling someone else's'. Tony was also to make friends among the local population, whose 'pleasantness' made his new situation all the more agreeable. 'Whenever one meets anyone on the road they have a word for you and usually a joke as well.' He seemed genuinely taken aback that 'everywhere you go they are friendly and cheerful. It makes it seem as if I had known the place all my life.' Finally, setting a benevolent tone over the whole institution was its founder-Head, Harry Watson, a lean, fit-looking man with thinning hair and a broad smile, who was both 'very pleasant' and 'a true Scot, both in accent and dress'.[11] Quick to take Tony under his wing, Watson was especially gratified when presented with a specimen from the

[9] Letters 3 and 5.

[10] Letters 4, 5 and 6.

[11] Letters 3, 5 and 6. Watson appears in a group photograph at https://www.forestry-memories.org.uk/picture/number3629/.

hills, a wild flower of great rarity that was 'usually only found about the snow line round Lake Constance'.[12]

The new intake were inducted into the classification of trees, being required to learn both their English and Latin names. They discovered that there were innumerable species of fir, and that, in the grounds of Benmore alone, there were some 1,400 different kinds of shrub. The boys were introduced to the techniques of planting, spending their days on a heather-clad hillside overlooking Loch Eck, where they picnicked and lit fires to boil water for their tea. The future forester had to know exactly what to do. The day might come, in some distant land, when he would have to instruct other men, and lead them by example.

At other times, sixty or more men would crowd into the sprawling nursery, and apply themselves to the meticulous work of seeding. The beds had to be thoroughly prepared, the seeds weighed out and treated with various chemicals to repel the birds and slugs, and sewn thickly into the ground before being covered with the fine gravel that would protect them against the winter frosts. About 84 per cent of the seeds were expected to germinate and would eventually be planted on the hills, the full-grown trees of the future.

The activities were too varied to be monotonous. One day it might be thinning and clearing a wood; the next, helping in a noisy saw-mill and learning how to operate its machinery. Once they were tasked with 'building a bridge over a deep burn, using a dry stone dyke and some felled trees'. Several days were spent 'surveying the line of a new timber chute above Strone on the side of Loch Long'. To measure a dead straight line through dense woodland, Tony had to rely on compass bearings. He was also expected to know how to 'find the area of a field to the nearest 1/10 sq chain being given only the figures out of a Field Book'.[13] The surveying was the students' most challenging work, but, for

[12] Letter 5.

[13] Letters 3, 4, 5 and 6.

Tony at least, the most stimulating, and - as it proved - the most useful for his future career.

The boys were involved in more conventional agricultural activity as well. There was one memorable evening in which Tony helped a farmer to shear his sheep. The task proved to be 'quite easy once one gets the animal to stay in the right position'. Tony was impressed by the intelligence of the shepherd's three dogs, 'which know exactly what to do in any contingency'; in winter-time they were able to detect and dig out lost sheep from under heavy falls of snow. To get from one side of the flock to the other, the resourceful Collies would use the backs of the sheep as a bridge. The students later turned out *en masse* to help the same farmer with his haymaking, 'a fine operation in the traditional sunshine'.[14]

That summer, Tony dressed simply and practically in breeches and a shirt with attached collar. More often than not he dispensed with the shirt altogether. The tie came out only on Sundays and he rarely even wore shoes, although, when his father offered to send his old army boots, they were accepted most gratefully.[15] The boys regularly bathed in the loch and climbed the nearby hills, including Ben More itself, whose summit afforded the most stupendous views. A set of oilskins was on permanent stand-by, though, for tremendous rainfall would often sweep very suddenly down the loch. Even in July, the 'burning sun' might suddenly be obscured by a 'misty haze', often presaging torrential rain.[16]

The boys were sustained by four nourishing meals a day (including a 'large meal' at five and 'supper' at 8.30), 'porridge, meat and a very nice brown bread' being the staples. Tony's friend Garriod put on a stone in weight and he himself seemed to double in size. At least one bad habit was formed, that of smoking a pipe, which was to remain with him for the rest of his life but could

---

[14] Letters 10 and 11.

[15] Letters 7 and 10.

[16] Letter 11.

hardly be said to have shortened it. Wills's *Golden Bar* was the favoured tobacco.[17] Tony's wife was later to refer to his pipe as being the smelliest in the army.

Before long, Tony had acquired the characteristic, weather-beaten countenance of the true Highlander, and was supremely fit. Making the most of his free time - the students were at liberty to do as they pleased after 4 p.m., 'homework' permitting - he claimed to cycle 'an average of fifteen miles a day mostly over rough roads'. At one point he even lost track of time ('I am making a guess that today is Wednesday').[18] He was having the time of his life.

Church and State

Sunday worship, for which the parson's son needed no encouragement, was itself an eye-opening experience. The 'Free Church' establishments of the district, which were routinely packed, offered a considerably pared-down service compared to those he was used to. That at the kirk in Kilmun typically lasted nearly an hour and a half and, though now conducted in English rather than Gaelic, maintained the Highland tradition for fine singing. The 'broad Scotch' minister, Mr Gilchrist, would deliver a commentary on each reading, 'which everyone followed in their bibles', as well as 'a long sermon full of fire and wit'.[19] Tony eventually came to the conclusion that Mr Gilchrist was 'not up to very much but, at times, he is most expressive'. He also sampled St Cuthbert's in Dunoon, where the music reminded him of St Michael's, and the town's 'High Kirk' for contrast. He had heard that it had 'the best organ and "Minister" in Dunoon, a combination not to be missed'.[20]

---

[17] Letter 30.

[18] Letters 4 and 6.

[19] Letter 3.

[20] Letters 9 and 11.

All this would have made for lively conversation at his parents' Rectory. The students were released in May for a long weekend, and Tony considered it well worth the journey to spend nearly four full days at home. Applying to his parents for the return fare (as he did regularly for pocket money and other comforts), he wrote: 'If you consider it worth it I can get to York by 2.0 a.m. on Friday morning'. He would then complete the journey on his bicycle, 'and if I cannot get on to Barmston by breakfast time I am no longer an Englishman'.[21]

His duty to God and his parents duly observed, this fine specimen of his breed was soon to be an active contributor to the war effort. On 10 May 1940, the German Wehrmacht invaded Belgium, marking the end of the 'Phoney War'. Four days later, the Secretary of State for War, Anthony Eden, addressed the nation through the medium of the wireless. He announced the formation of the 'Local Defence Volunteers', later to be known as the Home Guard. Willing men over the age of 17 were invited to step forward. 'You will not be paid,' he said, 'but you will receive a uniform and you will be armed.'[22]

The main purpose of this citizen militia, which was perhaps never properly thought through, was to slow down the advance of the enemy in the event of an invasion, allowing the regular troops to regroup. They were 'aggressively to defend' key communications points and installations against possible capture by paratroops or fifth columnists, whose traitorous intervention was widely feared. It was even believed that the insurgents might disguise themselves as nuns. A further duty was to maintain order among the civilian population. In fact, the nation at that time was strongly united in its patriotism and loyalty to King George. Within the week, no fewer than a quarter of a million men had answered the call, signing up at their local police stations, and thousands of local units were being formed. By July, the number

---

[21] Letter 8.

[22] See S.P. Mackenzie, *The Home Guard: A Military and Political History* (Oxford, 1995), pp.18-33.

of volunteers had increased to a million and a half.[23] Among them were ten students from Benmore, including Tony Fowle.

The boys had been less than enthusiastic when the local 'bobby' had turned up at the school, and personally invited them to enrol. Tony was as reluctant as any of them. He had been enjoying himself too much and, having heard nothing from the War Office, was more than happy that he might 'not be wanted for another year'. He and all the boys were keen to complete the six-month or two- or three-year courses they had embarked on. The certificate Tony would gain at the end of it (mid-September) was 'half-way to the B.Sc.' The kindly Mr Watson promised to award it to him whatever happened, but, as Tony acknowledged to his parents, 'this must be miles better than the army', a view with which his war-veteran father must surely have concurred. 'I find that I come under the heading of "Civil Servant",' he wrote, 'and that I am doing work of "national importance".' It was as if he himself had been stamped by the Office of Works, like the very light-bulbs in Benmore House.

Towards the end of his time there the students were often engaged for twelve hours a day producing 'poles to stop 'planes from landing',[24] but that was the extent of their 'vital' work. To date, the only inconveniences of the war had been the activities of the minelayers in the Clyde, which sometimes impeded the steamers - and therefore the post - for days at a time. Yet Tony knew at heart where his duty lay, and reasoned that it would 'help keep up my [military] knowledge which will be a "good thing"'.[25]

Six weeks later, their uniforms had yet to arrive but, for the evening a week that they paraded in the nearby village of Sandbank, the Benmore volunteers were armed with Ross P14

---

[23] Penny Summerfield and Corinna Peniston-Bird, *Contesting Home Defence: Men, Women and the Home Guard in the Second World War* (Manchester, 2007), pp.26-7.

[24] Letter 11.

[25] Letters 8 and 12.

rifles (left-over Enfields from the Great War), and wore distinctive arm bands in the Black Watch tartan.

Tony 'had the honour to be in the first patrol', the men going out in pairs on four-hour shifts in the middle of the night, typically 'covering 22 miles of very desolate country roads'. In late June they had had nearly a month of 'brilliant sunshine and no rain'. In some places, including Sandbank, the supply of water had had to be rationed, and yet there seemed to be increased activity locally, perhaps because of the need to cart water about. 'Everyone on the road has to be stopped and identified, it is remarkable how many people are out. On Sunday morning we saw two cars without lights parked beside the road near a house and spotted someone flashing a light round the house. On going to investigate we found two policemen looking like miniature arsenals.' Apparently they were searching the wrong farm; the boys directed them to the right one.

A few days later, the Sandbank section took part in a training exercise with the Navy. A party of sailors were dropped in the hills, disguised as paratroops. The task of the volunteers was to scour the countryside and round them up. With such a large area to cover, it was not an easy challenge.

There was further activity in the Clyde. The R.M.S. *Queen Mary,* which had been anchored there at the time of Tony's first coming to Benmore, had set sail from the Clyde and had arrived on 5 April at Sydney, Australia, for refitting as a troop-ship. Exactly a month later she had put to sea again, but this time in convoy with five similar vessels, and with a draft of 5,500 Australian troops aboard. Tony witnessed their disembarkation at Gourock. The famous passenger liner looked 'simply colossal', but her portholes had been blacked out, her hull painted grey and black for camouflage. They were already referring to her as 'the Grey Ghost'.[26]

Even in remote Argyllshire, there was an air of increasing tension. 'On Friday night we had our first raid. Several bombs were dropped on Dunoon where there were a few casualties. One of the planes came very low over the school, caught in the search lights it was chased off over the loch with two fighters on its tail. Two of our boys who were out the other night had a fine time when, passing a very lonely saw mill, they heard noises going on inside. They went to investigate and, on giving a challenge, saw something sink back into the shadows. One remained upon guard with the rifle while the other went to get the "watchman" who slept in a little wooden hut about 100 yds away. They pursued the figure for about ten minutes without being able to shine the torch on it when suddenly it ran into a pile of boards and let out a long bleat!'

It proved to be all too easy for the failed actor but extremely successful scriptwriter Jimmy Perry to satirise his own experience of the L.D.V., later the Home Guard, in the perennially-popular television series *Dad's Army.* In the series, first aired in 1968, Perry himself is represented by the milksop Private Frank Pike. Perry's teenage ambition to be a film star had earned the reproof from his father: 'You stupid boy'. He had nevertheless kept up his involvement in amateur dramatics while serving, from 1940, with the Watford Home Guard, and using every ruse to delay call-up at the insistence of his protective mother.[27] Perry knew whereof he wrote. In reality, a collection of portly, bespectacled old men, shirkers and immature boys in shabby uniforms were indeed

---

26 Letter 9; https://queenmary.com/history/timeline/the-war-years/, https://warfarehistorynetwork.com/article/rms-queen-marys-war-service-voyages-to-victory/ and https://www.sterling.rmplc.co.uk/history/wartime.html. She went on to have a most distinguished record of active service and, immediately after the war, delivered thousands of European war-brides and their children to new lives in America and Canada.

27 Jimmy Perry's obituaries in *The Guardian,* 23 Oct 2016, and *The Times,* 24 Oct 2016.

presented as the first line of defence against the possible invasion of Nazi stormtroopers, dressed as nuns or otherwise.

That impression is corroborated by Sir William Hutchison's poignant and revealing portrait from 1940, now in the Scottish National Portrait Gallery, of Private Walter Rankin, a retired newsagent and member of the Skelmorlie L.D.V. unit in Ayrshire. Dressed in plain fatigues, L.D.V. armband and forage cap, Rankin is seated on a wooden chair, his rifle propped at his side. He is on duty, but one's eye is caught by the mundane objects on the adjacent table, including a mug of tea. A cheerful and willing hand, if only in his tea-making, Rankin appears, like many of the characters in *Dad's Army,* to be somewhat over the recommended upper age of 65.[28]

Nevertheless, as Perry remarked, *Dad's Army* 'reminds us of our finest hour … We were on our own and we didn't run away.'[29] The comedy-writer and the distinguished portrait painter both, in their way, capture the indomitable spirit and good humour of the British in the face of a dreadful threat. People Tony knew, albeit peripherally, were already being killed. His old headmaster wrote to inform him that two of his former masters were among them. In fact, the Cranleigh Roll of Honour suggests that only one had died by that stage. Gordon Gordon-Potts, a subaltern in the Royal Warwickshires, had been one of the officers in the school O.T.C., so would have been known to Tony. He and his brother Michael were killed in Belgium on the same day, 21 May, and are buried in the Calonne and Bruyelle cemeteries. Tony learnt from the same letter that his 'poor old house master' was missing. He expresses no emotion at the news.[30]

---

28 For the image and catalogue entry, see https://www.nationalgalleries.org/art-and-artists/3540.

29 Neil Clark, 'Jimmy Perry Turns 90', *The Daily Telegraph,* 20 Sept 2013.

30 Letter 9; *Cranleigh School Roll of Honour;* information from the Commonwealth War Graves Commission website, https://www.cwgc.org/find-records/find-war-dead/casualty-details/2254200/gordon-francis-allan-gordon-potts/.

Meanwhile, the Sandbank L.D.V. discovered that they were the outermost line of defence for the boom that ran from Dunoon pier to the fort on the opposite bank of the Clyde. Their role would be critical in the event of an invasion of that area. Tony's O.T.C. experience stood him in good stead, and he was promoted to Sub-Section Leader. 'Yesterday I spent two hours drilling 14 incredibly stupid men. I am sure that the lowest boy at Cranleigh could have put up a far better show.' The Benmore boys, on the other hand, all seemed to pick it up easily. Of course, half of them, having been to public schools, knew what to do already.

They realised now that their idyll was approaching its end, as Benmore was to close in September (happily not before Tony had finished his course) and would thereafter accommodate the evacuated office staff from the Commission's headquarters in Edinburgh. Tony had also received definite news from the War Office. He was told (in no uncertain terms) that he now had the option of joining up at 19, rather than 20, his birthday being in August, and as this coincided neatly with his plans, and seemed like a firm instruction rather than an invitation, he duly completed and returned the application form. 'So, with any luck,' he wrote, 'I shall have my commission by January.'[31]

The tedious night patrols continued, sometimes in driving rain, but in early July there was a moment of high excitement. According to Tony's account, 'we signalled to a car to stop by waving the red light across the road but instead of stopping the car accelerated, the man with the light had to jump for it. I, who had the 12 bore shot gun, let fly at the tyres with both barrels bursting one of them and bringing the car to an abrupt halt. Inside the car were two Italians who were beyond their five-mile area, they were both reported to the police and are now boarding at His Majesty's expense.'[32]

---

[31] Letter 11.

[32] Letter 10. Italy was not then at war with the U.K., but resident Italians were regarded with suspicion because of their Fascist sympathies.

Tony had reacted well to the situation and had given a rather impressive demonstration of his marksmanship.[33] The time would soon come when he was soldiering for real.

[33] Tony mentions in Letter 13 that he had competed for Cranleigh at Bisley.

CHAPTER II

6464804 PTE A.P.H.B. FOWLE

Basic Training

Being drilled, shouted at and deprived of sleep is for most people a disorientating and unpleasant experience, but for Tony it was 'ten times as good as I ever thought possible'. For his basic training he joined 29 Platoon, 'D' Company of the Infantry Training Centre at Elizabeth Barracks, Strensall, near York. He wore the insignia of a fine old local regiment, the King's Own Yorkshire Light Infantry, who ran the I.T.C. and in whose catchment his home parish, Barmston, lay.

The vast camp was like a giant playground. It had been established by the Victorians who had enclosed over 1,800 acres of common land and erected a cluster of red-brick buildings, including a church, gym, Y.M.C.A., N.A.A.F.I. and Salvation Army hut, that was strongly reminiscent of Cranleigh School. Tony compared it to 'a small town'. There were organised games and sports and the gym doubled as a concert- and dance-hall. The entertainment was regular, of good quality and free of charge. There was at least as much fun to be had at Strensall as at Benmore, except that it offered Tony greater opportunities, a greater sense of purpose - and vastly improved cuisine.

The recruits seem to have been broken in rather gently, perhaps because they had no uniforms at first and also because 29 Platoon was comprised exclusively, albeit unofficially, of 'Potential Officers',[1] apart from 'three corporals who are with us to be "smartened up"'.

The day's work began at 6 and ended at 4.30, but there was time to rest between each activity, as well as a generous hour-and-

---

[1] Tony implies in Letter 21 that he wore white shoulder flashes for the first time when he arrived at Catterick.

a-half break for lunch. The platoon sergeant was patient and kind, with a fund of tales with which to entertain the men. He knew his job backwards and, admittedly, had an easy task with the 'P.O.s', who were mostly public school and 'varsity' men, used to shooting (like Tony himself who had competed for Cranleigh at Bisley) and with other military skills from their O.T.C.s. They were also quick learners and within a matter of weeks, according to Tony, were 'miles ahead of our programme and … doing quite advanced stuff'.

Thus he writes on 25 November that he has 'mastered the Bren Gun and can take all its 124 parts down and put them together again'. At the same time he must have awed his instructors with his marksmanship. In a shooting test with their service rifles, the men had to put seven shots into a target at 200 yards. Tony achieved a perfect score, 'all seven actually touching each other right in the centre of the bull'.

A greater challenge was to accustom himself to the Light Infantry drill. The K.O.Y.L.I. and its sister regiments, whose forerunners had been skirmishers in the Peninsular Wars, took great pride in their 'quick thinking and quick movement'. Committed to reaching their destinations in a hurry, they routinely marched at 140 paces to the minute in 'quick time' (the rest of the army managing only 120), and 180 paces to the minute when marching at the double.[2] (They only ever 'slow marched' when Trooping the Colour.) The platoon had rapidly to attune themselves to the required tempo, doubling onto all parades and, indeed, performing most of their drill at the double.

The kindly sergeant saw the potential in Tony, and in the barrack-room, armed with a broomstick, personally tutored him in these arcana. The re-adjustment was, admittedly, 'a bit of a strain', but Tony was fully prepared by the time of his first full Church Parade, 29 Platoon quick-marching behind the band to the tune of 'With Jockey to the Fair'. To his amazement, the

[2] *Drill (All Arms) 1951,* Chap.XVIII, 'Light Infantry Drill'.

breathless band suddenly transformed itself into an orchestra and began to accompany the organ once inside the garrison-church.

Meanwhile, Tony made his mark on the rugby and hockey fields. Out of 3,000 men at Strensall, he was one of the 'fifteen' who were selected to represent the camp at rugby. Regular Saturday matches ensued, against a team from Beverley on one occasion and the West Yorks Regiment on another. He also represented the I.T.C. in a match against York City.

Apart from these conventional opportunities to keep up one's fitness, there was the usual Physical Training in the gym and 'runs' in full kit, sometimes in gas masks, which Tony describes as 'pretty grim'. The Physical Training Instructor, who had the P.O.s at his mercy for at least 45 minutes each day, was a 'terror', apt to bark at anyone 'not absolutely awake and on one's toes'. Higher standards were expected of the P.O.s, who were required to perform 'the most ghastly stunts over the horse', while the ordinary recruits were put through their far simpler paces in the open air. Apart from the P.T.I., the Regimental Sergeant Major was the only man to be avoided, the Officer Commanding, Major Harrison, being a 'fine officer' and his Non-Commissioned Officers all 'first class' men who were dedicated to getting the very best out of their charges.

The men of 29 Platoon had been amply prepared by their various public schools for the rigours of the barrack-room. Tony shared his with seventeen others, who in the cold winter evenings huddled for warmth around its two coal stoves. On either side of his bed, 'a proper sprung one', with the 'absolute luxury' of sheets, were men from Rugby and Eton. Tony and his particular friends - John, the Rugbeian, Watson, the Etonian, and James, a Salopian - donned their battle-dress after tea and went out for supper on camp (they could feast for next-to-nothing at the 'Y.M.'), followed by an 'entertainment' and perhaps a dance, so long as they were in bed by 10.15. Twice a week they availed themselves of hip-baths under showers of scalding water.[3]

By early December the men had 'passed out' of their preliminary training. The final test for Tony was to take command of a squad of thirty men, keep them busy for twenty minutes, and then give a lecture on the light machine gun, all under the watchful eye of the O.C.

The platoon's work was now of greater intensity, what Tony called 'concentrated training with a vengeance'. His home-letters become rather infrequent, though he assures his parents, with no hint of insincerity, that he is 'having a really wonderful time and enjoy[ing] it more every day'. The P.O.s were also being given their share of routine military duties, including night patrols and quarter guard outside the main guard room, which put paid for a while to their leisurely evenings. They did their turn in manning the Anti-Aircraft Gun guard room, a gruelling twenty-four-hour session of alternating two-hour shifts, throughout which they were forbidden to remove any equipment other than their steel helmets. Tony was eager to take a pot shot at the next passing enemy bomber, upon which they had permission to fire at will.

Having made a considerable impression, Tony was fast-tracked for an interview with the I.T.C.'s commanding officer. Temporary Lieutenant-Colonel Victor Henry Wells-Cole - Wykehamist, first-class cricketer and veteran of the Great War, in which he had been twice wounded and awarded the M.C. - was an officer of the old school, and had Tony stand rigidly to attention throughout the encounter.

There must have been some discussion of Tony's key attributes: his powers of observation, his experience as a surveyor, his marksmanship and his obvious intelligence. This was a young man whose idea of light reading was *The Expanding Universe* by Sir Arthur Eddington or *The Stars in their Courses* by Sir James

[3] Letters 12, 13, 14 and 15.

Jeans.[4] The unexpected but very satisfactory outcome was a recommendation that he be transferred to the Royal Artillery, the refuge of many thoughtful and ambitious officers, which also happened to have a survey branch.

Tony could see that the gunner's life was intellectually more interesting than that of the infantryman. Promotion, moreover, would be 'twice as quick', most second-lieutenants advancing directly to the rank of captain. Indeed, Tony was personally acquainted with four youthful gunners of that rank. A quick decision was made, and the path of Tony's future career was determined in that instant.[5]

Dinner with Ebor

The bright boys of 29 Platoon had raced through their course, and their passing out was scheduled for early-January 1941. Tony notched up another success, achieving, in the final test of his Machine Gun course, a First-Class certificate. Meanwhile, the men were being trained to the peak of fitness. There had been a series of route marches, all in 'quick time', but these had been increased in length from 15 miles to 28, and they were to finish with 'a 70 mile one which, of course, takes two or three days camping by the roadside'.

In the midst of an extremely harsh winter, this may not have been the most alluring prospect. The Yorkshire countryside was submerged under deep drifts of snow, with freezing temperatures for days on end. The parade ground was out of action, buried under a three-foot drift; and any roads that were clear of snow were like skating rinks, especially for men in nailed boots. The A.A. gun pit was 'almost full of snow', and the guard frozen stiff.

---

[4] Letter 19, with reference to Tony's treasured collection of Penguin books.

[5] Letters 14 and 15; C.P. Deedes, *The King's Own Yorkshire Light Infantry: Register of Officers* (London, 1945) and https://en.wikipedia.org/wiki/Victor_Wells-Cole.

Tony was very grateful for his scarf, a contribution from the Barmston Knitting Guild.

There were final exercises to be done, and Tony achieved his with panache. Ordered onto the snow-covered moors, he was to lead an attack on the 'enemy' in a wood. Map-reading his way to the position, he managed to capture an 'enemy' patrol en route. When they reached the wood it seemed deserted, but then, emerging cautiously from the trees, he spotted a party erecting wire. His scout reported that these men had put their rifles and machine guns to one side while carrying out their work, but had neglected to post sentries. Tony and his men silently grabbed the weapons and carried them off in triumph to H.Q. 'You should have seen their faces when they got in to find their rifles waiting for them,' he reported.

The men of 29 Platoon were rewarded at the end of their course with a brief period of leave, which Tony spent at Barmston. It turned out to be his last visit. Tony's father was to take up a new appointment at Ogbourne St George, in his native Wiltshire, and the family were looking forward to it - after years of primitive accommodation, they were at last to enjoy the benefits of electricity - though they had first to face a harrowing motor journey through the snow.[6] Back at Strensall, a farewell dinner was held at the Station Hotel, then all but two of the P.O.s dispersed to their Officer Cadet Training Unit in Dunbar, Haddingtonshire. Only Tony remained at Strensall, with a fellow P.O., destined for the cavalry, who unfortunately was 'a very dull dog'.[7]

The pair were nominally attached to 15 Platoon, but had no particular work to do. Vacancies at the Royal Artillery O.C.T.U., which offered a far more specialised course than that for the infantry, were less regular, but it was thought that Tony might only have to wait a week or two. The camp seemed 'empty and

---

6 Letter 19.

7 This was probably Allen Searle who, during the hiatus between the end of the course and his assignment to a unit, was put in charge of the 'Y.M.'

quiet without the others', although he was delighted when, passing a new intake of nervous recruits on the main road, he spotted Mike, his room-mate from Benmore, among them.

With time on his hands, Tony trained hard for the battalion boxing contest. His first fight took place on a Friday night. 'The ring was raised five feet off the ground in the centre of a crowd of about 500 officers and men. The fight before mine ended in a knock-out and the man being carried from the ring, an event which did not make things any better for me.'

His opponent was a snub-nosed miner with 'thick ears, eyebrows that meet in the middle and a chest that looked like a barrel bound with steel hoops. I tried out a little bluff by swinging on the ropes to warm up and in an attempt to look professional.' The gong sounded, and Tony swung as hard as he could at the man's jaw, which felt like 'a piece of iron'. Although the man seemed untroubled by the blow he went down twice after a second one and, in the third round, refused to come out of his corner. The victory was Tony's.

The finals took place a week later, in the presence of a 'massive crowd'. Tony and his opponent 'went hard at each other', the band played, the crowd roared its approval, and he eventually walked off with a money prize for being the 'best loser'.

These antics were interspersed with a rather heady social life. The wife of the Rt. Rev. William Temple, Archbishop of York, was a frequent visitor to the camp, doing her bit for the welfare of the men. Temple, a left-wing aristocrat with an acute social conscience, was to be translated to Canterbury in April 1942, being, as Churchill put it, 'the only half a crown article in the sixpenny bazaar'.[8] Attending a dance at the 'Y.M.', Tony had spent most of the evening with the 'Arch B's' fascinating (but unattainable) 'youngest daughter', though he was certainly mistaken about this, as the Temples had no children. It is possible

---

[8] Keith Robbins, *History, Religion and Identity in Modern Britain* (London, 1993), p.223.

that the young lady was one of the Archbishop's four nieces. The middle girls were already married and the youngest was only ten years old in 1941, so Beatrice Temple, born in 1907, is the likeliest candidate. Beatrice was soon to be commissioned into the Auxiliary Territorial Service and had seen Hitler when travelling in Austria before the war.[9]

As a result of this connection, and perhaps also because of his father's serving in the diocese, Tony was invited, with a friend from the camp,[10] to dine at Bishopthorpe Palace, the Archbishop of York's impressive medieval residence. In the course of a 'fundamentally happy'[11] life, Temple had been an habitué of such palaces, for his father had also been an archbishop - of Canterbury - and before that Bishop of Exeter. Mrs Temple did not appear, so the boys were to be left alone with the great man, whose official signature was '+William Ebor'. Tony wrote of being 'ushered through miles of corridors, with carved walls and ornate ceilings, into a fairly small sitting room with the most lovely furniture. Ebor soon appeared and the three of us went almost straight into dinner.' The amiable Archbishop, then 59 years old, was bespectacled and professorial, with neatly-combed hair. The dining-room, with a long table said to date from the fifteenth century, had an ornate stuccoed ceiling and was lined with the portraits of previous incumbents.

No doubt glad of some youthful company to distract him from current worries, the Archbishop directed them to a smaller table in front of the fire. Servants brought in a succession of courses that would 'beat any hotel into a cocked hat'. Soup was followed by roast turkey which 'was placed on the sideboard for Ebor to

---

[9] Letters 15, 16 and 17; *Burke's Peerage,* s.v. Earl of Harewood; *British Resistance Archive,* http://www.staybehinds.com/beatrice-temple#:~:text=Beatrice%20Temple%20was%20born%20on,Army%20and%20Frances%20Mary%20Copleston.

[10] The friend is named as Peter Scot.

[11] A.E. Baker and George Bell, *William Temple and his Message* (London, 1946), p.15.

carve'. He tucked into it with as much relish as the boys and between them they 'devoured quite half the bird'. Likewise, 'a first class boiled pudding … soon completely vanished. Coffee followed and we returned to the small sitting room to lie in arm chairs before the fire and have the most interesting conversation on every subject imaginable. We left soon after ten.'

Tony was also 'getting ahead with real war training'. Days after dining with 'Ebor', he led a night patrol of seven men, charged with locating and mapping the 'enemy's' wire and his section posts beside yet another moorland wood. Tony went ahead with the only 'intelligent' man, crawling for ages over ice, snow and mud until they were soaked to the skin. They 'got right up to the wire and crawled all round it, measuring it and drawing a map of it together with descriptions of the "enemy" strength and position.'

Tony 'sent the other fellow back with the message and map to collect the remainder of the patrol and return to HQ'. He then crawled under the wire, 'crept up, inch by inch, to the enemy post, the outline of the trench being just visible in the star light' - and threw a 'Thunder Flash' straight into the middle of it. 'It went off with a fine bang making the poor men in the trench nearly pass out with surprise. I lay low for a bit and then got away without even being fired at.'

Closely observed by the umpires, Tony was to be warmly congratulated by the Major, and asked to give an account of his escapade to the entire company. He left Strensall in a glow of approbation and it was clear that the army had done well by him, recognising and drawing out his qualities and steering him in an appropriate direction. Physically so fit that he now thought nothing of the fifteen-mile route march, fed almost anything he wanted by the kindly ladies of the A.T.S., and plenty of it, and having sampled so many different aspects of army life in a comparatively short time, Tony Fowle was the proverbial round peg in a round hole.[12]

The Nursery Battery

Tony's first posting as 'Gunner Fowle' was to 6th Field Training Regiment, which occupied a vast converted mill at Dairy, Ayrshire. In retrospect he was not sure what had been achieved there, but he seems to have enjoyed it thoroughly at the time.

The atmosphere at Dairy was highly civilised, the catering outstanding, though Tony was somewhat appalled by the range and quantity of the food. Civilians, his own parents among them, were already subject to strict rationing, and he was scandalised by the daily waste of butter. The men were responsible for their own turnout and time-keeping. There was no marching or drill (rifles were not issued), no sergeants barking orders, and minimal red tape, merely a constant round of lectures and written exercises, in such abstruse fields as trigonometry and ballistics. The day was rounded off with an entertaining, if physically taxing hour's gun drill with the battery's 25 pounder. The N.C.O. instructors were, without exception, peace-time schoolmasters. Tony asked for all his old geometry equipment to be sent up. It was much like being back at school, except that the work was the hardest he had ever done.[13]

There were, however, ample opportunities for travel and for re-connecting with Benmore friends. Aged nineteen and a half, Tony was 'easily the youngest in the squad. Always drawn to his seniors, he befriended Mike Brown, an inveterate traveller and a solicitor 'when he felt like it', who at 32 was by far the oldest, as well as being 'the most intelligent'. Together they went on adventurous trips and Tony wrote how moved he had been by the

---

[12] Letter 17.

[13] Letter 18 and Tony's note to Letter 17.

beauty of Largs, by the red mass of the sinking sun, and by its scarlet reflections on the snowy peaks and on the low clouds and the sea.[14]

Early in March, Tony paid his first visit to Ogbourne, a brief one, before finally donning the white shoulder flashes of an officer cadet and embarking on his O.C.T.U. at Catterick. 'A' Battery, 123 O.C.T.U., including all his old friends from Dairy, were impressively housed in Bourlon Barracks, a modern, neo-Georgian monstrosity that 'looks like a cross between a hospital and an Oxford college', complete with quad and clock-tower. Unlike Dairy, the discipline was 'very strict' and the red tape 'lying around in rolls', but the food was said to be 'the best in the country'. Indeed it was something in which the Colonel, a gourmand who would have got on famously with the Archbishop of York, took a personal interest, to the extent of carrying out daily inspections of the kitchens and the massive dining-hall, where white-coated waiters were in attendance. Tony wrote later that 'the whole kitchen is the Colonel's pride and joy and is boasted to be the best equipped and best staffed in the British service'.[15] There were also sprung beds, with linen. Tony compared the place to a 'luxury hotel'.

The course, however, was tough. Within weeks the cadets were expected to have mastered the general principles of Leadership (the Colonel prized smartness and military discipline above all else), Military Law and, egregiously, Motor Transport, the focus of the latter being the three-ton Bedford Truck. To that end, they must fully grasp the intricacies of the Solex carburettor, the gear box, the A.C. pump and the Coil Ignition system. They would also be tested on their proficiency with the .38 pistol, in P.T. and foot drill, and on logic, military history and rudimentary tactics - all before they had even touched a gun.

---

[14] Letter 19.

[15] Letter 25.

At the end of their probationary period, the cadets were transferred to 'B' Company, and for some weeks Tony was too busy to write home. The Battery Commander was a hard task-master, and when Tony was rated 'a good average', it was the highest compliment he could expect to receive. Several cadets were deemed to be 'below average' or even 'hopeless' and were not expected to last the course.

The C.O., Colonel Waller, unlike the Battery Commander, was a man after Tony's own heart, with whom he discovered a shared interest in ornithology. The Colonel explained that gunner officers were not like other officers. Their expertise was not only in the highly specialised fields of gunnery and survey, but also in every aspect of infantry work, artillery units being responsible for their own ground protection. Inevitably, the average fall-out rate on the artillery courses was far higher than on those for the infantry, 35 per cent compared to 5 per cent. Most of the failures were N.C.O.s who had been recommended for commissions. Tony disapproved of 'ranker-officers', believing that the foremost qualification for an officer in the Royal Artillery was that he be a 'gentleman'; also, perhaps, the view of the esteemed Colonel. Tony had revised that opinion within months, referring with some reverence to his then Battery Commander, an ex-sergeant-major who had been commissioned from the ranks.[16]

Tony now wore his brass gunner cap badge - an old-fashioned cannon with a revolving wheel and the motto *Ubique,* 'everywhere' - with intense pride. Even the regimental band was, in his view, 'the best bar none'. Unlike other regiments, he wrote, the Royal Artillery was 'leaving more and more to the personal initiative of its officers'. He had moved to a new shared room on the upper floor, with fine views of Richmond Castle and the hills beyond; and he enjoyed the services of a batman, an efficient Scotsman who had been been Chief Steward on a cross-channel ferry, *The Maid of Kent.* Tony had scored high marks in the recent

---

[16] Letters 19 and 23. See Letter 62 for his very favourable impression of Captain Rickards.

exams: 89 per cent in Law, 71 per cent in M.T. He was now being given practical lessons in the three-tonner over some punishing terrain. The recruits had to negotiate the vehicle over a narrow bridge consisting of a few planks. Happily, none of them went over the edge. They were also required to give impromptu lectures before the C.O. and his board of officers. Tony's subject, handed to him on the platform, was 'the principles of true rolling and the Ackerman steering linkage', happily one that he had thoroughly revised beforehand.[17]

On 21 May, Tony completed his first six months in the army, and was half-way through his course. By way of celebration, the squad experienced their 'first real shoot', out on the moors with batteries of 25- and 18-pounders. Tony describes the satisfaction of seeing one's target, a patch of bushes and trees some 5,000 yards away, suddenly vanish in a cloud of smoke and dust. The 18-pounder shell made a terrific noise like a thunder clap as it whizzed through the air. 'It seemed ages and ages before the final "thump" of the burst could be heard. After that we put down a smoke screen using some of the new type of smoke shells which were most effective.'

Tony relished every moment and had resolved to put in for a peacetime commission, when army life would be even more fun than it seemed to be in war. He had come to the conclusion that the regular officers were 'much nicer' than the 'civilian' ones, and certainly more considerate to the men. Some of those he met in the mess, 'excellent fellows in all respects', were veterans of the old horsed artillery regiments, but even the Royal Horse Artillery was now mechanised. All that remained were the muled Mountain Regiments, on which Tony had set his heart. His sense of serving in an elite regiment had been intensified by the dramatic shrinking of the squad. Of the original 37, only 14 remained, and not all of those were expected to complete the course.[18]

---

[17] Letters 24 and 25.

[18] Letter 26.

Returning from home-leave in mid-June, Tony witnessed the bomb damage in central London, and there was some brief excitement at York, where he observed a party of captured German airmen on the platform. 'All of a sudden there was a great uproar, we saw a man fairly flying down the platform with three soldiers after him with fixed bayonets, everyone on the station shouting and join[ing] in the chase'. The train pulled out before he could discover the outcome.

The members of the squad were now 'senior cadets', entitled to wear an extra white shoulder flash, but had been reduced to only ten men; a further four had been deemed unsuitable. Now in the last lap of their training, they spent much of their time in anti-gas lectures and, in the course of a 'rather grim half hour in the gas chamber', they were exposed to the effects of the real thing. Eventually they were put to work in a concentration of mustard gas, the terror weapon of the Great War. Whilst safe in their protective clothing from the gas, they almost expired from the heat.

Tony passed his driving test at the end of June, and submitted in early July to a 'running repairs' test. Presented with a broken-down car, he fiddled under the bonnet and got it started in 22 minutes, earning a score of 85 per cent. He gave his final lecture on one of his favourite topics - calibration - 'which is a beautifully mathematical subject consisting of writing streams of figures on the blackboard'. No doubt the Colonel was impressed, announcing vaguely that he had been placed 'in the top six'.

Tony was then given signed permission to order his officer's uniform. The regimental tailor, Bernard Weatherill of 55 Conduit Street, Mayfair, had an agent locally, who took Tony's measurements.[19] Tony asked his father to send up his old Sam Browne belt as 'my man will make it look like new. The present-day ones are like cardboard and look simply ghastly, but yours

---

[19] The tailor's son, also Bernard, just commissioned into the 4th/7th Dragoon Guards, was the future Speaker of the House of Commons *(Supplement to the London Gazette,* 6 June 1941, p.3314).

will be more than a good belt - it will be an heirloom.' Tony's father agreed and promptly made a gift of it.[20]

Passing-out was now scheduled for 1 August, but the squad had still to face the ordeal of a 36-hour 'drill order'. As Troop Leader, Tony was charged with safely delivering four guns, six lorries, an ambulance, cooker and cable-laying trucks to a particular position, on time. The journey was to be made by night, there was a heavy mist, and the route took them over a steep hill. By 2 a.m. they had set up camp on the summit. Tony slept soundly, and at 6.30 a.m. led the procession down the other side through dense fog. Colonel Waller, who accompanied the convoy, ordered frequent 'emergency actions' against the invisible enemy, but Tony's main challenge was to maintain the speed and the distance apart of the various vehicles, a task that was especially difficult in the fog. The pressure was extreme and the whole exercise exhausting.

Finally, on 26 July, Tony was notified of his first posting - to the 65th Field Regiment R.A. at Aylesham, Kent - but hoped to be soon 'sent to a Mountain Battery as I have so often applied for one'. First, however, he would have to attend a four-day course at the School of Artillery, Larkhill, which was said to have 'the best mess in the country'. Tony's troop performed exceptionally well in their final gun drill. The Colonel, not normally a man for compliments, told them he had 'nothing but praise'. The long awaited commission came through at last, and was gazetted on 19 August 1941, two days after Tony's twentieth birthday.[21]

---

[20] Letters 28 and 29.

[21] Letters 30, 31, 32 and 33; *Supplement to the London Gazette,* 19 August 1941, p.4790.

CHAPTER III

A SUBALTERN'S LOVE SONG

'The dickens of a lot to do'

The recently-re-formed 65th (8th London) Field Regiment, which Tony duly joined as a Troop Leader in August 1941, was a Territorial unit. To be posted to such a unit seemed at first the 'worst luck' for an ambitious young man. The other subalterns may not have been 'very keen', but, as Tony soon discovered, the regiment was beefed up by regulars, the higher-ranking officers were all excellent men, and it had seen some serious active service, having been evacuated the previous year (minus almost all its guns and equipment) from the beach at Dunkirk.[1] Indeed, Tony's Battery Commander, Major Richard de Carteret Yeo, was an officer from the T.A. General List who had taken part in that action. A 'very quiet and pleasant man who remained unruffled by whatever panic was going on', he was to be awarded the D.S.O. in 1944 for his services with the 24th Mountain Regiment in Burma. As for the newly-appointed C.O., Lieutenant-Colonel Roy Mews, he had been the holder of a regular commission since 1918, and was to be the recipient of not one but two D.S.O.s, the first awarded in 1943, after he had led the regiment to North Africa, and the second (in the form of a bar) in 1944. He was to end the war as a Brigadier.[2]

From Egypt and Libya the 65th would go on to serve in Italy, but its role in the autumn and winter of 1941 was to guard the coastal districts of Kent against the German invasion, which was

---

[1] Letter 34 and Tony's notes appended to Letter 38.

[2] Tony's annotations to Letter 38, in which he mistakenly refers to 'George de Yeo' and credits him with an M.C.; *The Half-Yearly Army List* (Jan 1939) lists both Yeo (p.821) and Mews (p.621). See also *Supplement to the London Gazette,* 27 July 1944, p.3502, and 24 August 1944, p.3925; National Archives, WO 373/33/1, WO 373/24/276 and WO 373/7/273.

still believed to be imminent. To that end, the batteries were scattered widely across the east of the county, many of the men living permanently under canvas, whilst the officers messed in a succession of old rectories and vicarages.

Tightly and efficiently run, the 65th worked Tony harder than ever - to the extent that he was unable to keep up his weekly letters home - and provided him with further valuable experience and training. For that he had to thank the Commander of XII Corps (of which the 65th was part), one Lieutenant-General Bernard Law Montgomery. On his appointment in April, 'Monty' had, with characteristic vigour, instituted a regime of continuous training. Officers unfit to command in action were ruthlessly sacked. Monty insisted on high levels of fitness for both officers and other ranks; and he strove to promote among them an offensive spirit, even re-naming his command 'the South-Eastern Army'.[3]

Monty struck many who encountered him as a fussy, pedantic little man, and Tony was no exception. He recalled how all the officers in the corps were assembled for a talk in a large cinema in Maidstone. Monty forbade them to cough for as long as he spoke, though at regular intervals he allowed 'two-minute coughing breaks'. Tony remembered nothing of the talk, only the forced and unnatural coughing that took place during the breaks.[4]

Tony had an early stint as orderly officer for his battery, the 258th, which meant living with them for 24 hours in their camp near the village of Ash, the only officer present. His duties included drawing out and distributing the men's pay, mounting the guard, signing passes and permits and 'arresting suspicious characters', for whom he was constantly on the look-out. Much of the civilian population had been evacuated, but the Field Security Police were known to plant fake 'Fifth-Columnists' to catch out the unwary. Tony, who swore later that he would lock such a

---

[3] Richard Mead, *Churchill's Lions* (Stroud, 2007), p.303; Tony Heathcote, *The British Field Marshals, 1736 - 1997* (Barnsley, 1999), p.216.

[4] Tony's annotations to Letter 38.

provocateur in the guard room until someone came to claim him, had other, more pressing concerns. On the straight road back from Ramsgate with supplies, he encountered one of the regiment's lorries in a ditch, and placed its drunken driver on a charge. Returning to the town later, he had to dive into a gutter as a bomb went off two streets away.[5]

Monty's policies were rigorously enforced in the regiment and included 'officers' P.T.' every morning at six, for a whole hour, and constant classes and tests on gunnery. Even Major Yeo had to turn out at the crack of dawn in his P.T. kit, invariably grumbling about his being 'too old for that sort of thing'. (It might not seem so today. He was, in fact, 37 years old.) There was also plenty of live firing at ranges of five or six miles, including dramatic weekly barrages onto the beach south of Ramsgate. Tony had become extremely proficient at his gunnery and usually took charge. The other 'subs' were mostly junior to him anyway and 'quite U.S.' in his opinion, unable to operate except under supervision.[6]

Colonel Mews was suitably impressed and, by 2 September, had promoted Tony to Gun Position Officer. This was normally a captain's job. Tony was now responsible for the maintenance and deployment in action of four guns, twelve lorries and three motor-bikes, and for the training and efficiency of 53 men. It took a steady hand to ensure that 'no shells land where they should not', such as on the sea-front at Ramsgate. Being at the receiving end of a well-aimed barrage was unnerving enough for the locals.

Mews, one of Monty's appointees, was keen to keep up the required tempo. On one occasion, while Tony was leading his little convoy along a country road, an order came through on the wireless for the rapid destruction of a particular target, a post on the mud flats about five miles away. It took a mere 4½ minutes for Tony to pull his guns off the road and destroy the target.

---

[5] Letters 34 and 36.

[6] Letters 35 and 36; *The Half-Yearly Army List* (Jan 1939), p.821, on Yeo.

Now an aspiring Troop Commander, he cheerfully took on additional responsibilities, including command of an 'Anti-Paratroop' squad, which he trained in the use of Tommy guns, Bren guns, grenades and rifles, just in case those airborne 'nuns' ever arrived. Another role was as Battery Sports Officer. Compulsory games were played three times a week after lunch, and Tony made sure that there was a wide choice of activities, including squash and badminton. He set a fine example in November by finishing first in the regimental cross-country run. He claimed to be fitter and healthier than ever and was loving every moment.

The greatest excitements were the 'practice invasion flaps' that were regularly launched by H.Q., usually in the small hours. The one in October lasted an entire week, the roads for 'quite literally hundreds of miles' being thronged with military vehicles. Tony had barely any sleep and that was 'in the valise underneath my truck'. For five days, the troop lived off haversack rations, their lines of communication cut off, but it held together, despite movements on unfamiliar roads on dark, foggy nights, 'when units were branching off all along the way'. On the final day they were put out of action by a squadron of 'enemy' tanks and had to sit it out until the whole regiment was ready to march home. 'Within ten minutes,' Tony wrote, 'there was not a soul awake other than myself.'[7]

While under canvas the men (most of them fresh from 'civvy street') had yearned for a hotel. Tony was therefore delighted to settle his troop into a large, country house on the edge of Broadstairs, 'where it was just like being back at Cranleigh in charge of 1 North'. Tony was determined that, while in his care, the house should be 'the cleanest and tidiest in Broadstairs'. The officers' mess was indeed 'like a hotel', the cuisine excellent. However, Tony slept with his troop in a little room of his own.[8]

---

[7] Letters 35, 36, 38.

[8] Letter 38.

It was not long before he received his hoped-for promotion to Troop Commander, of 'C' Troop - though only 'acting', and on top of his duties as G.P.O. When out of battle-dress (which was not often), he cut a particularly fine figure in his father's old 'Sam Browne', which even 'beats the Colonel's into a cocked hat'. He had become well-known in the regiment for his professionalism, integrity and self-belief. On one occasion he was required to rain down ordnance from six miles away in a divisional competition. Having fired his last round, he received a furious 'phone call from the umpire. It had landed on top of the Observation Post, to the discomfort of three generals, two colonels and some other senior officers. The man was 'very rude', and accused Tony of ordering the wrong fuse length. 'The next day, I took out a party and found the fuse band and sent it to him.' As Tony suspected, it was faulty. The other officer came over in person and made a handsome apology to the bold twenty-year-old. The faulty batch of ammunition was, of course, withdrawn.[9]

Shortly afterwards, Tony was able to resume his acting command of 'C' Troop while the incumbent, Captain 'Rick' Rickards, took ten days' leave. Tony came to revere Rickards, an ex-Sergeant-Major, writing later that 'he taught me nearly everything I know about looking after men'. 'Old Rick' found on his return that everything had gone 'beautifully' and the guns were firing merrily from the playing fields of St Peter's School, much to the discomfort of the residents. Another 'practice invasion' was launched at 5.30 the following morning, in the course of which Tony had to 'take all my guns and vehicles over a pontoon bridge across a really wide and deep river, at 2.30 in the morning in a thick fog, which was not at all funny'. It was an uncannily prophetic rehearsal for events that would take place on a real field of battle just over a decade later. On this occasion, a

[9] Letter 37.

single lorry tipped over the bridge into the river, to be extricated by an obliging tank.[10]

With 'the dickens of a lot to do', there was limited time for a social life. A keen rider to hounds, and former Superintendent of the Riding Establishment at Woolwich, Colonel Mews had managed to procure a pack of beagles for the brigade, but no horses, so the riders - including all the officers below the rank of Major - were mounted on motor-cycles. These were as much 'motor-scrambles' as hunts, the bikes having to be forced through hedges and over ditches. Tony noted how the more senior officers wore battle-dress blouses with old gunner-pattern breeches and highly-polished field boots, a display of old-fashioned elegance which must have piqued his interest in the concept of horse-drawn batteries. Meanwhile, he relished his role as second whip to the 'hunt', which convened twice a week, the place being 'thick with hares and the hounds in very good form'.[11]

Meanwhile, he became romantically involved with a 'robust and rather pretty' girl called Rachel Drake-Brockman. Her father was Colonel Paris Drake-Brockman, known as 'D.B.', late of The Buffs and now C.O. of the 50th Anti-Tank Regiment R.A. Though he was described as 'the finest type of regimental officer who inspired great affection amongst all who knew him', 'D.B.' was extremely garrulous and Tony could barely get a word in edgeways, let alone address the serious business of paying court to his daughter.[12]

Not surprisingly, his eye wandered elsewhere. It began to be noticed that Tony was repeatedly volunteering to be orderly officer, which meant taking sole charge of the camp near Ash. He had encountered a retired sapper who lived nearby, the jovial,

---

[10] Letter 42. Rickards re-surfaces in Egypt in August 1942 (Letter 62).

[11] Letters 38 (with Tony's annotations), 39 and 40 (on beagling); *The Half-Yearly Army List* (Jan 1939), p.621, on Mews.

[12] See https://www.queensroyalsurreys.org.uk/colonels_and_co/commanding_officers/east_surrey/lt-col-ph-drake-brockman.shtml; Letter 36 and Tony's annotations to Letter 38.

somewhat bibulous Major McDonald. Major 'Mac' had suggested that Tony forsake his bell-tent in the camp, and bivouac instead in his own drawing-room at Christian Court. The equally charming Mrs McDonald (a fine pianist, despite being very deaf) seconded the plan. Apart from the home comforts that were available there, the McDonalds had a pretty daughter of their own. A tall, slim blonde, Isa McDonald had been a pre-war repertory actress (Tony had photographs of her playing Queen Bess in an outdoor production), though was now involved in some 'secret project' at Bletchley Park. Isa rapidly superseded Rachel as 'number one girlfriend'. The couple embarked, indeed, on a serious relationship, which was to culminate, a couple of years later, in their engagement, but inevitably it failed to withstand Tony's prolonged absences, first in the Middle East, and then in India.[13]

During ten days' leave that November, Tony managed to visit both Ogbourne and his old school at Cranleigh, where 'everything seemed just the same as usual'. However, on returning to East Kent and a round of ever more intense invasion exercises, he must have felt that change was afoot. 'Another batch of officers and a large number of men have left for service overseas,' he wrote at Christmas, 'and more are going soon. The last lot had only 24 hours notice before being rushed off on embarkation leave and only a very small percentage of them had volunteered to go, the rest being detailed.' The future seemed most uncertain. Tony only knew that his turn would come, probably sooner rather than later.[14]

---

[13] Letter 34 and Tony's notes appended to Letter 38.

[14] Letters 40, 41 and 42.

'The ship of a thousand romances'

The future was no more certain in February 1942, when Tony found himself in a holding-camp at Burton-on-Trent, one of a draft of a hundred officers waiting to be shipped overseas. They were never told where. Orders to move were expected at any moment, but the C.O. was as much in the dark as everyone else. Consequently, there were no parades of any sort, merely an endless round of form-filling, medical examinations, inoculations and interviews.

Tony made the most of an extremely comfortable billet, which was in a private house on the edge of town. He and another officer, Richard Grieg, had rooms to themselves, and the good people who lived there could not do enough for them. They tolerated the daily visits of their batman and even the presence of Grieg's wife, with whom he was on honeymoon. Grieg professed to be glad to have Tony around, in case he became 'too sentimental'. The three of them went for long walks in the snow, even as far as Repton, and dined in country inns. The whole experience seemed somewhat surreal.[15]

The next they knew they were embarked in the Armed Merchant Cruiser *Mooltan* at Liverpool. She was, in fact, the requisitioned P. & O. liner that used to ply between Tilbury, Bombay and Sydney. Billed as 'the ship of a thousand romances', she was an enormous vessel for the time and one of striking elegance and luxury. The first-class cabins, with their panelling and antique furniture, resembled the bedrooms of a grand country house.

In her new role, the *Mooltan* had been fitted with two pairs of six-inch guns, fore and aft, together with a number of light A.A. guns and two banks of 3-inch rockets, which rose vertically when launched, releasing a barrage of wires attached to parachutes. To improve the arc of the guns, the ship's second funnel had been

---

[15] Letters 47, 48 and 49.

reduced in size, so she had lost some of her pre-war allure. Tony noted ominously that every porthole and hatch had been battened down, and predicted uncomfortable levels of heat if, as was likely, they ventured anywhere tropical.[16]

The *Mooltan* set sail from Liverpool on 11 February and initially headed north, not because that was her ultimate direction of travel but because the deep, sheltered waters off Orsay, an island of the Inner Hebrides, were a convenient assembly point for a large convoy. This was 'WS' convoy no.16 (after Churchill's initials), and there were to be 21 ships in total, with their attendant naval escort, which included the carriers *Eagle* and *Argus.*[17]

The convoy (parts of which were to split off at various points) set off from Orsay on 17 February, a day of perfect sunshine. It was like a pleasure cruise on a summer's day. Tony had already discovered the excellence of the cuisine, which was varied and extraordinarily plentiful and was served on silver dishes by the ship's pre-war attendants. Mostly Indians, they were dressed in 'white ducks with red turbans,' and looked 'very smart'. Tony had the pleasure of female company as well, there being several Women's Auxiliary Air Force aboard.

As the fleet headed west into the Atlantic, however, the passage became progressively less smooth. The following evening there was 'quite a wind blowing' and soon they experienced the uncomfortable sensation of the ship climbing up over the swell and dropping down into the trough on the other side. Dicky Grieg retired to his bunk and remained there for four days. Meanwhile, the sea 'lashed clean over the forward deck'. Enormous waves tossed the ship to ever-more precipitous heights

---

[16] Letter 49; the 'Magnificent Mooltan' page on *The Old Peninsular and Oriental Steamship Company* website, https://www.pandosnco.co.uk/mooltan.html, which has much historical information and copious illustrations.

[17] See the *Naval History* website, https://www.naval-history.net/xAH-WSConvoys05-1942A.htm, for the composition of the convoy and its movements, and Les Pivnic and J.M. Pattinson, 'Durban Harbour, 1942 to 1945', *The South African Military History Journal,* Vol.16, No.3 (June 2014), available online.

and there were disconcerting scenes in the dining-room, with chairs and tables 'being flung all over the place … The storm kept up for a week, the mess growing more and more deserted.' Immune to sea-sickness, Tony sat alone at his table and, with admirable sang-froid, grimly held on to his plate to prevent its sliding down to the other end.

The squadron sailed as far as the coast of Newfoundland and then dropped south, before heading almost due east to Sierra Leone. Their ultimate destination remained a mystery, but was the subject of constant rumour and speculation. The Mooltan's captain knew only to follow the destroyer ahead of him.

Eventually the wind fell and a pale sun emerged. The sea took on extraordinary hues, varying from 'deep purple to the purest white'. It was suddenly hot, though mercifully with a pleasant, cooling breeze. Skin burned red and began to peel. Two days later the men were ordered into their tropical kit. Thenceforth they were required to wear their solar topees (the standard-issue pith helmets) whenever they were on deck, as a necessary protection against sunstroke.

Apart from the lavish meals (five courses for breakfast and lunch and seven for dinner), the daily routine consisted of P.T. under a Royal Marine instructor (he had the men running round the decks, eight circuits to the mile) and looking after the guns. Tony was assigned those at the stern, which were mounted perilously over the propeller, whilst Dicky Grieg took care of the forward pair. The gun crews were variously Maritime Artillery and Royal Marines. Tony wrote drily that it had been no fun negotiating a darkened ship at night during the height of the storm, especially as he had to climb 'outboard' in order to visit his station.

Every fifth day Tony also served his turn as Gunnery Officer, responsible for all the ship's guns and defences, spending much of that time on the bridge. These exploits qualified him later for the Atlantic Star, an unusual award for a soldier. Otherwise not overwhelmed with duties, he was determined to keep his mind busy. In the evenings he played chess with a coterie of regulars, including the ship's doctor and a formidable Queen Alexandra's Royal Army Nursing Corps nurse, who sat on chintzy armchairs in the Reading Room and ignored the swell, the pieces being fastened into holes in the board. Tony also read copiously, took up bridge, and tried to get to grips with Hindustani, which he practised with the waiters. One evening at dinner, he asked in perfect Hindustani for roast duck. The waiter seemed pleasantly surprised, but his response was unintelligible. Tony asked him to repeat it in English. 'It turned out he was asking whether I wanted braised celery with the duck. After that I gave up the unequal struggle.'

Tony's friends among the waiters gave him a tour of the galley, and another showed him the engine room, which was normally out of bounds. The cooks, the engineers and the stokers were all lascars (Indian sailors), and accustomed to the 'almost overpowering' heat of their work-places. After a tour of the lowest decks, Tony emerged with relief and had to wring out his shirt. Occasionally he cooled off in a salt-water bath.

His greatest pleasure was to lean over the railings on deck, smoke a pipe or two (Player's 'Navy Cut' was obtainable for next to nothing), and observe the abundant wildlife. 'Clouds of flying-fish dart over the bows looking like dragon-flies as they shine in the sun … Nearly all the time we are escorted by a school of porpoise which slide in and out of the water round our bows then race off to play round those of one of our sister ships. Yesterday I spotted the great grey fin of a shark cutting silently through the water beside the ship; luckily for the shark it was not mistaken for a conning tower!'

On 1 March, the steward who brought in the morning tea announced the sighting of land. After breakfast, Tony observed from the deck an unfolding vista of coral reefs, bright blue waters and palm trees until suddenly, rounding a headland, they swung into a broad bay with a hazy, mountainous backdrop. The soil of the hills was red, like that in Devon; and in the foreground there was 'the most odd looking town', modern apartment blocks mingling with 'mere shacks', and 'curious shrubs' and palm trees growing all around.

The convoy dropped anchor and was immediately assailed by scores of dug-out canoes paddled by 'massive-looking negroes'. There was much 'shouting and haggling' and a brisk trade in 'oranges, mangoes, pineapples and coconuts', along with 'knives, mats, baskets and even long curved horns'. The passengers threw down their pennies and the doughty canoeists 'flopped into the water' to catch them.

Having never been abroad or indeed anywhere more exotic than Bridlington, Tony was utterly entranced. That night, the whole town was lit up and even the decks of the ships were floodlit, as if the war had been suspended. 'The ship's band came up and we danced on deck by the light of the arc lamps.' A bright red moon rose out of the sea, 'tinting all the hills with crimson'. From the shore, they could hear 'strange singing … with a lovely deep note and stirring rhythm'. Tony slept on deck; down below, it was quite unbearably hot, although, in any case, he was far too excited to do otherwise.

The chief city and port of Sierra Leone (then a British Crown Colony), Freetown had been founded in 1792 by a British Abolitionist, and settled not by the local tribes, but by liberated slaves from America. (As an ethnic group the Sierra Leonians, being of indeterminate ancestry, are termed 'Creoles'.) Mindful of the censor, Tony never refers to it by name, and his parents would have been left guessing by his evocative account of the 'curious town with its strange mixture of houses and shops', that had clearly cast a spell on him.

Regrettably, there were to be no 'runs ashore', as yellow fever was rife in the town. However, Dicky Grieg had a connection with P. & O. (his father was a director of William Cory & Son, suppliers of the oil that fired the Mooltan's boilers), and cadged for them both a tour of the bay and surrounding coastline in a motor launch. Tony reported that the waters were still, clear and perfectly blue, broken only by 'the white wash from the launch'. Otherwise, he discovered plenty of new wildlife to occupy him. He saw sea-eagles and vultures and, once, 'a lovely bird with a long thin tail flew over us with a flash of green and red'.

On the morning of 6 March he awoke 'to the throb of the engines to find that the land had vanished into the haze from which it had come'.[18]

Local Colour

The *Mooltan* soon sped over the Equator, though Tony makes no reference to 'crossing the line' or any of the attendant ceremonies. Oddly, a strong wind blew for a while and the passengers felt rather chilly in their tropical kit. Tony was in awe of the birdlife, much of which he could not identify, and especially of the albatross that glided effortlessly around the stern of the ship, keeping a beady eye out for any fish that might be thrown up by the propellers. Eventually, the main body of the convoy skirted past Cape Town and entered the Indian Ocean, bound for Durban. It had been necessary to divide the fleet at this point, as neither port was large enough to accommodate them all.[19]

Land was sighted on 21 March, and the *Mooltan* glided into Durban harbour. The gunners were disembarked at last and taken by train to a large camp on a nearby hillside, where Tony noticed the same red soil as at Freetown. It was surrounded by banana and eucalyptus trees. Tony shared a tent with Grieg and they were attended by a 'very good native servant who looked after us well and, funnily enough, did not help himself to any of our kit'.

---

[18] Letter 50, the longest and easily the most evocative in the whole collection, illuminated by Tony's later annotations. Tony adds further small details of the voyage, and finally refers to Freetown, in Letter 55. In Letter 51 he compares the Indian Ocean with the sea at Bridlington.

[19] Pivnic and Pattinson, 'Durban Harbour' (http://samilitaryhistory.org/vol163lp.html).

Initially they were kept awake by the nocturnal carousing of the wildlife, especially frogs, toads and crickets, but they soon got used to the noise and found that it lulled them to sleep. On offer for breakfast were 'water melon … fried eggs, rump steak, toast, marmalade and home-made butter, coffee and cream'. It all seemed too good to be true. There were route marches and P.T. until lunch, after which they were free to explore.

Tony found Durban, with its distinctive white buildings, to be a most attractive town. Scores of rickshaw-pullers plied its broad, tree-lined streets, steely Zulu warriors to a man, magnificently attired in horned and feathered headdresses. Restaurants were 'amazingly cheap' but, as Tony noted ominously, there was 'a very strict colour bar', so 'one has to be very careful what one does'. Tony met more Zulus (some of them fully armed) on a day trip to the Valley of the Thousand Hills, whose varied flora seemed to have been 'taken from a fairy story'. The officers spent most of their time at the luxurious Durban Country Club, of which they had been made honorary members. It looked over the beach and Tony tried his hand with a body-board in Durban's famously powerful swell, the waves having had 'an uninterrupted journey for half way round the world'.

Tony's friend Joan, one of the W.A.A.F.s from the ship, invited him to spend a week with her in the Entumeni district of Natal. It proved to be 'one of the most memorable weeks' of his life (so far). Their hosts, a family called Suivelle, were friends of Joan's father. They lived on a remote sugar-plantation, high in the hills. Tony took an overnight train to Eshowe, the capital of Zululand. Thence it was a thirty-mile drive by 'the most awful road' to the Suivelle homestead. 'On either side there were miles and miles of wattle trees, gums and bush with thick undergrowth hiding buck, water buffalo, wild dogs and the most lovely birds of all the colours of the rainbow.'

The Suivelles' comfortable bungalow was set at an altitude of 4,500 feet, 'on the edge of a valley with the most wonderful view in all the world, they said they could see for 200 miles!' They had a swimming pool, a tennis court, a putting green and a horse, and every single comestible was home-produced, apart from salt, tea and olive oil. On a drive through the nearby game reserve, Tony saw 'lions, buck, antelope, zebra and one giraffe'. As the 'sun sunk over the hills the valley turned a really deep purple, with every hill taking on a different shade and the sky becoming a wonderful crimson. We used to sit on the terrace and just watch it for the half hour it lasted, till everything was quite dark except for the stars which shone very brightly and clearly'.

After nearly three weeks in South Africa, Tony re-embarked on another vessel that was no less graceful than the *Moolta*n. This was the *Île de France,* fresh from her refit in Port Elizabeth, another vast and luxurious passenger liner. Packed with anxious American tourists, she had, on 3 September 1939, been the last civilian ship to leave France before the declaration of war. France had no sooner fallen than she was seized by the British and put to use as a troop-ship.

The *Île de France* set sail from Durban on 9 April 1942. There were 5,000 British troops on board, as well as the small contingent of W.A.A.F.s from the *Mooltan,* nearly four times her usual complement. Tony found her 'very overcrowded' and elected to sleep on deck, the heat below decks being unbearable. By day, he observed the movements of the dolphins, the flying-fish and the sharks on the glassy surface of the sea. As they headed north, they began to encounter not only British merchantmen but dhows. They were entering the Arab sphere. A rocky island crowned by a great castle, with a domed roof and white walls running down to the sea, seemed to Tony like a scene from *The Arabian Nights.*

Eventually the ship arrived at her final destination, the port of Suez, where the troops were disembarked and entrained. Tony's draft of about seventy men had a train to themselves. The heat struck one like a hammer. After a long, dusty journey, they were welcomed in the small hours to their latest, temporary home-from-home, a collection of tents on the outskirts of Cairo.

Known as the Base Depot, Royal Artillery, the encampment at Almaza was where freshly-disembarked troops acclimatised themselves and awaited posting to their various units. The tents were dug in to the ground, to a depth of about six feet, to keep out the sand, and were large enough for ten men, though Tony shared his with only two other officers. They had to adjust quickly to the intense, dry heat, the cold nights, and the 'millions of flies', for which 'everyone carried a fly whisk made of horse hair attached to a short piece of cane'. There was, however, an abundance of good food, especially eggs and fruit. Moreover, Tony's enterprising batman had acquired some coconut matting and a few sticks of furniture, so their tent was 'really quite comfortable'.

Tony went off with Dick Grieg to nearby Cairo, where they explored the narrow streets and bazaars. They toured the Giza plateau on horseback, and marvelled at its complex of ancient buildings, including the Great Sphinx and the Great Pyramid. They planned later to sail down the Nile to Luxor and the Valley of the Kings, but, all of a sudden, Dick received his posting. It was to somewhere rather pleasant, with fewer flies. He was given two hours in which to pack up and leave.

Tony's other close friend, Bob Shenton, followed soon afterwards. That left Joan, who was employed at the R.A.F. hospital in Cairo. Tony had no news of his own posting but had been interviewed by a general and by a relatively youthful colonel (he was 41) called Robert Mansergh. The latter had a keen sense of humour and he and Tony had got along famously. 'Do you have any relations in the Indian Army,' asked Mansergh, 'and do you know the Fowles at Chute?' Tony's transfer to Mansergh's own regiment of the Royal Horse Artillery, one of the oldest and proudest, was assured.

Apart from building up their physical fitness, the officers were required to attend a week-long navigation course, which culminated in a gruelling test in the field. Small parties, each of them mounted on a 15cwt truck and a four-wheel-drive gun tractor, were stranded deep in the trackless desert for four days. Using only a map and compass, they had to find their way to various points. This was quite an initiation. The landscape was incomparably grand, except when obscured by a sandstorm. Picking one's way through soft sand was a particular challenge. The surface of Tony's vehicle was 'too hot to touch', and the 'intensely dry wind' left everyone with a raging thirst. On Tony's initiative, a missing party was sought out and retrieved, their vehicle being 'hopelessly stuck', and all returned safely to camp. It had been an adventure similar to that evoked in the film *Ice Cold in Alex* (released in 1958), not least the scene at the end where the parched officers quench their thirst with ice-cold lagers at the nearest bar.[20]

Tony was detailed for a guard of honour that formed up in the sweltering heat to greet a visiting 'Royal' (unnamed, possibly foreign), and was relieved that it did not last too long. In the absence of any 'real work', he preferred to spend his time studying Arabic. His only other job was command of the 'riot squad', which he considered rather a lark, taking pleasure in 'bagging' drunken soldiers who misbehaved on their evenings out. Fascinated by the local colour, he describes the famously importunate pedlars, whom he fended off with a stick and some 'idiomatic Arabic', and the crowded electric trains that ran down the centre of the street, with hordes of passengers perched on the roof or hanging off the sides. He was himself a passenger on the train when, a few weeks later, it came off the rail. The leading car crashed into a shop-front and overturned. Luckily no one was

---

[20] Letters 51, 52, 53; Ross Dix-Peek, 'The S.S. *Île de France* in South African Waters, 1940 - 1945', https://peek-01.livejournal.com/11746.html. On the BDRA, see https://www.bbc.co.uk/history/ww2peopleswar/stories/49/a4046249.shtml. Tony writes later that Grieg knew 'nothing whatever about gunnery but is very good at organising things and at sitting in an office looking busy'; hence his promotion by August 1942 to Captain and Adjutant of his regiment. 'His wife is all right, still doing her hush-hush work for the War Office.' (Letter 62, and *cf.* letter 115.)

killed, though there were a number of broken arms and other injuries.

Naturally suspicious of 'the foreigner', Tony was generally open-minded and revelled in the experience of being abroad. 'The natives,' he wrote, 'are usually very small and very untrustworthy but have a wonderful sense of humour.' According to a Pathé newsreel of the time, they ingratiated themselves with soldiers of every rank by addressing them (not without sarcasm) as 'Captain', or even as 'Captain Mackenzie'. Cairo was a melting-pot, with Copts, Greeks, Jews, Turks and Arabs all living in close proximity and conversing in their various languages. Traditionalists of every class still wore the distinctive red tarboosh or *fez* of the Ottoman era, which added colour to the scene. A symbol of reactionary Islamism, the fez had been banned in Turkey in 1925 and for similar reasons was to be banned in Egypt in 1958, by the revolutionary government of Gamal Abdel Nasser.[21] Tony admired the elegant European quarter, its streets and squares lined with hundreds of flowering trees, but the city mostly consisted of a maze of 'little narrow winding streets where the upper storeys almost shut out the sky. Every now and again one has to get out of the way … as a mule cart, with high wheels and narrow axles, comes by, or as a string of camels, led by a boy about two feet high, plods slowly down the street'. Apart from the proud Bedouin, whom one encountered quite often, all had something to sell; and whatever product or service was on offer, it would invariably be advertised as 'very nice, very cheap, very clean'. Tony concluded on reflection that the Egyptians were 'only half civilised' and that the upper-classes were generally rather unpleasant, and 'very effeminate' with it.

Not surprisingly, there was simmering resentment against the British, whose ambassador, Sir Miles Lampson, had effectively taken over the government of the country. Indeed, Tony never went out without a revolver or indeed unaccompanied, and there

[21] Beverly Chico, *Hats and Headwear Around the World: A Cultural Encyclopedia* (Santa Barbara, California, 2010), pp.175-6.

were parts of the city where it was 'very dangerous and against all rules to go singly or at night as lots of people have failed to come back.'[22]

The Base Wallah's Jaunt to Knightsbridge

To Tony's great delight, his selection for the 2nd Royal Horse Artillery was confirmed. The regiment 'pride themselves on doing everything twice as fast as anyone else and with superior results'. However, the wait to be sent to his unit seemed interminable. Tony played tennis and swam in the camp pool, which was like a warm bath, and was looked after by a wonderful Indian bearer. He received occasional cables from home, but a morale-boosting batch of four letters delivered on 26 May were the first he had received since February.

Introduced at last to 2 R.H.A.'s mess, he immediately encountered old friends from his various training camps and even a couple of men from Benmore. The world suddenly seemed incredibly small. His fellow officers, mostly regulars, were friendly and approachable, a 'really first rate crowd'. Colonel Mansergh himself was 'one of the nicest men I have ever met'.[23] They were also highly professional, and were currently getting to grips with the latest gunnery drills. The regiment had already had to adapt to mechanisation in August 1939; now it was having to familiarise itself with a brand-new fleet of 25-pounder howitzers, a weapon much feared by the Germans. Tony wrote that his

---

[22] Letters 51, 52, 59, 60, 65; 'On Leave in Cairo', Pathé Newsreel 1942, available on YouTube. In Letter 61 Tony refers to the Egyptians as 'still savages' and hopes they will stay out of the war.

[23] The future General Sir Robert Mansergh (1900 - 1970), promoted to Major-General in 1944, was appointed on retirement the Master Gunner of St James's Park, the senior post in the Royal Regiment of Artillery. In a note to Letter 78 Tony remarks that he attended Mansergh's funeral at Westminster Abbey in 1970 and that this was the last time that he wore his full dress uniform.

'horse' was an armoured car and the Observation Posts were tanks.[24]

He was soon sent up to Palestine by train, a four-day trip, to take charge of a convoy of guns and tow them back to Egypt. The landscape of the 'Holy Land', which 'every Christian wished he could visit at some time', was refreshingly different - rolling hills and mountains, their sides thick with the blue jacaranda and other flowering shrubs, and grassy valleys. They drove their three-tonners through the night along a dead straight road, Tony swapping shifts at the wheel with a dependable Punjabi soldier. The bedding arrangements were in the back, a form of discomfort that his father had often experienced in the Great War. Their diet of Bully Beef and biscuits, with a little fresh fruit, was also a little wearing. Tony had been spoiled for too long.

When activity in the Western Desert 'flared up again', as was widely reported in the newspapers, Tony yearned to be with his regiment at the front. Instead, he languished at the School of Artillery in an instructor's role, where he worked 'fairly hard', but it was 'not the same as being where the fun is'. Auchinleck's Eighth Army was struggling to hold the Gazala line, west of the vital port of Tobruk, against Rommel's Afrika Korps. Tony went up for ten days to deliver some guns and was present at the Battle of Knightsbridge, which commenced on 2 June. Knightsbridge was a defensive box, close to the ominously-named 'Cauldron'. There is a graphic depiction by the war artist, Terence Cuneo, of a battery of 107 R.H.A. in action at Knightsbridge on 6 June, the sweating gunners pounding away for dear life at the advancing Panzers. Characteristically, Tony refers later to his enjoyment of 'the few days fighting we had there',[25] which would have been his first taste of action. Later still, he was able to be more specific, describing his first 'baptism of fire' as being 'from shells and a

---

[24] Letters 52, 54, 55, 56, 57; Lt-Col. H.F. Joslen, *Orders of Battle, Second World War, 1939-45* (London, HMSO, 1980), p.567.

[25] Letter 65.

dive bomber'.[26] Fully two years have passed before he admits to his parents: 'Though my orderly was shot by my side and my truck set on fire I do not qualify for the eighth army bar as some wretched clerk forgot to add my name to the list. Anyway, what does it matter?'[27]

Tony had evidently escaped the battlefield by 13 June, the infamous 'Black Saturday', when the Knightsbridge box was abandoned by the depleted Guards Brigade. A battery of the Natal Field Artillery defended the withdrawal with great gallantry, firing at the Panzers over open sights. The last gun in action was manned by Lieutenant Ashley and a signaller, who at length were overrun and captured by the cautiously-approaching Germans.[28]

By 17 June, the Eighth Army was in headlong retreat, the so-called 'Gazala Gallop'. Tony certainly missed the battle that was fought near the port of Mersa Matruh, well inside Egypt, in the last week of June. It was a total rout. He describes this cryptically as a 'spot of trouble' in which 'we gave more than we received', but, as a result, 2 R.H.A. no longer required his services. Actually the regiment had been severely depleted and had lost all its guns. Tony knew people who had been killed and others who had been captured, happily the greater number. Apparently the regiment had earned a special mention from the G.O.C. before being overrun. Tony describes these events as 'a shocking disgrace to the higher command'. The 'Auk' was soon to be sacked, and replaced by the unbearable, if ultimately unbeatable, Montgomery.[29] The now Brigadier Mansergh, who had escaped

---

[26] Letter 69.

[27] Letter 126.

[28] J. Greene and A. Massignani, *Rommel's North Africa Campaign, September 1940 - November 1942* (Conshohocken, 1994), p.163.

[29] When accepting the poisoned chalice, Montgomery is supposed to have remarked to General Ismay: 'After having an easy war, things have now got much more difficult'. Ismay urged him to cheer up, at which Montgomery replied: 'I'm not talking about me, I'm talking about Rommel.' (Winston S. Churchill, *The Second World War,* Vol.IV (London, 1966), p. 420. *Cf.* John Toland, *Battle: The Story of the Bulge* (New York, 1959), p.157.)

the rout, released Tony with apologies, promising that his next posting would be 'really good'.

When not instructing Poles and others in the intricacies of the latest gunnery, Tony was being 'a glorified policeman', or, to give him his official title, Liaison Officer to the Egyptian Police. His role was to concern himself in any offences involving military personnel. The compensation of being a 'base wallah' was the easy access to Cairo. Tony spent his free days at the Gezira Sporting Club in Cairo, an exclusive resort, founded by and for the British Army in 1882, on an island in the Nile, which in normal circumstances had an enormous waiting-list. Its lovely garden had been carved out of the former Khedivial Botanical Garden, and was a true oasis, where Tony could eat well, play tennis or chess with friends and lounge by the swimming pool, though that was 'as warm as a hot bath at Barmston when the range was being funny'. One day he came home to discover the charred and smoking remains of his tent. Luckily, someone had managed to pull out his steel kit-box before it was consumed. Tony had all his kit neatly stowed in the box, in readiness to move at a moment's notice. This included the two books that he prized the most, *The Pickwick Papers* and the Bible.[30]

The weeks passed and still there was no news. A language course was mooted, though he was not told what the language might be. He liked the idea of training native troops. The orders finally came in late-July. He was to report to the Indian Army Depot at Mena, which was some thirty miles away, in the very shadow of the Great Pyramids, and there to embark on a three-week course in Urdu.

The language course was intensive, one of total immersion. Tony and 25 other officers, 'mostly ex-cavalry and R.T.R. [Royal Tank Regiment] men', were completely isolated from other English-speakers. The camp servants and even the *munshi,* or teacher, seemed to speak only Urdu. These arrangements proved

---

[30] Letters 55, 56, 57, 58, 59, 60, 66, 67.

extremely effective. Within quite a short time the students were able to converse at some length with their servants.

The huts in which they were billeted were none too glamorous and infested with wildlife, including moths and bats. One of the Lancer officers found a giant, bottle-green scarab beetle in his bed, so large and threatening that it might have climbed out of a pharaoh's tomb. It was six inches long - the young men excitedly measured it - and somewhat of a distraction from their studies.

Tony thought Mena 'the most unhealthy place in Egypt'. There were no facilities for bathing and, inevitably, 'people started vanishing with malaria, sandfly fever and other tropical horrors till, by the end of the third week, a quarter were in hospital'. Tony learnt to his surprise that their attachment to the Indian Army had been back-dated to 1 July. The 'cavalry boys' were all destined for elite regiments like the Poona Horse and the Corps of Guides. As for Tony, he had, yet again, 'to wait around until a posting came through'.

On the very last day of the course, he, too, was carted off to hospital, having contracted sandfly fever. The 15th (Scottish) General Hospital in Cairo was a large, efficient and extremely pleasant establishment overlooking the Nile. The 'Officers' Mess Suggestion Book' survives from that time and includes such priceless comments as that 'a batman be available up to dinner time for cleaning shoes', that 'no newspapers be removed from the mess', that 'cream be provided for everyone when fruit tart is on the menu' and, from a regular and particularly dyspeptic contributor, T.R. Savage: 'That bread and cake be sent into the mess whole and uncut, thereby limiting handling by Wily Oriental Gentleman'.[31] It will be evident enough that Tony was very well looked-after and the effects of the fever, including loss of vision and hearing, had worn off within the week. The Medical Officer then dispatched him to a curious 'convalescent depot' some 150

---

[31] *15th (Scottish) General Hospital, Officers' Mess Suggestion Book, 1941 - 1945,* Wellcome Collection, RAMC/1079, comments from 10 April, 15 May and 15 Oct 1942.

miles away, on the banks of the Suez Canal. Tony did an hour's P.T. every day, played hockey and cricket, swam in the canal, which was like a hot, salty bath, explored the port of Ismailia, and went out on a yacht, returning guiltily to Mena after a week.

There he was assigned to the 2nd Indian Field Regiment and had the prospect of a proper job at last, one that was much sought-after and usually done by a captain. Tony had long dreamed of serving with a Mountain Artillery regiment. Indeed, he had been repeatedly applying for such a posting since Catterick, and could only credit this lucky appointment to Mansergh's influence. In the old days, the artillery in India had been equipped with the standard 2.5-inch, muzzle-loading 'Screw Guns' which could be dismantled and transported by mules, as celebrated by Kipling in his poem 'Screw-Guns' - 'With seventy gunners behind me an' never a beggar forgets/ It's only the pick of the Army that handles the dear little pets'. Tony was perhaps familiar with the verse; he certainly knew enough about soldiering on horseback to find it intensely glamorous.

Sadly, as he soon discovered, such regiments had mostly been unhorsed in 1940. The 2nd Field were not only fully-mechanised, but a brand new regiment, raised at Bangalore in May of that year. They had arrived in northern Syria in February 1942, and had almost immediately been sent into action on the Gazala line, where they had received a battle honour. Their discipline and morale were impressive, despite their heavy losses in the desert. There was a preponderance of Indian officers in the regiment, including Pram Singh Gyani, a Sikh from the Punjab. In 1932, Gyani had been the first Indian officer to graduate from the Royal Military College, Woolwich, known affectionately as 'the Shop'. Another was Major Paramasiva Prabhakar Kumaramangalam from Madras, who was commissioned from Woolwich a year later, but had previously received a very thorough English education at St Hugh's, Bickley, and Eton. Kumaramangalam's award of the D.S.O. for his bravery in Libya was gazetted on 30

August. Both officers, and several others in the same regiment, went on to achieve high rank in the army of independent India.[32]

Tony, who judged other races as he found them, held both officers and men in the highest regard. Liberated from the 'infested hut', he was now happily ensconced in a tent, complete with mosquito net, sharing it with an urbane, Tamil-speaking officer from the Deccan, a Cambridge graduate who proved to be 'the most pleasant companion'. Not only were the officers of exceptional calibre, but many of the other ranks had been educated at Indian universities. They were 'first class soldiers. Discipline is amazing and turn-out would do credit to any Guards' regiment.' They certainly seemed to be 'far cleaner than the average Tommy'.

Unfortunately, while Tony was convalescing, the bulk of the regiment had shipped out, to a location of which he was unclear. Languishing at the depot, with 'very little military duty to do', he brushed up his Urdu with the munshi, and his riding skills courtesy of the Royal Indian Army Service Corps, whose depot was full of horses in need of exercise. Mounted on a magnificent Arab stallion called Hawai (Urdu for wind), he accompanied two Royal Indian Army Service Corps officers and a groom to Egypt's oldest archaeological site, the Saqqara necropolis:

> 'We set off through the native villages of mud huts and flat-topped houses, with cows, water buffaloes and goats walking around in the narrow streets. Date palms grew from the middle of the courtyards from which half-naked children ran out to stare at us while the dogs ran after us barking and snapping at the horses. We went on along dusty tracks beside irrigation canals with farmers pumping water onto their mud-caked fields of maize and Indian corn. We passed groves of orange trees with their ripening fruit gleaming like golden balls in the

---

32 Letters 63 and 64; https://salute.co.in/2-indian-field-regiment-and-the-battle-of-bir-hachiem-pt-171/; https://en.wikipedia.org/wiki/Paramasiva_Prabhakar_Kumaramangalam.

afternoon sunshine. All kinds of birds flew out of the rushes beside the canal; snipe and brightly coloured Jays, large white birds like small storks and hundreds of others whose names none of us knew and whose colours and cries defy description. We passed farmers working in the fields with their age-old mattocks, chanting weird songs as they dug into the parched soil.'

In one of the hamlets they came to, the path was blocked by a large water buffalo; 'looking like a scolded dog', it swung around menacingly when the lead horse attempted to pass. Eventually the beast was 'led sulkily away'. Striking out into the desert, they had 'a fine gallop' through a deep valley, then looked back from a high ridge to distant Cairo. Thousands of miles of rolling wadis stretched before them, but 'away on the sky-line' they could discern three rocks that 'looked too symmetrical to be natural'. These were the famed pyramids of Saqqara.

Avoiding the steepest wadis, they completed their journey through the heat of the day in two and a half-hours, the horses seeming not to feel the heat at all. Saqqara was breath-taking. Even in the 'lesser' temples, the brightly-coloured carvings seemed 'truly alive'. In the Djoser complex, Tony experienced an 'air of intense mystery … as if hidden eyes were watching us as our footsteps echoed on the paved floor'. Their guide then led them into an enormous tomb some distance away, locking them all inside while, by the dim light of an old oil lamp, they paced the central hall and descended through a tunnel. A dozen chambers lined the sides, each with its enormous granite coffin. At last they came to the magnificent tomb at the end, where 'the coffin lid had been pulled aside by a pulley to reveal what lay within. We climbed up a sort of ladder and looked down; there below us was a mummy with its cover pulled aside and the body in its decaying winding bands open to view. The bandages had fallen from the face which gazed up at us like that of an old man with shrunken features and shrivelled hair. It seemed cold down there after the heat of the desert, the sandy floor deadened the sound of our footsteps and the dim flickering light made it seem very ghostly.'

It was 'fairly dark' when they set off home, 'but the moon was already starting to turn the night into day and, as the last light from the dying day faded to darkness, the sand was turned to a vivid gold and the sky in which the moon reigned supreme, blotting out all other stars, became a beautiful deep blue. A cool breeze sprang up over the desert, most welcome after the heat of the day, and the horses, having rested and knowing that they were heading for home, needed no urging.' They 'trotted through the farmyard where the resting buffaloes grunted up at us from beside the path', and followed the track along the canal, 'where thousands of frogs croaked among the reeds and crickets sang from the tall grasses which grew beside the path'. Presently, they peeled off towards a little village 'which glimmered faintly in the moonlight at the edge of a palm grove'. Here, one of the party had somehow procured an invitation to dinner. It was at a large private house with a courtyard, surrounded by a high mud wall. Their host was 'a very tall man wearing a turban and large flowing robes of pure silk'. They sat on couches around a 'long, low table', and feasted on curried meat and vegetables and all manner of fresh fruit, with coffee and 'a curious sweet wine poured from a large jug with a long curved spout'. The Arabian Nights had truly come to life. After cigarettes and chat with their host and his sons, the three officers and their groom galloped back to Mena where they arrived around midnight.

Tony certainly had some stories to tell in the mess, but felt that he was 'wasting time', however agreeably. Meanwhile, his new regiment was 'very short of officers'. By early August 1942, Tony was calling on the adjutant twice a day, impatient for the orders that never seemed to come.[33]

---

[33] Letters 61, 62, 63, 64, 65, 66. Tony says in Letter 67 that he 'last saw my regiment' (by which he surely means the 2nd Field) on 28 July and that he then languished at Mena 'for about ten days'.

Tony (standing) at Cranleigh School.

Barmston Rectory.

Tony's first serious love interest, the beautiful Isa McDonald, actress and wartime employee at Bletchley Park. They were almost permanently apart.

Tony (second left) in Zululand with his friends Dicky Grieg, Bob Shenton and Dick Marsh. Tony heard later from Bob that the others had been killed.

Sept 1942: from a pleasant camp on the banks of the Tigris, Tony would be ferried across to Baghdad in a rowing boat. He enjoyed a news reel and a film that were shown at an open-air cinema, despite their being in Russian.

1 Dec 1943: in a break from the Tehran Conference, Churchill receives a rousing 'three cheers' from officers and men of P.A.I. Force. On Tony's initiative, they presented him with a Persian miniature.

The location of this superior encampment in the Iraqi desert is not identified. Tony languished here during the harsh winter of 1943-4, when he was with H.Q.R.A. Its amenities included a hospital and a well-stocked N.A.A.F.I. On New Year's Day it was struck by a terrible storm.

From May 1944, Tony was stationed as an intelligence officer in Syria. Beyond saying that it was a 'Paradise' by the sea, he never reveals its whereabouts. 'Life here is far too pleasant,' he wrote.

From 21 Dec 1944, Tony was a mountain gunner at last. Among the perks: a palatial bungalow at No.11 Mall Road, Peshawar (above, with visiting snake-charmer); a stable at the rear that contained his own personal charger, in this case Henry; and opportunities to hunt with the Peshawar Vale, led here by the redoubtable Master, Marjory Diamond.

The Khyber Pass.

CHAPTER IV

DESERT SANDS

Cadillac versus Camel

The exasperated adjutant eventually caved in and, with the C.O.'s permission, issued Tony with a travel pass and instructions to go off and find his regiment. So off he went, after a 'wonderful party' in the mess, to a destination believed to be 'somewhere in Palestine'.

Tony had no idea where he would end up, which was a good deal further away than he thought, but the journey was epic. He travelled mostly by train, through 'wild desert' at first, then through a beautiful coastal plain. Ruined Crusader castles were juxtaposed with the prosperous houses of Jewish settlers. For much of the time the railway line hugged the shore, and Tony saw the 'great white waves beating against the yellow sand'. After 27 hours he arrived at Jaffa, which he described as 'a lovely little town almost falling from the steep mountain side into the sea', and consumed 'the largest and most juicy red beef steak I think I have ever seen'.

An ancient narrow-gauge train, 'drawn by a massive diesel engine', took him on the next leg of his journey. From Haifa, it headed south, through the flat, fertile Jezreel valley, then through increasingly rugged and mountainous country. There was a single, no-frills passenger coach, with an observation platform at the rear; the views were indeed magnificent. The mighty engine chugged its way up a mountain-side, then chugged its way down. 'On one station,' he writes, 'a notice informed us that we were 960 feet below sea level,' a misremembered figure, as the lowest town on the route was Beisan (Beit Se'an), which was a mere 394 feet below. At Beisan the line turned sharply northwards and they headed through the Jordan valley, coming at last to the 'little town' of Samakh, at the southern end of Lake Tiberias - better known as the Sea of Galilee. The train stopped there for an hour, so Tony 'went down to stand by the water's edge', reflecting on the significance of the place to a well-brought up Christian like himself.

Tony re-boarded the train and it 'snorted and puffed its way' out of the British Mandate of Palestine, into the French one, and on through the valley of the River Yarmuk, which was and is truly spectacular, 'the most beautiful country I have yet seen'. Clinging to vertiginous mountain-sides, the line followed the bed of the thundering Yarmuk as it twisted, turned and tumbled through amazing gorges. 'Ten times we crossed the river on high bridges slung between the two walls of the valley.' There seemed to be few houses, but occasionally Tony saw clusters of 'low black hair tents', with thousands of sheep and goats milling around.

At length they came to 'a fairly large town', where the train stopped for an hour. This was probably Deraa, infamous as the place where T.E. Lawrence, on a mission to reconnoitre the station, was captured and assaulted by Turks in 1917. It was dusk, but Tony and his companion, a fellow officer who had come up with him from Cairo, spotted a café in the distance, 'a little table spread out in front of it and lit by lanterns hanging from the doorway'. Tony made for the entrance, but his way was blocked by 'a massive Arab in a flowing head dress and a long cloak with a dagger at his belt. He was having a heated argument with a rather less distinguished looking fellow who was holding a sheep by its long brown fleece.' The tall Arab had his back to Tony, but as he stepped aside to let him pass, gave Tony a terrific slap on the back. 'My dear fellow,' he said, 'what on earth are you doing here?' It was an old friend, now serving with the 'native corps', which presumably refers to Glubb Pasha's Arab Legion. If he was on a secret mission like Lawrence, one hopes that his 'cover' was not blown.

Tony arrived at Damascus at 2 a.m. on 29 August 1942, after 39 hours in his various trains. He settled gratefully into a 'mud hut' in a transit camp; but learned in the morning that he was still hundreds of miles from his regiment, and must await the assembly of a convoy that would transport him there. Far from being 'somewhere in Palestine', it was deep in Iraq, on the farther side of Al Anbar, the Syrian desert. It would take him no fewer than five days to reach it by a 'very bad and difficult road'. At least he would have several days in which to explore the historic city.[1]

Watered by the river Barada, Damascus in 1942 was still surrounded by the oasis that, as early as the seventh millennium B.C., had been its original attraction; there was minimal development beyond its medieval walls, and it was crammed with historic buildings, some dating back to Roman times. Tony's immediate impression was that it was 'very much cleaner than Cairo and had really beautiful bazaars'. With his companion from the train, he scrambled up the nearby Mount Qasioun (3,776 feet) that spectacularly overlooks the city. They saw 'lots of birds; beautiful dark green things, larks and partridge, while lizards sat on the rocks and stared at us; there were also some of those things that change colour' (chameleons). From the top of the mountain

[1] Letters 66 and 67 give a vivid but somewhat confusing account of the journey. In Letter 76 Tony says that his train travelled south from Haifa and then ran 'right up the Jordan valley, stopping all the way and passing to the east of the Sea of Galilee where we stopped for over an hour'. Years later, he incorrectly annotates 'the oldest city in the world' as being Jericho rather than Damascus, but he also mentions seeing 'the house of an ancient oculist', presumably the Damascene Yuhanna Ibn Masawaih (*c.*777 - 857), and he is able to refer specifically to Damascus in Letter 76. The description of the town 'almost falling from the steep mountain side into the sea' better matches Jaffa than Haifa. Otherwise I have reconstructed Tony's journey using S.H. Stephan and Boulos 'Afif, *Palestine by Road and Rail. A Concise Guide to the Important Sites in Palestine and Syria* (Jerusalem, 1942). This was a pocket-guide for soldiers serving in the British Mandate of Palestine. I have referred especially to the fold-out map. Tony avoids naming not only Damascus but also any of the other places on his route, which I have attempted to identify from his descriptions. In letter 114 he confirms that the last leg to Damascus was indeed from Haifa, and that it was a journey he had no wish to repeat! In November 1917, T.E. Lawrence had failed in his attack on the Yarmuk bridges, but many of them were destroyed by Zionist paramilitaries on the night of 16-17 June 1946, the so-called 'Night of the Bridges', and have never been rebuilt.

(nowadays heavily developed) they gazed in wonder over the plateau, the city 'looking like a great white stone' in its midst.

The impending journey across Al-Anbar was a less daunting prospect than it might have been, thanks to the Nairn Transport Company, who had reduced it to a mere 24 hours. After service with Allenby in the Great War, the brothers Norman and Gerald Nairn, from Blenheim, New Zealand, had settled in the Middle East, initially dealing in surplus army vehicles, as well as running a taxi service between Beirut and Haifa, notwithstanding that much of the route was through ploughed fields. In 1923, with official British encouragement, they had pioneered a service from Haifa to Baghdad.

The caravans plying this ancient route had traditionally followed a well-watered path through Damascus, Palmyra, Muhaiwar, Rubaisa and Hit, but that road was infested with murderous Bedouin. The Nairns favoured a more direct route that took them through nearly 500 miles of desert. The country was desolate, featureless and virtually uninhabited, the only watering holes being at Rutbah and Ramadi. The summer temperatures were searingly high and there were frequent, blinding dust storms that might last all day. It could at least be said that the hard, sunbaked surface of the desert (apart from a forty-mile stretch of 'soft sand', east of Ramadi) was good for cars - except in the rainy season, when it turned 'greasy', or might even be inundated.

The Nairns had discovered that the only vehicles able to withstand these conditions were American Cadillacs and Buicks, largely owing to their superior radiators and cooling systems. Maintaining an average speed of 70 m.p.h., they travelled mainly by night in a strung-out convoy formation, navigating by compass, though the route was well worn by now by their own tracks. The drivers were colourful, highly-experienced individuals, who were adept at dodging both gazelles and hostile Bedouin, as well as carrying out roadside repairs.

In 1937, the brothers had added two stainless-steel, fully air-conditioned 'Desert Pullmans' to their fleet, the first such buses in the world. These former oilfield pipe carriers had been specially converted for the Nairns in Indianapolis. Each was sixty feet long and drawn by an enormous truck, or as Tony puts it, 'a mechanical horse with the most massive engine standing eight feet from the ground'. The Nairns had put their entire operation at the disposal of the armed forces for the duration, not least for transporting personnel to the R.A.F.'s enormous base at Habbaniya, between Ramadi and Baghdad, which included a flying school and a hospital.

Tony and his friend considered themselves lucky to be offered seats on the bus, as they were usually reserved for 'senior staff officers and nursing sisters'. Having inspected the gleaming sixty-foot Pullman, whose ten Firestone tyres were reputed to cost £300 each, Tony watched the five tons of luggage being loaded onto the roof. The eighteen passengers then took their seats and the convoy sped off. 'To our right a vast plain stretched away as far as the eye could see, with tufts of scrub and thorn where huge herds of camels were grazing.' Soon they came to a 'real toy fort with iron gates and a watch tower', where passes were checked. Then for hours 'we ran on across the desert, dead flat with very little scrub,' though 'even in this remote and desolate place we passed the occasional tents of Arabs living entirely on their herds, wandering in this vast wilderness owing allegiance to no one'.

There were a lavatory, hand-basins and 'a little kitchen in the back', for serving meals and drinks, and there was iced-water on tap. Tony settled comfortably for the night in his 'adjustable arm-chair which could be folded back to form a bed'. When he awoke, the worst of the desert was behind them, and they were soon passing through 'a plain of palm trees, orchards and villages with a fairly well made road'. The 'green blue' Euphrates was crossed by a 'long bridge' at Ramadi; then there was the forty-mile stretch of soft sand, 'unpopulated save for several very fierce looking men, in flowing cloaks and head cloths, carrying silver-embossed rifles across their backs'. Eventually they came to 'cultivated fields, palm groves and dried up fields where the corn had already been reaped. In the distance the domes and minarets of a large city shone in the afternoon sunshine.'

Rather than enter Baghdad, Tony and his friend alighted at 'a camp in a date grove' on the opposite (west) bank of the Tigris. Yet again Tony was obliged to wait 'while they find out where the regiment is'. Meanwhile, he was visited in his tent by a pair of mongooses and was grateful for it, as they warded off the 'large black snakes' that infested the place. He remarked that the 'sticky heat', in contrast to the 'dry heat' of Egypt, was 'very trying and - my goodness - what heat!'

The little encampment was pleasant enough, the mess consisting of four large tents with the sides removed, and the food was excellent. 'At night lamps are hung in the palms outside and we sit and read or exchange tales under the deep blue sky. There are banks of sweet-smelling rhododendrons about the place ...' The palms grew right down to the glassy river, the lights of the city being reflected in the water. Little rowing boats, each with a lantern at its bow, took passengers to and fro. The young men availed themselves of the service to visit an open-air cinema in town, much enjoying the news reel and film, even though they were in Russian.[2]

---

[2] Letter 67. On the Nairn bus, see especially Maurice D. Hendry, 'The Cadillac Versus the Camel', *Veteran and Vintage Magazine* (Feb 1968), pp.183-96; Imperial War Museum, Royal Air Force in the Middle East, 1944-1945. CM5691.jpg.; https://en.wikipedia.org/wiki/Nairn_Transport_Company.

O.C. Hillside

Once more chafing at the inactivity, Tony applied to the Brigadier for a temporary job. Late one evening, he was unexpectedly put on a very comfortable sleeper, 'which even had clean sheets', and transported northwards, in the direction of Mosul, for about 150 miles. He was then met by a truck and conveyed to the middle of nowhere, a hot, dusty encampment on a 'large, sandy plain below a ring of low sandy and rocky hills'. The unit to which he had been assigned was the 1st Indian Anti-Tank Regiment. The C.O. was an Indian, a kindly man, but very correct. Tony explained that he was there 'to polish up my Urdu'. The obliging colonel sent him straight to 2 Battery.

Tony was immediately handed the role of Mess Secretary, responsible for providing three meals a day for the five officers in the battery. Three of them were Indian, all regulars, all trained in England at the Shop. Their names were Major Habibullah 'H.B.' Khan, Captain Khulla and Lieutenant 'Sam' Sammanwar. The fourth was an Englishman whom Tony recognised from his schooldays, a Lieutenant Baker. They had boxed together and played on opposing sides at rugby when Tony was at Cranleigh and Baker a pupil at the rival Brighton College. The novelist Paul Scott makes much in his *Raj Quartet* of the network of public school men (from which Scott himself and his character Ronald Merrick felt excluded), especially the 'Chillingburians', and of their tendency to encounter old acquaintances in the most improbable situations. Tony certainly seemed to do so quite regularly.[3]

Despite being housed in a 'mud hut with a straw and mud roof', the mess turned out to be very congenial. Tony set about making it comfortable. He scraped together a few sticks of furniture, carpets and even a wireless. Under his supervision, they also seem to have eaten rather well. The staple evening fare was

---

[3] *E.g.* his meeting the former Cranleigh School Captain at Catterick (Letter 21) and another school contemporary, Elliot, at B.D.R.A. (Letter 60).

curried meat or chicken which had been 'bought alive for about 9d'.

The presence of the battery in this remote place was explained by the 'large steel towers and massive chimneys' that were scattered all around. Nearby were an oil refinery and a pumping station. The reddish glow of the burning gases lit the night sky. By day, it was too hot for the men to do anything other than play games, polish their armoured cars and guns, and wash their own bodies and clothes in the nearby well, which they did assiduously.

The British could not tolerate any threat to their land bridge between Egypt and India, nor to the vital oilfields and refineries. On 1 April 1941, pro-Axis Iraqi nationalists had seized power in a *coup d'état.* When they laid siege to R.A.F. Habbaniya, the Vichy French administration facilitated Axis air-raids from Mosul. The British responded swiftly, invading and taking control of mandated Syria and Lebanon, and toppling the nationalist government in Iraq. The 1st Indian Anti-Tank Regiment, raised at Hyderabad in 1940, had arrived in late 1941, specifically to help guard against any further invasion. It was soon to be subject to the 'Persia Iraq Command', established at Baghdad on 18 September, whose mission was partly to bolster the Russian supply routes from the Gulf, but above all to secure the oilfields and refineries from attack by air and land.[4]

As the danger receded, Tony enjoyed the lack of interference, the greater autonomy and authority that was allowed the British officer in the Indian Army, but he hated having so little to do. 'Occasionally we have a little fun when the local tribesmen try to get tough. The other night one of our sentries was shot and we had quite a lot of kit taken; we raided a local village and got it all

---

[4] General Sir Maitland Wilson, *Despatch on the Persia and Iraq Command Covering the Period from 21st August, 1942, to 17th February, 1943.* London: War Office, in *Supplement to the London Gazette,* 28 Aug 1946, p.4333. The first 'gusher' had been struck, near Kirkuk, as recently as 1927: C.J. Edmonds, 'The Kurds of Iraq', *Middle-East Journal,* Vol.11, No.1 (Winter 1957), p.54. On 2nd A/T Regiment, see http://www.rothwell.force9.co.uk/burmaweb/1st-Indian-aa-atk.htm.

back. We are now expecting to receive a counter raid. The men love it as they are really still savages at heart.' He was nevertheless very attached to them and could converse with them quite well in Urdu. 'The men are all regulars; when it comes to turn-out, drill and discipline they put any R.H.A. or Guards Brigade in the shade.' Their uniform consisted of khaki pugarees, khaki shirts, shorts and stockings, and short khaki puttees over their black boots. When off duty, they wore pugarees in the battery colours. Tony was struck by how intensely loyal they were to their officers, of whom they brooked no criticism, though they had always to be handled with tact. Their personal administration and hygiene were legendary. They were 'wonderful shots, even with the Tommy gun', and good drivers too, but unfortunately had 'no idea about M.T.', and were 'quite hopeless when it comes to looking under the bonnet'. They were, of course, quite new to motorised transport, being instead experienced handlers of mules and horses from their days on the North-West Frontier.

Tony was alone with them for much of the time, especially when commanding an outpost called 'Hillside' in the nearby mountains. Within a day of his arrival, the C.O. had applied to the Brigadier to have him formally posted to the regiment. This meant promotion, with immediate effect, to full Lieutenant and Troop Commander; but the Brigadier's ready assent to the C.O.'s request had caused him some anguish. To a dedicated practitioner like Tony, anti-tank gunnery presented few intellectual challenges, as it required 'very little technical knowledge' or 'brain work'. After all, 'one can always see the target and no maths or survey are involved'. Moreover, that coveted posting to a Mountain Battery now seemed more elusive than ever, though he was no doubt gaining the sort of experience that would prepare him for one in the future. He even kept up his riding, courtesy of a neighbouring cavalry unit, going out every day with H.B. and Sam 'so that after the war, or even before if we are lucky, when we revert to Mountain gunners and get the horses back we will still be able to ride - rather they will still be able to ride and I shall just be able to do so'.

He certainly relished his two weeks in mid-September as O.C. 'Hillside', where his men built him 'a little stone hut' with a beaten earth floor and a straw roof, whilst they themselves (there were well over a hundred men under his command) lived in similar huts along the valley. Tony's cook and batman occupied 'a little tent just outside', so he was well looked after. His Viceroy's Commissioned Officer or 'V.C.O.', in his case a Subedar,[5] handled much of the routine work, but Tony walked miles along steep tracks to visit the piquets, and the men all seemed very happy to have such exciting work. After all, priority on the 'Leave to India' list had been promised to the first of them to 'bag' a sniper. The Colonel came up one day and tried to surprise one, nearly getting shot for his pains. Tony thought this 'a very good show on the sentry's part and told the Colonel so'. It was nevertheless a tough time for the men, coinciding with the month of Ramadan. They were 'not allowed to eat, drink or smoke while the sun is up. Anyone who breaks the fast is very much looked down on by the others.' The camp was alive with 'scraggy' foraged chickens, which were being fattened up for the impending feast. Meanwhile, Tony observed huge lizards and snakes (believed to be harmless), and many colourful varieties of bird, including a 'lovely little vivid green bird with orange underneath who sings a very merry song'. There were gazelles and long-haired goats, and picturesque, if menacing natives, all with 'silver embossed rifles and long knives under their flowing cloaks'. By day it was scorching hot and the water had to be brought up each morning in a cart. By night there was the risk of attack by tribesmen, who on one occasion rained rifle- and machine-gun fire on the camp. This was Tony's 'second baptism of fire'. He

[5] A subedar wore two stars on his shoulder and was equivalent to a lieutenant: see Michael Creese, *Swords Trembling in their Scabbards: The Changing Status of Indian Officers in the Indian Army, 1757 - 1947* (Leicester, 2007), p.xiii.

took a patrol out to deal with them, but the tribesmen melted away.

Down on the plain, Tony availed himself of the swimming bath and other recreational facilities of one of the refineries, and made trips to the nearest town, which seemed to be very ancient indeed. It was on the near side of a dry river bed, beyond which, reached by an old stone bridge, an equally-ancient walled city arose from a rock. That city was clearly Kirkuk, which stands on an ancient *tell* or mound beside the Khasa. The river is virtually dry in summer, but becomes a torrent in winter. The city walls date from the Ottoman period, but the mighty citadel is of extraordinary antiquity, its foundations possibly dating back some 3,500 years, to the time when ancient 'Arrapkha' was part of the Assyrian Empire. To Tony, Kirkuk seemed to capture the essence of the Orient. 'The road winds round the base of a high cliff, on the left a spring pours out from beneath two stone arches, round the spring date palms and the most vivid green grass make the most striking contrast to the rocky desert and hills behind. On the other side of the river a huge rock rises from the bank crowned by the old walled town, like a cork of red stone, resting on its summit. Round the base of the rock there are more date palms with the now golden dates shining from below the green palm fronds while goats and camels wander grazing among the palms watched over by small boys who, at a distance, look very clean and colourfully dressed. Round the spring large columns of the pidgin *[sic]* houses, which adorn all native towns and villages, rise like huge fingers and flocks of pidgins call to each other from the perches. At the foot of the hill there is a lovely garden, full of all kinds of flowers and shrubs.'

So tantalising from a distance, Kirkuk was considered dangerous and was therefore 'out of bounds'. Its nearer suburb, however, was surprisingly good for supplies, including razor blades, tobacco and even polish for Tony's father's very superior Sam Browne belt, which he habitually wore, with his revolver in its leather holster. One day, visiting the town in quest of a dart board, a chess set and even, improbably, a gramophone for the mess, Tony was 'twice saluted by majors who thought my red pips, lanyard and the now beautifully polished Sam Brown[e] must belong to a Lt Col'. Young for a Lieutenant, Tony now aspired to a full-term commission, with which he felt he could 'get up to Colonel or Lieut[enant] Colonel fairly easily'. Apparently he already looked the part.[6]

He hated being back with the regiment, however, as there was so little to do. There seemed to be 'less chance of seeing any real fighting than ever before'. Some of his fellow officers had never yet heard a shot or even seen the enemy. Offered the role of Assistant Adjutant, he characteristically declined. 'I told the C.O. that in civil life I would rather be a farm worker than a bank clerk and the same went for the army.' The regiment was now dispersed over a large area and Tony lived in a hole in the ground, dispensing with the poles from his tent and using the canvas as a roof. Temperatures were dropping and the nights were cold. There was talk of his going back to Cairo for an M.T. course, when at least he would be able to collect his winter clothes. He organised hockey for the men and found them 'extremely clever with their sticks, which seems very odd to me as they are usually rather clumsy, always moving with the slow methodical deliberation of the East'. The officers were required to entertain each other with lectures on any subject. Tony chose 'Forestry' and 'the Flash Spotting Battery of the Survey Regiment'. There were rumours of a return to the regimental station in the Punjab which would have made for an interesting overland journey.

Then suddenly, in late September, Tony was summoned to the Colonel and told that he had at last been reclaimed by his regiment, the 2nd Indian Field. He had had the briefest of introductions to the regiment in August, before succumbing to sandfly fever. By the time he recovered, they had already moved on. Tony knew only that they were east of Cairo, but he had no

[6] Letters 68, 69, 70, 71, 72.

notion of quite how far. It is astonishing how, in an age of advanced communications, the regiment and one of its officers had completely lost track of each other for over a month. Their C.O. was apparently incensed at Tony's being poached by an 'inferior' anti-tank regiment (whose hapless colonel must have felt the sting of his ire) and demanded that he be returned forthwith. Tony, of course, was delighted.[7]

The Burra-Khana and the Wonder of the World

As it happened, the 2nd Indian Field Regiment were also part of 'Persia and Iraq Force' and not too far away, although it took Tony two days in the train to get there. He arrived on 1 October 1942. Their camp was romantically positioned in the desert west of Musayyib, a large, ancient city that straddles both banks of the Euphrates, some forty miles south of Baghdad. The country was very wild and inhabited by nomadic, or semi-nomadic tribes, some of whom were authentic Bedouin.[8]

Along the river bank, which was thick with palm trees, was the occasional ruined settlement, the haunt of jackals and wild dogs and of magpies that darted in and out of the thorn. Away from the river, the palm soon gave way to thick, thorny scrub and then, after about a mile, to the 'usual dusty plain' which, disappointingly, was the site of the camp. The small tents of the officers were pitched around some larger ones, which housed the

---

[7] Letters 72, 73, 74.

[8] With the censor's permission, Tony subsequently locates the camp 'in the desert west of Musaiyib on the Euphrates' (letter 94). On the tribes, see Gertrude Bell, *The Arab of Mesopotamia* (Government Press, Basrah, 1916), pp.1-10, 84 *et seq.* The Bedouin of that region were originally 'immigrants from the deserts of the Arabian peninsula'. Despite their turning cultivator and being only 'half-nomad', their 'tribal law and customs hold good and tribal blood feuds continue to be a terrible scourge ... A periodic reversion to tents is common.' The authentic Bedouin is determined by his genealogy, of which the Arabs are as knowledgeable as they are particular.

battery commander and the battery office as well as the rank and file. It was usually more comfortable to sleep outside. The officers' mess consisted of a pair of large tents put together, with tables down the centre. Its forty or so members, many of them Oxford graduates, would sit there chatting into the night or listening to music programmes on Radio Berlin, as the B.B.C. seemed to broadcast very little music on any channel, being dedicated instead to interminable discussions about football or the progress of the war.[9] Thus for many an evening would the cultivated voices of the officers and the strains of 'Lilli Marlene' ring out across the desert, the gazelle and the wild pig pricking up their ears at the unwonted sounds.

Tony's battery, number 7, of which he was G.P.O., was entirely composed of Sikhs, a noble warrior race with a fine sense of humour. With eighty men under his command, he was left to his own devices. So pleased to 'get back to a real gun regiment', he was soon helping to strip down a gun (covering himself in oil and grease in the process), or shooting all night in the desert. He found that he and the Sikhs were alike: they 'have to be kept busy to keep them happy,' he wrote, and 'the same goes for me'.

In command of the battery, and for a time the senior officer in camp, was the seemingly very youthful Major James Hepper, a regular R.A. officer who was actually aged 33, not 26 as Tony supposed.[10] In his first week with the regiment, Hepper detailed Tony to join him for a very special experience. They were invited

[9] *Cf.* letter 105. Tony adds that neither subject is 'of the slightest interest to any of us'.

[10] The future Brigadier James Mortimer Hepper, D.S.O., O.B.E. He was born on 24 March 1909, educated at Wellington School, Somerset, and at 'the Shop', and commissioned in 1929 (*The Half-Yearly Army List,* Jan 1939, p.914-9, https://www.thepeerage.com/p75277.htm#i752765 and Tony's notes to Letter 74). Married since 1938 with two small sons, one of whom he had probably never seen, Hepper was mentioned in dispatches for his services in Burma. He later commanded a Gurkha artillery regiment during the Malayan Emergency and served in the Cyprus campaign. He and Tony kept in touch (letters 188, 216) and were present at the same investiture in 1952. Hepper retired to Morchard Bishop in Devon, and died in 1987 (Probate Register).

to what the old India hands referred to as a *burra-khana,* a 'big feast' laid on by one of the local sheikhs. Mounted on a Jeep, they drove eastward into the desert for about fifteen miles, as directed by a guide. Suddenly they were surrounded by what seemed to be thousands of horsemen with rifles and swords, who started firing into the air and yelling. The cavalcade led them in a great cloud of dust to a fortified village. It had stout mud walls and tall wooden gates. A great throng of warriors had arrived for the gathering. They had come with their flocks and their womenfolk and had pitched their tents below the walls. The two British officers were escorted by an interpreter (whose command of English was 'fairly good' and who obligingly advised them at various points on the appropriate etiquette) to the most prominent house in the village. It was 'a large hall-like building with thick mud brick walls, small barred windows without glass and a thatched roof supported by a row of beautifully carved wooden pillars'. This was the house of the Sheikh, who awaited them at the door.

The dim interior of the building, which was pleasantly cool, was exactly like a medieval baronial hall, except for a small recess to the left of the door, which contained an iron stove and a chimney. As with the Western counterpart, there was a dais at the far end for the prominent people. This was sumptuously carpeted, as were the walls, and low couches lined the sides. A small fire crackled in the middle of the room, the smoke drifting up to the roof 'to find its way out the best it could'.

Arriving just before 11 a.m., Tony and Hepper were directed to the places of honour on each side of the Sheikh, various chiefs occupying the remaining seats. The interpreter sat at his feet and the tribal elders sat cross legged around the walls, 'their rifles resting between their legs and their daggers showing from beneath their long cloaks'. They drank some exceptionally delicious coffee that had been roasted in front of them over the open fire, then ground in a wooden bowl at their feet. Processions of tribesmen came in to stare at them for a few minutes before going out again. There were no women in sight, but they must have peered inquisitively at the visitors when they first arrived, through gaps in the sides of their tents. The interpreter explained that T.E. Lawrence had once sat in that very room. That might have been in April 1916, when Lawrence, a staff officer based in Cairo, as yet unproven as a warrior, navigated the Tigris in a paddle-steamer-turned-troopship from Basra to Wadi, and returned the same way. His mission was not to recruit, but to offer a hefty bribe to the Turkish general besieging the British at Kut. That mission had failed, but according to Tony's interpreter, he had so charmed their friend the Sheikh, on this or another occasion, that the Sheikh had been persuaded to send two hundred of his warriors across the desert to participate in the Arab Revolt, which had been launched in June of that year.

After their coffee, the company went outside for a 'war dance', of which there are variants throughout the Arab sphere, always accompanied by an insistent drum-beat. 'The men all charged around in circles chanting the most weird songs, waving swords and daggers and firing rifles into the air. This lasted for two hours with the last half hour being like the dance of fiends in hell; they all shed their cloaks, covered their hands and faces with red paint and went really mad. The climax came when the Sheikh mounted a horse and rode into their midst brandishing a long curved silver sword. After this they gave us a demonstration of horsemanship with the only visible means of controlling their mounts being the waving of a stick, rifle or sword in front of its eyes … [T]he horses turned almost within their own length while not paying the least attention to the bullets that were still whistling around.'

Returning to the hall at about 1.30 p.m., the party finally sat down for the feast, which was 'burra' indeed. 'Never have I seen such mountains of food; we had a low table before us with a line of massive silver trays down the centre, each filled with rice crowned by half a sheep with lumps of fat seeping down into the rice. All round these large dishes, which were about three feet high, there were rows of smaller ones holding vegetables swimming in gravy, whole chickens and pigeons. There were huge bowls of curds made from goats' milk and great slabs of bread made from unleavened flour.' Without the benefit of a knife, fork or spoon, Tony claimed to have devoured, among other things, 'three whole chickens, which were most beautifully roasted over [the] wood fire, simply tearing off the legs and sucking off the meat. I had great chunks of mutton, torn off the bone and dripping with fat; there were lambs stuffed with raisins and dates as well as mountains of rice and vegetables.' The rice was eaten 'by pressing lumps of it together into a ball and then soaking it in the gravy with the vegetables. This was followed by every imaginable type of fruit, the table being literally covered with it.' These scenes were repeated among the men in the centre of the hall. How different, he must have thought, from the home life of the dear Archbishop of York! The meal was finished off with delicious Persian tea, yet more coffee, and cigarettes 'made from tobacco grown in the mountains'. At last, barely able to move under their own steam, the pair 'were given an escort of about a hundred men to see us all the way back to our camp.' Their arrival in such style must have created quite a stir, but is reported without further comment.[11]

Hepper got them both back into shape by sending the entire battery, including its mascot, a 'beautiful, long-haired white Billy goat, with immense curved horns', on a 25-mile route march. Tony thought it 'very good fun'. They set out at 2 p.m. and returned by the light of the moon, having stopped for a meal 'in a date grove by the side of a spring'. The following evening, that of 17 October, a terrific storm blew away half the camp. Tony writes that his bath was retrieved from about 400 yards away. The storm presaged 'a very violent change in the weather', with torrential, 'almost horizontal' rain accompanied by 'howling winds which carry all before them'. The 'thirsty sand' of the desert would rapidly turn to 'squelching mud'. In the intervals, it was 'warm

[11] Letters 75, 76; Michael Asher, *Lawrence, The Uncrowned King of Arabia* (Harmondsworth, 1999), pp.145-8. I have been unable to identify the Sheikh.

enough for just an open shirt and shorts' under a cloudless sky, but the threat of further storms was constant.

On 18 October, when the storm of the previous night had cleansed the palm trees of dust and even encouraged the growth here and there of patches of grass, Tony went out in a truck to the site of Babylon, the famed city of Nebuchadnezzar. Accompanied by Derek, the senior lieutenant in 7 Battery, Tony drove along a rough track through miles of flat, lush countryside, and hardly saw a soul. There was a single, Bedouin encampment, notable for its herd of white, humpless camels. Tony's experience of the ruined city, which rises out of the plain, was 'most disappointing', the main palace complex 'being only a pile of rubble', but the site covers a large area and he can barely have seen a fraction of it. He mentions the well-preserved 'main street' (the so-called 'Processional Way'), and a series of vaulted chambers under the palace 'which were said to have been used as potting sheds'. The 'Hanging Gardens' of old were a lush, rooftop terrace, and are indeed described by classical writers as being over a vaulted substructure; the celebrated 'Wonder of the World' had otherwise entirely vanished. Tony learned that the German Oriental Society had excavated the site before the war, carrying off many treasures, including wall decorations, so there was less to see than there might have been. The baked bricks, of which the city was largely built, had been systematically robbed over the centuries by the locals. Perhaps the difficulty of the journey had left him hard to please.

There was little else on offer by way of recreation other than hockey in the evening or going out into the desert with a shotgun. Wild pig was the most alluring game on offer but the best shots in the regiment had failed as yet to bag one. Tony at least managed to bring home a brace of sand grouse for his supper.[12]

---

[12] Letter 76.

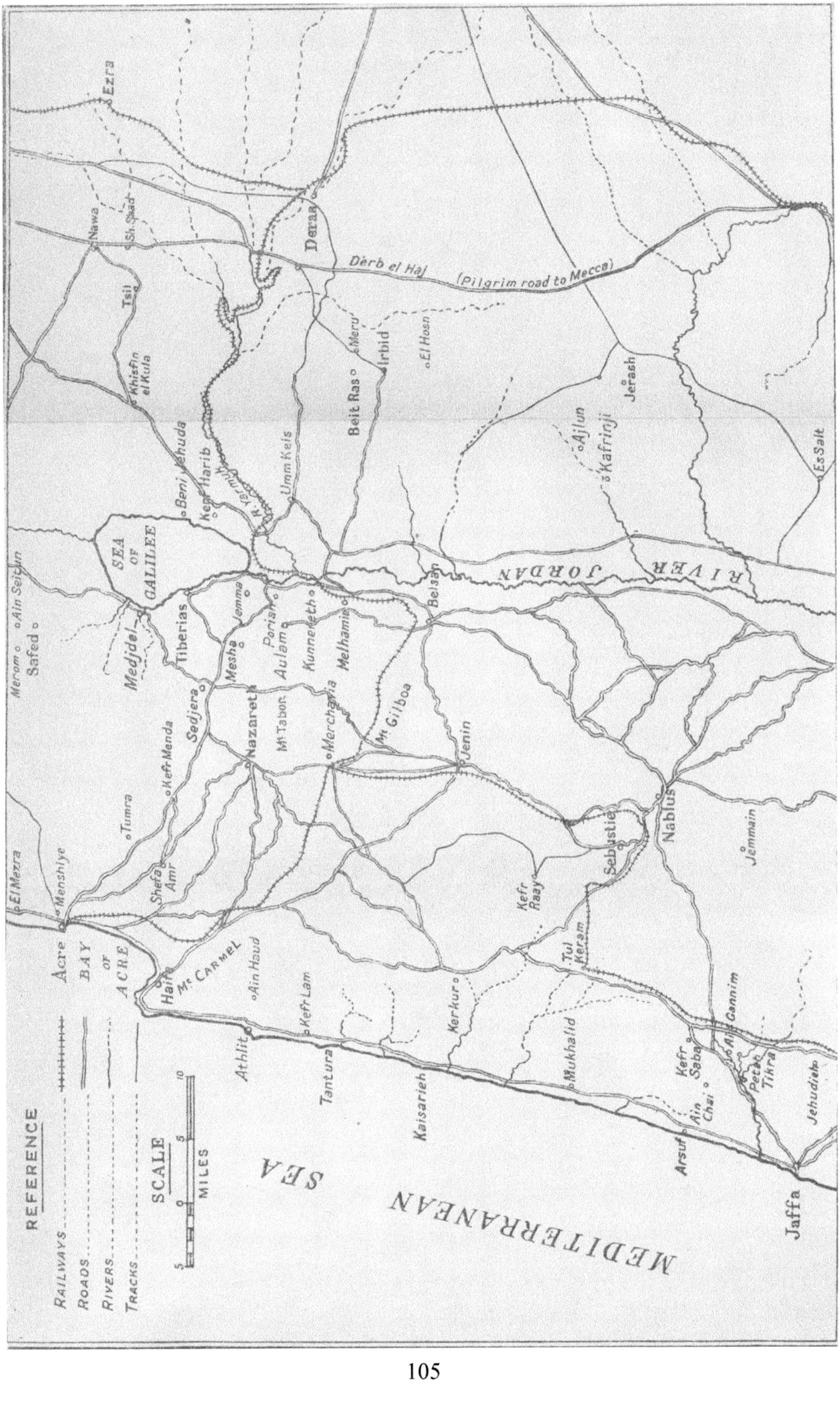
REFERENCE
RAILWAYS
ROADS
RIVERS
TRACKS
SCALE
5 0 5 10
MILES
MEDITERRANEAN
SEA
BAY OF ACRE
Acre
Haifa
Mt CARMEL
Athlit
Tantura
Kaisarieh
Arsuf
Jaffa
Ain Haud
Kefr Lam
Kerkur
Mukhalid
Ain Chai
Kefr Saba
Ain Gannim
Petah Tikra
Jehudieh
Tul Kerem
Kefr Raay
Sebustie
Nablus
Jemmain
El Mezra
Menshiye
Shefa Amr
Tumra
Kefr Menda
Sedjera
Nazareth
Mt Tabor
Merchavia
Mt Gilboa
Jenin
Merom
Ain Seitun
Safed
Medjdel
Tiberias
Mesha
Jemma
Poriah
Aulam
Kunneleth
Melhamie
Beisan
SEA OF GALILEE
RIVER JORDAN
Beni Jehuda
Kefr Harib
R. Yarmuk
Umm Keis
Khisfin el Kula
Tsil
Nawa
Sh. Saad
Ezra
Deraa
Dèrb el Haj
(Pilgrim road to Mecca)
Meru
Irbid
Beit Ras
El Hosn
Ajlun
Kafrinji
Jerash
Es Salt

SYRIA & LEBANON
Railways
Main Routes
Oil pipelines
Land over 5000 ft
0
50
100
Scale of Miles
N
SEE INSET
TURKEY
SYRIA
IRAQ
TRANSJORDAN
EGYPT
CYPRUS
TAURUS MOU
BERLIN BAGHDAD RAILWAY
EUPHRATES R
Tigris R
Great Zab R
Little Zab R
Khabur R
Balikh R
Firat R
Orontes R
Kara Sou R
Jordan R
Litani R
Sea of Galilee
Dead Sea
Salt Lake
Jebel Druse
Cilician Gates
Kirkuk
Baghdad
Mosul
Haditha
Ana
Abu Kemal
Rutba
Ras el Ain
Deir ez Zor
Raqqa
Hamman
Sukhne
Meskene
Palmyra
Djerablous
Gaziantep
Bab
Kilis
Azaz
Aleppo
Idlib
Harim
Antioch
Alexandretta
Latakia
Hama
Selemiya
Homs
Forqloss
Qaryatein
Djedeide
Damascus
Qatana
Tripoli
Beirut
Sidon
Merdjayoun
Tyre
Baniyas
Acre
Haifa
Tiberias
Nazareth
Nablus
Tulkarm
Tel Aviv
Sarafand
Jericho
Jerusalem
Bethlehem
Amman
Ajlun
Beersheba
Gaza
El Arish
Port Said
Kantara
Ismailia (Moascar)
Suez
LEBANON
Ras Baalbek
Baalbek
Labouie
Bekaa Valley
Riyak
Zahle
Batrun
Bourouch
Mt Hermon

Baghdad

The regiment had ticked along happily under Hepper's command but a new C.O. arrived on 26 October. Lieutenant-Colonel Johnny Willans made an immediate impression. 'When Jonny Willands *[sic]* yells one does not hang about,' wrote Tony, but he was 'a first class man who really knows his stuff'; nor did he care 'what the old conservatives think'. He seemed the ideal C.O. for 'a really crack regiment', although, as Tony concedes, he was not the easiest man to get along with. Better still, Tony's old friend Bob Mansergh, 'a really great man with large ideas', had re-entered the stage as a Brigadier, the local Commander Royal Artillery. Tony, meanwhile, had become senior lieutenant in the regiment, his friend Derek (a pre-war Territorial) having been promoted to captain.

Willans required a high level of proficiency in Urdu from his officers and, to that end, organised thrice-weekly visits from a *munshi,* although the poor man, serving with the Indian Army Education Corps, had to be driven in from Baghdad and the journey took about three hours. Preparing for written exams in January and April, Tony was a diligent student and put aside an hour a day for homework, practising both spoken and written Urdu and augmenting his vocabulary.[13]

Willans ordered an immediate 'operation' to test the mettle of his men. Tony drove all night through the desert with his guns, navigating by the stars and compass. The stars were often invisible, however, owing to the frequent heavy rain and sandstorms. The following morning, dug in and camouflaged, the

---

[13] Letters 77, 83, 84. John Harte Harris Willans, born 29 May 1902, commissioned in 1922, had served in Burma in 1930-32 and on the North West Frontier in 1935 *(The Half Yearly Army List,* Jan 1939). He retired as a Brigadier. In a note to Letter 77, Tony says that he was known as '"Jasper" to his friends, of whom he had very few', but he clearly thought highly of him at the time. In letter 104 (23 November 1943), he writes of his being not an easy man to live with.

guns opened fire and continued to do so until about 2 p.m. The skies were clear that night and they followed a dead-straight compass course over the firm sand, firing at further targets during the third day, and returning early in the morning on the fourth. Tony was relieved that his knowledge of Urdu had proved more than satisfactory, 'quite complex orders' being 'understood and acted on without questions or misunderstanding'. Willans would have been pleased.[14]

Then suddenly, on 6 November, the regiment packed up the camp and journeyed northwards. Their new position was only about 25 miles away, but the drive was exhausting, there being no roads other than the deeply rutted cart-tracks and camel routes of the locals. A new camp took shape on the now familiar plain. It was low, flat and 'desolate beyond belief', for nothing grew there, apart from a few patches of thorn. It was enlivened for Tony, however, by its abundant birdlife, including eagles, water-wagtails, larks, and the flocks of sparrows that gathered on his tent in the daytime.

The rows of tents formed three sides of a square, the fourth being formed by the tightly-packed guns and vehicles. Each tent was dug in to the ground to a depth of three to six feet, the first task for the weary gunners, as the winter nights were unforgiving. The camp was rounded off by a wire fence with tin cans hanging off it, to ward off thieving Arabs. There seems to have been a veritable epidemic of robbery from British camps, especially of firearms but also of any kit the thieves could get hold of. The four-man night-patrols had orders to shoot on sight, but the pilferers were prepared to take extraordinary risks, and Tony felt it prudent to sleep with a loaded revolver. At the end of the first week his was the only battery not to have lost any kit or weapons, which he mainly attributed to the vigilance of his Sikhs.

Tony's tent was tiny, a mere six feet by eight, its floor covered with coconut matting and the little flat-woven blue rug or 'Dhurri'

---

14 Letters 77, 78.

that was issued to all Indian troops. His camp bed was set up at the far end as one went in. The opening was normally 'shut tight to exclude the freezing wind. On one side I have my camp table, with books and a lamp on it, and a small bookcase made from a gelignite box which holds all my clothing, ledgers, account books, training manuals, vehicle log books, gun history sheets and such like. On the other side of the tent I have my tin trunk which followed me up here, taking two months over the journey, and my now very battered and faded suitcase. Under the bed I have an ammunition box full of tinned food, two weeks' supply, an eight gallon cask of water, a tin of oil for my lamp and stove and the rolled up valise. It is really very comfortable and quite warm as I have a little oil stove which heats the tent and boils a kettle at the same time.'

By late November the men wore Battle Dress against the cold, and had been issued with sheep-skin coats. These were 'made out of the whole fleece and lined with leather'. Tony was soon having to break the ice on his water to shave; by December, the wind coming down 'over the mountains from Russia' cut through both battle dress and greatcoat 'like a knife'. At least, with the coming of winter, there were fewer flies to plague one.

The rations in their new camp were disappointing, though Tony acknowledged that he had been spoilt, and that conditions were probably far worse at home. There was, however, an abundance of fresh game, particularly pigeon and sand-grouse. Tony and three other officers returned from one early-morning shoot with a bag of 24 pigeon. Tony had accounted for four of these, and the C.O., fittingly, for twelve. Two games of hockey per week kept Tony fit, and he was even selected to play for the regiment. Despite his claims to have kept 'very well indeed', conditions in the camp were neither comfortable nor healthy. Short bursts of torrential rain would leave the entire camp-site a sea of mud, which loosened every tent peg. There was frost in the morning and occasional snow, as well as the incessant wind, all of which was very debilitating. Tony no doubt understates the effects of 'the local disease' - 'desert' or 'bush sores', which were 'very unsightly' and would have earned him time off had he been able to spare it. Every cut or scratch seemed to become infected. In addition, a scorpion sting had left him with a severely swollen hand.

The purpose of re-locating had probably been to accommodate an intake of 150 recruits, men plucked from their villages and farms to replace the battle casualties of the previous May. Like all the colonial troops of the Second World War (of whom India alone provided more than two and a half million), these men were volunteers, not conscripts.[15] Most were illiterate and had never seen the sea, let alone a car or an aeroplane. Tony's job was 'to try to teach sixty of these and transform them from uneducated Indian farmers into soldiers worthy of the best battery in the Indian Army'. Tony was also Battery Education Officer and as much time was spent doing 'office work' in his tent as on the parade ground. By 10 December he felt able to report that his men, though not 'perfect', were 'nearly all twice the size, walk upright, know how to fulfil their job in action and a majority of them can write,' as well as perform simple sums of addition and subtraction, which sounds like an extraordinary achievement in so short a time.

With the backing of both Mansergh and Willans, Tony had already submitted his formal application for a regular commission. As if not busy enough, he was also sent on a three-day course in demolition, blasting and sabotage, which he found 'most entertaining'. The emphasis was on blasting 'really large lumps of rock ... from drilling the holes and setting the gun cotton or gelignite to firing the fuse'. The gunners would thus be equipped to construct their own gun pits in the mountains, without recourse to the Sappers. Though they yearned to have 'another crack' at the Germans in North Africa, the men of the

---

[15] Nigel Biggar, *Colonialism: A Moral Reckoning* (London, 2023), p.273.

Battery sensed that there were 'other things in store for us', very possibly involving proper mountainous terrain.

Meanwhile, Willans had decided to reduce the punishing workload. No further work was to be done on Saturday afternoons or on Sundays. Though the camp was only five miles from Baghdad, Tony had rarely had time to visit. When the moon shone on the Tigris, it looked 'as romantic as its reputation demands', but he was put off by the smell and the fact that it was home to all the thieves who beset the camp. On Sunday 6 December, however, he and an officer called Allen drove into the city in 'a lovely little 8cwt Morris with four wheel drive and a top speed of 70 mph', in order to attend the morning service at St George's. Built in 1936, a monument to the dead of the Great War, St George's was an Anglican church serving a vast parish, and was located on Hayfa Street, a stone's throw from the Tigris. Tony describes it as 'a lovely little church, quite modern but very well designed and beautifully appointed with lovely rugs and carpets and a very good little organ'. It was the first time he had been to church since July.

After a 'pleasant' service, the vicar invited the two officers into his garden for coffee, and from there they went, unexpectedly, to lunch at the American Legation. The first and second secretaries treated them to a bath in their impressive quarters before regaling them with a 'wonderful meal served by a Turk and cooked by an Italian'. This was followed by coffee and *crême de menthe.* They even stayed for tea, the Minister at the Legation and an official who advised the local air force having 'turned up', along with a couple of 'very presentable' English girls, 'the first I have seen, much less spoken to, since June'. Tony was entirely won over by his new friends, who were 'quite civilised for Americans', and was even offered a regular free pass to the Minister's bath. Unfortunately, he doubted that he would have the opportunity to follow up these connections, or indeed make further use of the bath.[16]

In the absence of proper roads, Baghdad was simply too far out and indeed was invisible from the camp. However, in the very near vicinity, the evidence of its former glory was plain to see. A system of canals and irrigation channels had been dug in the reign of Khosroes (A.D. 531 - 79). These were repaired and expanded under Harun al-Rashid (786 - 809), the Abbasid Caliph who is said to have inaugurated the 'Golden Age' of Islam. Harun founded the legendary 'House of Wisdom', the greatest library in the world; and his glittering court was the inspiration for the *Thousand and One Nights,* a work which had fed the imagination of the young Tony. Famed for its magnificent markets, mosques, palaces and bath-houses, medieval Baghdad was unrivalled in size and wealth.

Whilst supplying the medieval city with water, the canals and channels had also served to irrigate the surrounding plain, which had become its bread-basket. Now, as Tony observed, the canals were all dried-up, the once-fertile plain a desert. The disaster that had befallen Baghdad was apocalyptic. In 1257, an enormous Mongol host under Hulagu, grandson of Genghis Khan, had arrived before its walls. Hulagu had demanded tribute. When snubbed, he had, in accordance with Mongol custom, ordered the total destruction of the city, brick by brick, and the massacre of every man, woman and child inside it. Their blood, flowing into the Tigris, is said to have stained it as red 'as the verse of the Koran'. When the contents of the House of Wisdom were also tipped into the river, the red waters had turned black from their ink. The city walls were pulled down, the moat was filled in and, of course, the canals and dykes of the irrigation system were totally destroyed. Baghdad never recovered from the calamity; nor, indeed, did Islam. The city had declined thereafter into an

---

16 Letters 79, 80, 81, 82, 83.

insignificant provincial capital, the charmless, chaotic and rather noisome town of Tony's experience.

Tony had heard vaguely of the Mongol invasion, of how they 'broke down all the canals and locks and burnt the cities', and of the killing in Baghdad alone of 'more than a million people', after which it was 'never really rebuilt'. He had even come across the remains of some forgotten city, deep in the desert, that was only half-buried in the sand and still strewn with broken pots and other debris. He did wonder why the locals had never bothered to reconnect the abandoned channels to the Tigris and restore the fertility of the plain. He assumed they were 'too lazy', although in fairness to the present population of Bedouin tribesmen, who were not successors to the previous inhabitants, they were generally uninterested in settled lives and the pursuit of agriculture, let alone grand engineering projects.

Much like the Persian chronicler who had described the dawn of Hulagu's attack, 'when the orange of the sun was placed at the rim of the dish of the horizon', Tony was profoundly moved by the landscape and by his reflections on history. 'Early in the morning and again just before sunset,' he wrote, 'when the sun rests flaming like a giant furnace on the horizon, the long shadows make the mound and ditches of the ancient and long disused irrigation canals stand out black and the clay shines like gold. Just for those few moments the whole country looks really wonderful. The sunset and more specially the sunrise are miracles of colour and beauty far outreaching any picture post card.'[17]

---

[17] Letter 83. For a vivid account of the destruction of Baghdad, see Frank McLynn, *Genghis Khan* (London, 2015), pp.xxxiv - xl. *Cf.* Letter 51, where Tony refers to the 'Arabian Nights'.

CHAPTER V

IRAQ AND PERSIA

An Incendiary Situation

At 3.30 on a typical afternoon, Tony is to be found in his 'office', tapping away on a typewriter. For a large tent in the desert, albeit one that is dug deep into the ground and sandbagged, it has the reassuring ambience of an English sitting-room. There are a rush mat, two armchairs, three tables covered in carpets (in the best military tradition) and a brick fireplace which, in the midst of a bitter winter, keeps it reasonably snug.

There are three telephones next to the typewriter. A neighbouring table has the regiment's 'fighting maps' pinned to it. The third, Tony's desk, is strikingly free of clutter. The only objects on its surface are a large sheet of blotting paper and two bottles of ink, a black and a red. Tony could not begin to contemplate the intricacies of double-entry book-keeping, and apply those coloured inks correctly, without a clear desk in front of him.

He is accustomed to the to-ing and fro-ing of his three clerks but, as they have little English, he finds it easier to do his own typing. Apart from the regimental accounts, there are disciplinary matters to be dealt with, amongst the junior officers as much as the men. He is also in charge of collating intelligence and has to type up his reports.

Wearying of the task, he checks his watch, and is suddenly aware that the horse and groom who come for him daily will be waiting outside. He leaps joyfully from his seat and, moments later, springs into the saddle of his favourite mount. Both horse and groom belong to a neighbouring Mountain Battery. The Battery Commander keeps an immaculate stable and is delighted to have someone willing to exercise the animal, so Tony rides out for an hour each day, practising his jumps with the groom and becoming an ever more proficient equestrian. It is his escape from the penance of being an office wallah.

On his return, Tony turns to another of his duties, that of mess secretary. Dug in a full ten feet below the surface, the mess is efficiently heated by a large, red-brick stove. This ingenious contraption, eighteen inches high and six feet long, was designed and built by Tony. It is fuelled by a mixture of crude oil and water, which is channeled through burnished copper pipes onto a metal plate within the stove. The drip of the oil and water is controlled by a pair of taps, so the heat is adjustable.

Colonel Willans, who from long days in Africa 'feels the cold', developed an early attachment to it. When conditions in his own office can no longer be endured, Willans tends to seek refuge in the mess. Arriving there one day and finding the fire apparently out, he barked at the mess waiter with impatient displeasure: 'Re-light this at once,' he said, 'and then fetch me a cup of tea'.

The waiter nervously ignited the largest lump of gun-cotton waste that he could find and tossed it into the stove. He then scurried off to fetch the Colonel's tea. Far from being extinguished, however, the fire was merely set at a low heat. As the colonel bent over it, expecting to warm his behind, the flaming gun-cotton ignited the incendiary vapour. Willans was hit by the full force of the resulting explosion. The metal top blew off and caught him squarely on the seat of his trousers, followed by a shower of oily soot.

The bedraggled Colonel duly presented himself at Tony's doorway. He was thoroughly coated in soot, but the face beneath was livid with rage. 'Tony', said he, 'your [expletive] stove has gone wrong.' 'It just shows,' thought Tony, 'that one should not go to the mess when one should be working.'[1]

---

[1] Letter 84. Willans served with the King's African Rifles for three years (1926-9) *(Half Yearly Army List,* Jan 1939).

'Like an extended Cook's tour'

Though still in the unglamorous role of assistant adjutant, Tony was about to embark on one of the most exhilarating periods of his life. First, with a driver, cook and two soldiers (whose main task was to put up the tents at night), he was sent on a ten-day 'road recce' into the mountainous north-east of Iraq, an area largely populated by Kurds. It was the wildest, grandest country he had ever seen, a land of towering snow-clad mountains, hill streams in full spate and the odd native village, where peasants in sheepskin coats brandished silver-embossed rifles, but were generally well disposed to the British.

Tony took part on his return in a couple of exercises and attended a Counter Battery course, in which he achieved a distinction. But then the order came, early in February 1943, to strike camp at a moment's notice, and the whole regiment set off in the direction that Tony had recently reconnoitred, he himself travelling the whole way not in a staff car, as before, but on a motor-bike. 'There was no road worthy of the name and for a hundred and twenty miles we saw no one - not even a village, a house or a tent - while all the time the country became steeper and steeper.'

Leaving the distant snow-clad mountains to their right, the regimental convoy headed through the Kifri Gorge, which Tony likened to 'a picture from a fairy story'. It was a stupendous landscape of steep red cliffs, pitted with innumerable caves, and deep ravines. The water from a hundred mountain streams flowed across their path, though the river bed itself was virtually dry. After periods of heavy rain, a raging torrent would gush through the gorge, inundating the narrow track and leaving it utterly impassable. No human beings lived there, but the wildlife was abundant. Gazelle and buck scampered over the steep rocks above, and flocks of exotic birds darted in and out of the caves. On the fertile banks of the streams, clusters of tulips, forget-me-nots and 'huge white daisies' added to the enchantment.

From the top of the pass they had their first glimpse of the vast, undulating plain beyond and its protective wall of mountains. These snowy monoliths appeared to be close at hand, but some of them, peaking at 18,000 feet, were actually hundreds of miles away. At length the regiment established its base 'at the foot of a range of wild and forbidding hills', Tony's tent being pitched 'further up the hillside than any other'. It was a fearful place, apparently deserted by humanity. From his perch below a sheer, thousand-foot wall of red granite, Tony looked out in the clear winter sunshine over the vast plain, which stretched for hundreds of miles in every direction. The silvery River Kifri snaked its southerly course as far as the eye could see. There were no towns or villages, just the occasional nomadic encampment. The silence at night, broken only by the howl of the wind or the clink of a sentry's rifle, was overwhelming.[2]

Tony was soon sent off on another, two-week reconnaissance mission, with orders to write a detailed report. His party consisted of two Indian soldiers and two vehicles, a 15cwt truck and an American jeep. They explored and mapped the grassy plain, fording its innumerable rivers, living off the land, and encountering only a few nomads with their flocks. In one encampment they were offered tea and home-made tobacco. Tony noticed a collection of Persian lambs stuffed into a sack near the fire, ready for slaughter. There was plentiful game, however, including gazelle, wild duck, Egyptian geese, bustard and snipe, so fresh meat was always available. All sorts of creatures roamed the plain freely without fear of man, as if it were the Garden of Eden. It was cold in February, yet the whole plain for miles around was carpeted in flowers - wild tulips, pansies, an exotic version of a snowdrop, lupins and daisies, among others, all adding to the illusion of a Paradise on Earth.

These were normally days of invigorating, bright sunshine, but the weather was apt to turn, dramatically and without warning.

---

[2] Letters 85, 86.

Suddenly Tony's party were caught in a terrific thunder storm, 'with purple lightning', just as they were crossing a broad but normally shallow river. The rain came down 'in buckets'. It must have been terrifying for the driver of the Jeep as it was carried downstream by the resulting torrent, but Tony had no wish to alarm his parents by expanding any further on the incident. It was enough for them to know that he returned safely to camp.

Tony resumed his routine of office work, but enjoyed the task of writing up his route reports, or accounts of what he likened to an 'extended Cook's tour'. He was receiving an extra £100 a year for his trouble (his total salary now exceeding £500). There were other compensations. He took a day off for climbing with the second-in-command, Major Hepper, with whom he had built up a good rapport: it was Hepper whom he had accompanied, the previous October, to that memorable feast with the Sheikh. Their first attempt had to be abandoned when their Jeep slipped off the track into a river. The only way back was on foot. Tony remarks almost casually that the distance was 25 miles, and that there were some serious obstacles in the way, including 3,000-foot hills and 'some quite big rivers'. For most people, that trek alone would have been the adventure of a lifetime. Returning the following day with a gun tractor, they were able to winch the Jeep back onto the road, and on 15 April had 'another shot' at the mountain, managing to get to the top without mishap. Tony had caught the bug and longed to scale even greater heights.

Tony's Sikhs were as happy as he with their surroundings, experiencing the true contentment of being in a wild and sequestered place. They entertained themselves at night with their own 'strange' music. Tony, now qualified with a 'Distinction' in spoken Urdu, communicated quite easily with the Kurds, whose dialect was similar. He admired their beautiful woollen tents and thought they were a fine race of men, who recognised no borders, paid no taxes and acknowledged no authority other than that of their own tribe. They certainly cut a ferocious figure with their long red hair and beards, their terrific hooked noses, the long curved knives in their belts and the silver-embossed rifles that they slung over their shoulders. He found them all to be 'very friendly', perhaps because the British, not least Churchill himself, had been vocal supporters of Kurdish nationalism.[3]

Quite suddenly, at the end of April, everything changed. First, the regiment embarked on what Tony describes as a 'wild goose chase', but the letter in which he detailed those events seems never to have arrived.[4] On their return, they took up a new position on the edge of the plain. The luxuriant green grass and the carpet of wild flowers had been replaced by 'a sea of golden hay'. The sun would be high in the sky by 5 a.m., and the temperature, already soaring, would typically reach 110 degrees in the shade, of which, however, there was very little. The surrounding rocks would soon be too hot to touch. On their way up to the new camp, someone had knocked over an oil lamp and, within seconds, '800 yards of grass was ablaze and a six feet high wall of flame was sweeping down towards the guns and vehicles'. Thankfully, the fire petered out when it hit the dry bed of a stream, but the men had learned their lesson, and there were now strict controls on smoking and even cooking.

To add to their discomfort, a fierce wind would blow up around midday, fanning the cauldron of the valley, and driving before it 'clouds of fine dust', which was evil-smelling (of dried clay) and all-pervasive. Mini tornadoes tore up tents and sucked loose objects into the atmosphere. There were also ferocious storms, one of which uprooted half the campsite, the debris having to be retrieved from a good mile away.

Most of the birds having flown off, the wildlife that caught Tony's eye was now of the noxious kind: black scorpions, non-hooded cobras, vipers and massive tarantulas that lurked in the grassy valleys and the dried-up river beds. There were also

[3] Robert Owen, 'The Second Time Around: British Policy towards the Kurds (1921-22)', *Die Welt des Islams,* N.S.27, No.1/3 (1987), pp.91-102.

[4] The 'gap' is between letters 87 (15 April 1943) and 88 (2 May 1943), which opens with a reference to 'the wild goose chase I told you about'.

monstrous reptiles at large. Tony probably refers to the carnivorous Desert Monitor, which can grow up to two metres in length.

He also observed the harvesting by the locals of their meagre crop. 'They cut the stalks with a sickle, not with a sweeping motion but with a distinct pull. The cut corn is then stacked onto a donkey and carried in long platted mats to the threshing floor where all the ears are placed in a circular pile about six feet high. Cows, horses and mules are then driven round on top of the pile in order to knock out the grain. The richer farmers have massive wooden sledges that are pulled round the threshing floor by horses. These sledges are carved with the most beautiful designs and are said to be very old indeed as they are made from a type of wood that no longer exists in this country.'

A combination of the unpleasant, parched conditions and the inactivity drew from Tony an uncharacteristic outburst: 'There is absolutely nothing whatever to do here; we are all getting very bored.' Occasionally he took time off to swim in the wide river that was not far off, sometimes joined by his regular companion in adventures, Major Hepper, and the Signals Officer. Their favourite spot was a tiny settlement called Kala'ka, with its curious medieval watch-tower, the origins of which were a mystery, even to the locals. The river was 600 yards wide and there was a fierce current, so the swimmers were swept across diagonally. The murky water, formed of melted snow from the mountains, was deliciously cold.

When the sun set at 8 it came as a blessed relief, though it took another couple of hours for the air to cool. The men had their meals in the open at 10, by the light of an outsized moon and a panoply of unfeasibly bright stars. It was too hot ever to sleep under a blanket.

Tony comments, as so often, on the excellence of the fare, including fresh fruit, vegetables and eggs, and plenty of meat that was sent up 'on the hoof', and looked after on the outskirts of the camp by the regimental herdsmen. During a head count one day,

Tony discovered that they were ten animals short. 'Ah well, Sahib,' explained the large Sikh in charge, 'those sheep have been eaten by tigers.' 'I managed to make it very clear to him that there were no tigers about and that I expected to find the correct number in the flock when I next counted them. Three days later there were six more than there should have been.'

Another recalcitrant soldier was arraigned before a court martial. Tony appeared for the defence, and, despite the garrulity of his client, managed to get him off. His duties as mess secretary continued to occupy much of his time and were the source of great pride. His meals were legendary and he even procured an ice-box, from which iced puddings and fresh orange juice could be served throughout the day. Working from an 'office truck', the vehicle being 'tucked into an over-hanging ledge in the rock', he continued to write his 'route reports', but was deeply frustrated at being under-employed and so far removed from the theatre of action. 'We all do so wish that we could have been in at the "kill" in Tunisia; we who took the blows in the early days are now forgotten while those who arrived at the turn of the tide have had all the fun and also have the chance to go on to the next stage - we can only hope that our turn will come again soon.'[5]

Into Persia

Tony's toiling away in an office for six months - most recently in a tent 'whose walls are almost too hot to touch' - had been for a purpose. When the adjutant, David Meredith, went off on a course in early June, Tony had already been groomed for the role, which meant having to 'write out all the regimental orders, give out the operation orders and deal with the criminals'. His new office was 'bigger than the C.O.'s with five clerks and two orderlies at my beck and call'. It was fun for a while, but when Meredith returned, Tony begged the C.O. to let

---

[5] Letters 88, 89, 90.

him 'please go back to the guns, forsaking the pen for the sword'. 'All right,' said Willans, 'but you're not going back to the bearded men in 7 Battery.' Instead, Tony was given command of the worst troop in the worst battery in the regiment, 4 Battery. The men were tough Marathas from south-west India, who were considered to be ill-equipped intellectually for the mathematics of gunnery.

It is evident that Willans and all his superiors thought very highly of Tony, entrusting him with the adjutancy and supporting his application for a regular commission, and his being given a further difficult assignment was a mark of their confidence. Tony resolved that they would 'not be the worst troop for much longer'. Their strict daily regime began on the parade ground at 4.30 in the morning. They broke off at midday but were drilled again between 4 and 6 p.m. Their speaking only Hindi put Tony at somewhat of a disadvantage, but he relished being back with a troop and they seem within weeks to have built up a good rapport.[6]

The new encampment seemed less remote than the previous one. In mid-June, the C.O. and Tony, again being singled out for special favour, were invited to dinner with the Corps Commander Royal Artillery. Brigadier Basil Trappes-Lomax was not merely a regular soldier but also a Catholic squire and a passionate collector of bookplates.[7] He had many Yorkshire friends in common with Tony and even claimed to have seen him at a house party. There was much talk of Wavell and his imminent appointment as Viceroy of India, of which they all approved.

One could imagine for a moment that one was back in England, were it not for the infernal heat. A month later, the temperature would rise to 126 degrees, that in a place where there was barely any vegetation, let alone shade. Even by night it never fell below 100 degrees. The daily visitations of a 'strong wind' were like 'a blast from a furnace'. The pillars of fine dust that

---

[6] Letters 91, 92, 101 (describing the Dussehra celebrations in October), 102.

[7] *Burke's Landed Gentry,* Vol.I (1965), p.455; https://www.ulricofengland.com/prodshow/Waterloo_Bookplate/b001890.html.

settled on everyone and everything were, to say the least, irksome. There were also 'dust devils' that 'rush about like huge water spouts of dust rising several hundred feet into the air', carrying off tents and boxes. A cold bath was out of the question, 'as even if the water is left in the shade it becomes almost too hot to get into'. This was still, however, a place of wonder. Around that time the camp was beset by a pack of wolves which carried off several of the regimental sheep. They came close enough for Tony to observe their powerful necks and enormous teeth. Happily, they had more tact than to confront the humans.[8]

In the first week of July Tony was sent up north to do some work with the R.A.F., who were surprisingly 'civilised', though they had 'some very odd ideas of how to behave in a mess'. The details were unfortunately deleted by a censor who was no doubt keen to preserve inter-service relations. Tony enjoyed a daily swim in the 'very large river nearby', which ran through a steep gorge. About 400 feet above him, a rope bridge swung perilously in the wind.

After returning briefly to camp, Tony embarked by road and rail for Baghdad, in order to attend the Regular Commissions Board at G.H.Q. Late one evening, having travelled for nearly 24 hours, he settled into a very reasonable, clean, romantically-situated hotel. The staff were 'very uncouth', but the food was plentiful, and it was served on a floodlit lawn by the side of the Tigris.

The five-day Board 'consisted of written exams, physical and practical tests and interviews', the exams being particularly gruelling, especially in the intense heat. Tony passed the Board and celebrated with a couple of days' leave. He swam at the Officers' Club, a shady 'piece of England' on the outskirts, exercised the G.O.C.'s horses and explored a city that, once again, struck him as 'quite uncivilised', most people being armed with guns or knives. 'There is only one street worthy of the name and

[8] Letters 91, 92, 94.

that is only just wide enough for a double stream of traffic. All cars are constantly blowing their horns and everyone walks in the middle of the road which is littered with hawkers, donkeys and the occasional camel.' It surprised him that no one ever seemed to get knocked down or run over. The club, however, had not only a pool but a cricket pitch. Tony ran into a stream of military acquaintances, and even met two senior officers who had taken tea with his parents at Barmston. They stood him a very good dinner on the strength of it.

Back at the camp, Tony had the 'interesting' experience of going forward under a fierce barrage, the whole ground shaking with the concussion of the shells. It was good practice for a real battle. His face burned from the blast. Then suddenly, at the end of July, it was time to 'up sticks' again and, to Tony's delight, to move on from what had become 'a sweltering hell'. The regiment was to embark on another thrilling adventure. This unit of Persia and Iraq Force would at last be going to Persia.

They set off across the plain in a procession of vehicles and headed into the mountains. Their second camp was in 'the most wonderful spot' in the foothills of the Zagros range, with green bushes and a refreshing breeze that came down the valley. There was even a chance for a swim, the river that watered it being 'really deep'. The next day, they entered the steep 'Paitak' Pass that was the gateway to Iran. This was the ancient Khorasan Highway, a miraculous thoroughfare, albeit only a track in places, which over the centuries had been 'followed by any number of travellers: nomads, caravans - and the armies of conquering kings'. The kings of Assyria had campaigned relentlessly against the wild 'Aryan' tribes that dwelt there; but in 615 B.C., the tables had been turned, the Assyrian colossus being toppled by the Aryan Medes. From their gleaming palace at Ecbatana (modern Hamadan), which was on the highest point of the road, a full mile above sea level, the kings of Media had, for a season, commanded the trade between East and West, until in 550 B.C. they in turn had been toppled by other, more durable Aryan nomads, the

Persians of Cyrus the Great. The convoy of vehicles climbed a road that clung vertiginously to the mountainside, with a sheer drop below, then zig-zagged through woods of holm-oak that seemed to grip the side of the cliff for dear life. Tony wrote that 'one could always be certain of seeing a lorry which has gone over the side'. Meanwhile, 'the plain lay spread out below us like a gigantic map, pale blue in the gathering mist'.[9]

It was a thoroughly nerve-wracking journey. Brakes failed, towing ropes broke and engines over-heated. The next day they found themselves on a better road, but forced to dodge the speeding ten-tonners that were *en route* to the Red Army with supplies. These were British-built vehicles, each laden with sacks and boxes that had been brought up by ship and rail from the Gulf. For some reason, their running-boards were crammed with 'Ivans' in their unfamiliar uniforms. Accidents were inevitable. One of them, racing round a hair-pin bend, struck one of the lorries of Tony's regiment, knocking its body 'clean off the chassis', and sending it hurtling off the cliff. 'It bounced only once on its 2,000 foot drop,' Tony remarks drily. Miraculously, both cab and driver had been left i*n situ* on the road. The driver would no doubt have needed to have a 'lie-down' afterwards and probably a change of pants. On the fifth day, the weary gunners arrived at their new camp in the neighbourhood of Kermanshah. It

[9] See Tom Holland, *Persian Fire* (London, 2005), pp.1-20, on the Khorasan Highway. In a subsequent annotation, Tony refers to it as 'the Pass of Pytak' and in letter 149 calls it 'Pai-Tahk'. The established road route was from the border town of Khanaqin, where the trains from the Gulf were unloaded of their supplies, through the Paitak Pass into Iran, and on through Kermanshah, Hamadan and Kazvin, whence it veered north-westwards to Tabriz, a total distance of 1,200 miles. See the Ministry of Information film, 'The Road to Russia: The Story of PAIFORCE' (1944), Imperial War Museum CVN 232, and Edward Bowden's evocative watercolour of the scene, Art.IWM ART LD 4397. These can be viewed online at https://www.iwm.org.uk/collections/item/object/1060022077 and https://www.iwm.org.uk/collections/item/object/1726. As Charles Fowle points out, 'Paitak' may be typical military nomenclature - 'PAI Tac, as in Persia and Iraq Tactical (Pass)'.

lay under a snow-capped mountain. Tony and Hepper, joined this time by the Quartermaster, lost no time in climbing it.[10]

On 16 August, Tony and a friend were given the use of a Jeep and sent off on a week's leave. Tony had 'the most wonderful seven days' in Tehran, 'some of the best days I have had since leaving home'. He was only moderately surprised to jostle with Germans in the streets, and seemed to have no sense of being part of an invasion. The requisitioning by the Allies of much of its transport infrastructure had caused severe disruption in neutral Persia, or 'Iran' as it was now known.[11] Famine had spread after a bad harvest in 1942, and many people had died. The streets of Kermanshah had recently been thronged with starving people, and an outbreak of typhus in February 1943 had been catastrophic.[12] The Iranian Shah, Reza Pahlavi, had an old affinity with Germany and had been skilfully wooed by the Nazis, who had promised to build him a steel factory. He currently harboured about a thousand German nationals, ranging from 'simple technicians to sinister

---

[10] Letters 93, 94, 96, 98, 149. In letters 101 and 111, Tony refers to an ancient carving in a cliff about seven miles away'. By 'Bisitoun' he presumably means the Behistun Inscription (now a U.N.E.S.C.O World Heritage site), which is in the province of Kermanshah. XXI Indian Corps had been formed at Kermanshah on 6 June 1942 - hence Tony's being only half an hour away from the nearest N.A.A.F.I. See Robert Palmer, *A Concise History of XXI Indian Corps* (2019) - https://www.britishmilitaryhistory.co.uk/wp-content/uploads/sites/124/2020/08/XXI-Indian-Corps-History-Personnel.pdf.

[11] 'Persia' is the Greek name, favoured in the West, for the country that was traditionally known as 'Iran'. In 1935, Reza Shah had 'asked the world not to call it Persia, but to use the country's own name for itself': see Abbas Milani, 'Revealing Errors. Iran, Jews and the Holocaust: An Answer to Mr Black' (23 Feb 2006), http://www.iranian.com/AbbasMilani/2006/February/Black/index.html. It was from the 'Parsua', however, an Aryan tribe of the Zagros, that Cyrus the Great, founder in 550 B.C. of the Persian Empire, had originally sprung (Holland, *Persian Fire,* p.9).

[12] Mohamed Gholi Majd, 'The Three Famines and the Makings of a Malthusian Catastrophe in Iran, 1869 - 1944', *Journal of Iranian Islamic Period History,* 12 (27) (2021), pp.97-101. The reference to the privations in Kermanshah is in a Wikipedia article, https://en.wikipedia.org/wiki/Iranian_famine_of_1942%E2%80%931943, where it is also stated that the Soviets released grain supplies (previously banned) only in 1943.

spies', as well as the leaders of the former pro-Axis Iraqi government, whom the British had deposed in 1941. To his credit, Reza Shah had also provided refuge to 1,388 fugitive Jews from Poland, and, as a *quid pro quo,* had obtained protection for all Iranian Jews living under the Nazi yoke.[13]

The presence of even a small number of Germans in Persia was nevertheless an affront to the Allies, whose sole priority was the transfer of lend-lease *matériel* to the Soviet Union, thereby hastening an end to the war. Reza Shah was aware of the recent arrival of Allied reinforcements in his country, of which the 2nd Indian Field Regiment was a not insignificant part. On 17 August, a final ultimatum was delivered to the Persian government, requiring the expulsion of the Germans. A proud and stubborn Reza Shah had no intention of complying. As a result, the British and Russians launched a joint invasion on 25 August that met with little resistance, the Persian army apparently being taken completely by surprise.[14]

Meanwhile, Tony and his friend had been preoccupied with the comforts of their hotel, the sights of a very modern, cosmopolitan city and the company of two nubile Wren officers, on leave from the naval base at Basra, with whom they went dancing and for swims in mountain streams. They even drove north one day to catch sight of the Caspian. On the day of the delivery of the ultimatum (17 August), Tony celebrated his twenty-second birthday. In his letters it is very rare for him to discuss politics, a matter apparently of little interest to him; nor does he remark on the effects of famine and disease in the locality, although he does comment later on the scenes of poverty that he witnesses in Iraq. He was still very young and, understandably, had other things on his mind. By 25 August the pair were back in camp. That happens

---

13 Milani, 'Revealing Errors'.

14 See 'Iran during World War II' in *The Holocaust Encyclopedia* (United States Holocaust Memorial Museum) - https://encyclopedia.ushmm.org/content/en/article/iran-during-world-war-ii.

to have been the day of the invasion, in which, however, 2nd Indian Field seems to have played no particular part.[15]

Now Command Post Officer of 4 Battery, Tony relished the role, as it involved computation and survey as well as command of H.Q. Troop - giving the orders rather than receiving them. There was time to swim in the local rivers and for mountaineering, with Hepper his constant companion. On 25 September, the pair scaled one of the highest peaks in the area, measuring 12,000 feet. There was a moment in the descent when Hepper froze, unable to extricate himself from a narrow ledge. Tony wrote later that he 'had to cling to the rock below him to show him the next foothold'. Tony also visited, and photographed, the nearby archaeological remains. The most spectacular of these was the Behistun inscription, only seven miles from the camp. A lengthy recital, in cuneiform script, of the achievements of Darius the Great, it dates from the sixth or fifth century B.C. The inscription and associated bas-reliefs, depicting Darius and twelve other figures, are carved on the sheer side of a cliff, about 100 metres above the plain. They would have been visible from the ancient road below, but a close inspection means climbing the cliff face and traversing a narrow ledge, something Tony would have taken in his stride.

The festivities marking Dussehra, in early October, were a welcome distraction for both officers and men. There were thrilling war-dances, wrestling matches and a massive feast. Tony had never eaten so well. He had become a connoisseur of the Maratha cuisine and was fascinated by their music - rousing chants accompanied by a cacophony of drums, pipes and bells.[16] He also fostered relations with the officers of a neighbouring unit. After one convivial evening he was walking back to the remote camp when he heard the howl of a wolf. Thrilled and alarmed in

15 Letter 98.

16 The Marathas are described in the *Encyclopaedia Britannica* as 'yeoman warriors and champions of Hinduism' (https://www.britannica.com/topic/Maratha).

equal measure, Tony cautiously primed his revolver. There were lion in the area and also black bear: the C.O. had recently shot one, and was keeping the skin as a present for his wife.[17]

The outcome of the invasion of Persia had inevitably been the deposition, on 16 September, of Reza Shah, who was invited by the British ambassador to 'kindly abdicate in favour of his son'.[18] Tehran was occupied by the Soviets, and the Germans fled to Turkey. The invasion having had a satisfactory outcome, the regiment was free to return in mid-October to Iraq, reprising its hair-raising trek across the mountains in the opposite direction. The C.O. travelled with a driver and two soldiers in a seven-ton armoured car, whilst Tony made the whole journey on a motor-bike, at liberty to overtake other vehicles, or to stop and admire the view.

The procession of guns, trailers and three-ton lorries snaked its perilous way up the same steep pass. Inevitably there was another terrifying incident, when the secondary gearbox on the lead armoured car failed on the descent, slipping out of low gear into neutral. The brake was unable to hold the vehicle as it rapidly gathered speed. There were 'hairpin bends every hundred yards or so and a drop of over 2,000 feet' on their left-hand side. The quick-thinking Colonel saved the day. Pushing the driver aside, he grabbed the wheel and steered the vehicle 'into the wall of the cliff', which stopped it very effectively. Four very shaken occupants emerged from the crumpled vehicle, lucky indeed to be alive.[19]

The Colonel's dicing with death may have helped to improve his mood. He was, by now, deeply unpopular in the regiment, known for his short fuse and tendency to criticise. It seems, however, that he had been extremely worried about his wife and

---

[17] Letters 99, 100, 101, 102, 111 (enclosing photographs of the Behistun inscription).

[18] Ryszard Kapuscinski, *Shah of Shahs* (Harmondsworth, 2006), p.25.

[19] Letter 103.

children who had been stranded in India. It was a great relief to him when they managed to arrange a passage back to England and he seemed to be 'much more amenable' thereafter, even 'quite human', to the extent that the officers were prepared to give 'Jasper' the occasional dinner in the mess. To Tony, fretting as usual about the lack of any opportunity for 'real fighting', he was a dependable ally, though Tony's desperate application to become a parachutist was firmly refused.[20]

Staff Officer

Tony was far too useful to the regiment, not least as a stand-in adjutant. His services were again required from the end of October, when David Meredith took sick. Unfortunately, Tony had soon to take to his own bed, when a scratch from a tent-peg turned septic.[21]

A week or so later, however, the General having asked for him by name, Tony embarked on a three-month staff attachment at the R.A. headquarters. Tony offers few clues as to its whereabouts, other than that it was an encampment in the Iraqi desert, close to that of his own regiment, and that a hospital and a well-stocked N.A.A.F.I. were at hand.[22] Far from being confined to an 'office', Tony was mainly responsible for the care of the men, whose discipline was poor, probably because the previous officers in the role had not had a word of Urdu. The mess was tiny, just the very amiable Brigadier, the Brigade Major, the staff captain and Tony, who endeared himself by building a concrete floor to the mess-tent and brick walls all around it, 'with proper wooden doors and glass windows', along with one of his bespoke fireplaces (this one

---

[20] Letters 99, 102, 103. Tony recalls in letter 131 that he had 'put in for a special job which would have involved a parachute drop, I was accepted but the Brig said he could not spare me'.

[21] Letter 103.

[22] Letters 104, 105. In letter 109 he also mentions a fortified police station being in the middle of the bazaar of the nearest town.

fuelled by wood and coal from the railway) to keep them all warm that winter.[23]

Not surprisingly, Tony was soon considered indispensable and was invited to make the attachment permanent, which meant leaving the 2nd Indian Field. It was a difficult decision, 'but the chance of getting some real action clinched the issue'. No doubt the endless office work and an overbearing colonel also played their part. By the end of the year he was firmly ensconced in divisional headquarters as Intelligence Officer, R.A., promoted to the temporary rank of captain, and recognisable by a red armband marking his attachment to the staff.[24]

The 'great excitement' of this period was Tony's involvement in the Tehran Conference, which convened in the Persian capital on 28 November. Tony alludes to it in the letter to his parents dated 10 December. The meeting between Churchill, Stalin and Roosevelt (the latter having travelled 7,000 miles, despite being confined to a wheelchair) was, of course, highly sensitive. The main topic of discussion was the impending invasion of northern France ('Operation Overlord'). Tony allowed himself a mere three lines on the subject, one of which was deleted by the joyless censor. However, his role was purely ceremonial. 'There was a great deal of jealousy over the guard of honour,' he writes, 'and the presentation of the sword.' A photograph in the Imperial War Museum documents the event, which took place on 1 December 1943. Churchill, in his Air Commodore's uniform, inspects British soldiers of P.A.I. Force, who stand stiffly to attention. He is accompanied by Major-General Selby and by the British Minister in Tehran. Tony adds that, as the Prime Minister had just

---

23 Letter 106.

24 Letters 107, 109.

marked his 69th birthday, a present was made to him of a Persian painting, no doubt on Tony's initiative.[25]

Tehran was by then under the brutal rule of the Soviets, from whom many of its citizens had fled. Tony and a group of British friends, including the Provost Marshal and two girls, went for an evening out in the centre of Tehran, which must have been eerily quiet. They were sitting in the courtyard of a café, sipping Vodka and Vermouth, when a Russian officer strode past them. Halting at a nearby table, he curtly addressed a group of Russian soldiers. He accused them of being drunk, and ordered that they return to their barracks immediately. The men took no notice, and were still drinking twenty minutes later, when the officer emerged from the café. Without a word, he took out his revolver and shot one of them in the head. Returning the revolver to its holster, he calmly walked out into the road, leaving the shocked soldiers to deal with the corpse.

The Provost Marshal, who spoke Russian, explained that a Soviet officer could not be seen to tolerate drunkenness and disobedience. The unfortunate 'Ivan' had been sacrificed merely for the sake of appearance. After another drunken Russian soldier had been picked up by one of his patrols, the Russians had asked: 'Do you want to shoot him, or shall we do it for you?'[26] Tony admitted later that he quite admired their approach, and thought the Americans might learn from it.[27]

Back in Iraq, part of Tony's routine was to tour the native villages and camps in his Jeep, accompanied by an Iraqi interpreter and by his two armed 'thugs' for backup. He found the villages to be 'quite unbelievably squalid', the people 'very dirty and poorly dressed'. Those in the tribal centres fared better, being

---

25 Letters 98, 106, 130; Imperial War Museum, ref. A 20740, https://www.iwm.org.uk/collections/item/object/205153161. Churchill was born on 30 November 1874. Tony was at this time a keen collector of Persian miniatures (*cf.* letter 111).

26 Tony's annotations to letter 98, though they properly belong to letter 106.

27 Letter 126.

'dressed more like the Arabs one sees in pictures', and still brandishing arms despite an embargo. There was plenty of riding and shooting in his spare time, he and Hepper even swimming their horses to an island in the middle of a river, a new and agreeable sensation.

Tony also went down to Baghdad on official business, driving alone across the desert. On arrival, he was irked to discover, yet again, that 'no one ever seems to look for traffic before crossing and everyone walks down the middle of the road', not to mention the throng of horse-drawn carts, wooden buses and speeding taxis. Tony completed his business in an hour and a half, but the Brigade Major had allowed for an absence of three days. Tony shopped for additions to his collection of Persian miniatures; and he made a 25-mile excursion to Ctesiphon, the former winter capital of the Parthian and Sassanian kings, who in the third century A.D. had enlarged it into a sprawling metropolis. The site covers thirty square kilometres, but the only standing structure is the famous 'Archway of Khosroes' *(Taq Kisra),* actually the remains of a magnificent vaulted hall, which is thought to date from the sixth century A.D. Tony thought it 'wonderful … like a gigantic aircraft hanger. It is made entirely of sun baked brick and is a marvel of constructional ability.'[28]

The H.Q. staff made the best of their Christmas under canvas. Tony attended mass, played in a hockey match, helped to serve the British 'other ranks' with their Christmas dinner (turkey and plum pudding) and sat down with the officers to their own dinner at 8.30 p.m. It seems to have been a considerable feast. They then gathered contentedly round Tony's fire, listening to the wireless. The nights were, by now, freezing, and the New Year was marked by a quite terrifying storm. It struck up in the small hours, blowing down many of the tents, and the ensuing heavy rainfall had created by morning a two-foot river through the centre of their lines. Sheets of corrugated iron were blown into the air; one

---

[28] Letters 105, 106. Tony refers in letter 109 to the 'two armed "thugs" on my payroll'.

man was struck by a passing bed. Even the parked vehicles were blown forward, one three-tonner by as much as 75 yards. The torrential rain gave way at tea-time to a hailstorm. Then the sun came out. Generally the days were lovely, 'with bright, warm sun making it unnecessary to wear a greatcoat'.

Tony spent most of January 1944 away on exercise, including an ambitious one in the foothills. He slept when he could 'in the back of the Brig's car', and wrote intelligence summaries for the divisional commander. He reconnoitred the 'enemy' lines by night in a staff car, turning off the headlights to avoid being seen by either the 'enemy' or the umpires, and was cross-examined by the G.O.C.-in-C. himself on their positions. The Brigadier drove off a pack of wolves by firing his pistol into the air. In a letter to his father dated 26 February, Tony wrote of life going on 'almost too happily'. When others were embroiled in terrible battles, 'we at the very worst only have a few wild tribesmen to deal with'. In truth, the clergyman's son felt almost guilty to be enjoying himself so much, for his life had become a glorious, intoxicating adventure.

> 'The colour of the mountains,' he wrote, 'was really wonderful; deep snow except where the cliffs were too steep for the snow to lie, so they were cut up by great streaks of red rock. The few towns we passed were like glimpses of another age, all were dominated by forts with high towers and massive walls guarded by sentries standing by their great brass studded gates. One such town had a squad of prisoners outside, they were being marched round by an armed guard who looked far more bloodthirsty than the prisoners themselves. Other than this the only other people we saw outside the small towns were a few farmers ploughing with oxen and wooden ploughs and the occasional shepherd with his flock of goats. The shepherds wear long white felt coats with pointed shoulders and very long thin sleeves reaching almost to the ground. They all carried embossed rifles and long knives. Occasionally a party

> of horsemen rode by with their rifles resting on their saddle bows, they wore long brown cloaks edged with gold braid. Once we saw a long caravan of camels and donkeys loaded with bales of wool plodding their way to market.'

They returned to camp just in time. The very next day, the rain started again, 'transforming the country into a huge marsh impassable to any wheeled traffic'. As they sat over their roaring log fire, it was impossible for the officers to believe that, in three months' time, the thermometer would probably be standing at 125 degrees in the shade.[29]

[29] Letters 107, 108.

CHAPTER VI

THE CEDARS OF LEBANON

Policing the World

Tony's main duty as Intelligence Officer was, quite simply, to keep a beady eye on the locals. There were occasional disputes between ethnic Kurds and Bedouin which required his intervention. One day in February 1944, an Arab headman, whom he had managed to pacify, offered him coffee by way of thanks. The rival Kurdish headman caught wind of this and, not to be outdone, invited Tony to a meal. He being 'a rather superior sort of chap', they sat on Tabriz carpets in front of his tent, and feasted on various delicacies that Tony describes in detail. He thought highly of the Kurds, who were pleasant but idle. As it transpired, they feared that the profits of any effort or enterprise on their part would simply be taken away in taxes by the government, so saw little point in making the effort.

Tony liaised with the local Chief of Police in his fastness, a defensive building in the middle of the bazaar. Each booth in this maze of alleyways seemed to be presided over by a villainous-looking individual with a hooked nose and a long knife. Arriving at the enormous gates of the police station, Tony's bodyguard had to address the occupants forcefully in order to gain admittance. Entering a large courtyard, they saw the line of barred windows on one side, from which the faces of 'what must have been hundreds of incredibly wretched looking men' stared out at them. The Chief proved to be hospitable enough, 'kicking out all his relations who were squatting in his office'. A charcoal fire was produced, and offerings of tea and Players cigarettes.[1]

---

[1] Letter 109. There are no clues to reveal the location of the police station and bazaar.

Tony claimed to travel at least a thousand miles a month on his tours, often spending nights or even whole weeks away. There were also the periodic visits to unlovely Baghdad, which might offer Tony the temporary comforts of a bath and a sprung bed, but never failed to rile him. It was not merely the chaos in the streets that got on his nerves, but the population of ragged shopkeepers, beggars and thieves.

At the age of twenty-two and a half, Tony had seen more of the world than most people will ever see. As a result, he had learnt to appreciate so much that he had previously taken for granted, especially British codes of 'behaviour and morality'. He had acquired an intimate knowledge of the Middle Eastern lands, which he clearly loved. He was eager to discover their antiquities and to learn their languages. But he understood something that 'the great British public' did not: that their 'way of life is so completely different from our own'.

Tony especially deprecated the lectures that the Americans were apt to give on British overseas policy, as if they occupied the moral high ground or even knew what they were talking about. He might not have been to India, but in his service with the Indian Army, he had been privileged to know Punjabis, Tamils, Sikhs and Marathas at close quarters, all of whom had less in common with each other than a Swede does with an Italian. He had discovered that Indians will lie shamelessly for their own advantage, especially in disputes between castes. Had not the trusted regimental herdsman, one of his beloved Sikhs, recently lied to his face about the disappearance of his sheep? The same went for the disparate tribes of Iraq. The Egyptians were 'still savages', a mongrel-race 'who are always begging' and 'cannot look after themselves',[2] whilst the Persians were 'a most miserable looking lot of people' who were 'shockingly badly ruled'. Above all, he recognised that the races of India were

---

[2] Letters 40, 61, and 64 on the Egyptians.

endemically corrupt, and incapable of uniting as a nation.[3] Tony was prophetic on both points. At the time of writing (2023), ethnic violence has again erupted in India, this time between Hindus and Christians in the state of Manipur. What is more, Tony's own division, re-raised in post-independence India as the 6th Mountain Division, was the subject of a corruption scandal in 2006, for which the divisional commander, Major-General Gur Iqbal Singh, was tried and dismissed the service, two of his brigadiers being also implicated.[4]

Such expressions of British 'superiority' might savour of 'racism' today, but there is never the slightest suggestion of Tony's treating any individual as inferior on the grounds of his race. On the contrary, he had been brought up to treat all men as equals. When he joined the 2nd Indian Field Regiment in 1942, he was in awe of its officers and men. They were 'first class soldiers' he wrote. 'Discipline is amazing and turn-out would do credit to any Guards' regiment.' They also seemed to be 'far cleaner than the average Tommy'.[5] These are not the reflections of a 'racist'.

On the contrary, Tony's instinct, and, indeed, that of the average Briton, was to 'accept a man for his personal worth'. That had been the conclusion of Roi Ottley, an African-American journalist who had reported on the arrival of U.S. troops in 1942. By 1944, over a million and half U.S. servicemen had been posted to the British Isles. The 150,000 African-Americans among them

---

[3] Letter 105.

[4] 'Two Indian Army Brigadiers being tried for corruption', *Indo-Asian News Service,* New Delhi, 27 June 2007. It is relevant to mention that the infamous wartime famine in Bengal, which Wavell worked tirelessly to relieve, is also now blamed less on the 'heartless' colonial government than on the elected local administration. It is said of the Minister of Civil Supplies in that administration, Huseyn Shaheed Suhrawardy, that he 'siphoned money from every project that was undertaken to ease the famine, and awarded to his associates contracts for warehousing, the sale of grain to governments, and transportation'. (Thomas Keneally, *Three Famines: Starvation and Politics* (New York, 2011), p.97.)

[5] Letter 64.

were officially segregated, in accordance with the 'Jim Crow' laws of their own country, and largely confined to service and supply roles. The U.K. government had, however, refused to accommodate the American practice, knowing that the British people would have none of it.[6] Despite the bafflement and disapproval of their white comrades, many of them unreconstructed 'Southerners', black personnel were welcomed into British pubs and cafés without discrimination, and were even at liberty to court white women, without the prospect, very real at home, of being lynched.

'Thus the Negro has social equality here in more ways than theory,' Ottley writes. 'To put it in the language of the Negro soldier, "I'm treated so a man don't know he's colored until he looks in the mirror."' The experience of black servicewomen was equally positive. According to Evelyn Clarisse Martin-Johnson, who served as a postal clerk in Birmingham in 1945, 'we were well received by all the English, whatever city we visited ... They appreciated us. They treated us royally.'[7]

Tony's own attitude to segregation is clear from some remarks in one of his letters, dated 23 November 1943. 'What a grim incident that was with the negro; with the British Isles "out of bounds" and filled with those half-civilised Americans it is not really surprising. I am glad to see that they are at last finding out what little they really know about the races and nations of India; they were always so ready to make suggestions as to what we should do and condemn our policies ...'[8]

---

[6] See Christopher Thorne, 'Britain and the Black G.I.s: Racial Issues and Anglo-American Relations in 1942', in *Border Crossings: Studies in International History* (Oxford, 1988), pp.259-74.

[7] See https://www.iwm.org.uk/history/they-treated-us-royally-the-experiences-of-black-americans-in-britain-during-the-second-world-war, which quotes from Roi Ottley's article for the *Negro Digest* and includes the filmed interview with Mrs Martin-Johnson.

[8] Letter 105.

It is likely that he is referring to the so-called 'Battle of Bamber Bridge' in Lancashire, which had been discreetly reported in the papers. On the evening of 24 June 1943, U.S. Military Policemen had attempted to arrest a group of black servicemen in Ye Olde Hob Inn, ostensibly for wearing the incorrect uniform. In the ensuing confrontation, one of the M.P.s had shot and killed Private William Crossland, who is presumed to be the 'negro' of Tony's letter. A full-scale gun battle had been fought throughout the night, leaving seven people injured, and bullet scars which can still be seen in the walls of the town's bank. Though the higher command privately acknowledged the very poor leadership and 'racist' attitudes of their officers, twenty-eight black soldiers were subsequently convicted and imprisoned for mutiny. Tony had probably read a report of the second trial which concluded on 18 September.

Ye Olde Hob Inn is a typical English pub, with its half-timbered frame and thatched roof. According to the novelist Anthony Burgess, the locals were entirely sympathetic to the blacks. When the commanders of the nearby base had demanded the imposition of a colour-bar, all three pubs in the town had responded defiantly, posting 'Black Troops Only' signs at their doors. On the evening of the 'battle', the regulars, including British servicemen, had been vocal in their support of the harassed blacks. When the M.P.s initially challenged them in the pub, they were asked: 'Why do you want to arrest them? They're not doing anything or bothering anybody.'[9]

Racial hatred was far from being the very essence of the British Empire, as is often stated today. The opposite is true. It had been built on the premise that 'there is no hatred of brown skin', and its policies since the early 1800s were driven - notwithstanding individual lapses - 'by the conviction of the basic

[9] See https://en.wikipedia.org/wiki/Battle_of_Bamber_Bridge, and references therein. The incident inspired the plot of the 2022 film, *The Railway Children Return.*

human equality of the members of all races'.[10] It was, nevertheless, perfectly reasonable for a British officer serving abroad to contrast his own codes of 'behaviour and morality' with those of the foreigner, especially the peoples of the chaotic Middle East.

Thus Tony writes of Tel Aviv and Haifa that they were 'very modern in appearance[,] having been built with American money[,] but are in fact very eastern[,] with their full quota of baza[a]rs, beggars, thieves and bandits.' However, his remarks about the Orthodox Jews, with their outlandish hairstyles and costume, leave one wincing.

Comparing them unfavourably with the Arabs, who were dependably 'pleasant and friendly', he says they are crafty, acquisitive and treacherous, and 'make one think that there is a lot to be said for the Nazi point of view'.[11] In fairness to Tony, the Zionists of Palestine were themselves as contemptuous of the British as they were of the Arabs, and by the time he wrote those words, in September 1944, he had witnessed their own atrocities at first hand - the bombing of the Land Registry Office in Jerusalem on 14 July.

Moreover, the extent of the Nazi genocide was only revealed to the world in April 1945, after the liberation by the Americans of the Buchenwald Concentration Camp.[12] Tony, who had no sympathy whatever for the Germans and thought 'the man in the street and the man in the firing line were just as much to blame for it all as the Party Bosses',[13] would have been utterly horrified.

---

[10] Biggar, *Colonialism,* pp.91, 224-5, citing Lord Canning's expression of his and Queen Victoria's views.

[11] Letter 127.

[12] 'How the World Discovered the Nazi Death Camps', *The Times of Israel,* 14 January 2020.

[13] Letter 129.

On the Move

By March 1944, Baghdad seemed to be growing on Tony slightly, as there was 'quite a lot of "life" down there'. He travelled first-class on the sleeper train, was put up in the best hotel, went for afternoon rides and evening dances and had his meals at the Officers' Club. One visit was to attend a final, four-day board for his regular commission, which was 'stiffer' than the previous one as it included physical tasks, such as the swimming of rivers. Tony passed with flying colours, and awaited what he hoped would be an ante-dated commission, preferably to 1 August 1941, which would boost his post-war prospects no end. In fact it was some years before he received that commission (9 August 1947), and there was to be only a niggardly allocation of ante-dated seniority, to 17 February 1944, which was the date of his passing the board.[14]

Tony returned to H.Q., now encamped in a verdant little valley, miles from anywhere. There was no padre to remind them of Easter, which came and went. The Indians and the British competed in a hockey match and Tony stalked gazelle in the hills, with two Indian 'other ranks' for company. Having spent the night under the stars and crawled for miles by day, as if he were back in the Highlands of Scotland, Tony bagged five fine buck and drove back with them in triumph in his Jeep. The gazelle meat tasted like mutton, but was incredibly fine and tender.[15]

Much to his excitement, Tony was soon afterwards sent off to Cairo on 'a sort of course'. He much enjoyed the reverse journey across the desert in the luxurious Nairn bus, but declined to board the train at Damascus. That had been too convoluted a journey. He and another officer resolved instead to hitch-hike their way to the coast. An Arab lorry took them first to Tiberias, on the Sea of Galilee. After spending the night in a 'little hotel' that overlooked

---

[14] Ministry of Defence: *A.P.H.B. Fowle's Service Record.*

[15] Letters 112, 113.

the lake, they climbed onto the back of another truck, this one with a load of oranges. It took them, by way of Nazareth and Mount Carmel, all the way to Haifa, where they arrived in time for the midday train. At nine o'clock the following morning, they were having breakfast in Cairo.

The teeming, sweltering city was no more appealing than it had been on Tony's last visit. He particularly disliked the fashionable, over-priced Shepherd's Hotel, describing it as 'dark and dingy'. Luckily, his own quarters were a simple wooden hut that directly overlooked the Nile. Tony re-connected with old friends, including one of the girls he had met in Baghdad. The course went well. He passed out first in a field of 36, scoring 98% in one exam, and earned himself 'a pat on the back from the General'. He was further rewarded with ten days' leave, during which he had planned an excursion to Luxor, but there is no account of it in his surviving letters.[16]

By 15 May, Tony was comfortably installed in the palatial, N.A.A.F.I.-run Officers' Club, Beirut (all the main military centres had them), after 24 hours in a train that, for much of the way, had run 'within a few yards of the sea'. He describes Beirut as a quaint, hillside town of winding, cobbled streets, where there were electric trams and everyone spoke French. For an oriental town, it was 'almost unbelievably clean and tidy'. This was a convenient place for Tony to eke out his leave, as it was on the way to Headquarters Royal Artillery's new, secret location. The Brigadier, who happened to be passing through, described their mess as being 'in a house in an olive grove surrounded by mountains', with 'a little snow still lying about'. Tony alludes to the 'hush-hush' nature of his work, a subject on which he had become unusually reticent. Meanwhile, he relaxed by bathing in the warm Mediterranean Sea, and by going for long walks among the famed cedars of Lebanon.

---

[16] Letters 112, 113, 114, 116 (on Cairo).

The lush trees and grass of this sunny place seemed to Tony like 'part of a dream'. He kept running into old friends, including Bob Shenton, his old shipmate from the *Île de France,* with whom he had subsequently shared a tent at Almaza. Shenton imparted some sobering news. Of the four men who had shared that tent, two had recently been killed in action in the desert. One is believed to be Dick Marsh. Another was Tony's good friend Dicky Grieg, with whom he had 'shared' a honeymoon in England, manned the guns on the *Mooltan,* and taken a pleasure jaunt around Freetown harbour, among other adventures. Shenton himself had been wounded, and had only just emerged from hospital. On 21 May, a chastened Tony went to a service at All Saint's, the tiny Anglican church that seemed, literally, to overhang the harbour at Beirut (and is today dwarfed by tower blocks) - and thanked God for his superior luck.[17]

That run of luck continued. Within the week, Tony was ensconced in the new camp, which was, indeed, 'a Paradise'. After nearly two years in the desert, the headquarters staff now lived in 'real' houses, with plumbing and electric light. Beyond the lovely, shady garden attached to the mess, which was mercifully free of flies, there were orchards, olive groves and meadows. The people around them lived like Europeans, and were fluent in European languages. Both officers and men relished the opportunity at last for a social life. Best of all was the nearness of the sea, in which Tony and his friends bathed almost daily. Tony would also ride for an hour before breakfast with the Brigadier, enjoying 'some very fine gallops over turf and also some good jumps'. Everyone felt fit and well, and rejoiced to be no longer serving with P.A.I. Force. Tony adds, however: 'We all

---

[17] Letters 115, 116. Shenton is not named. However, he and Grieg were Tony's closest friends at Almaza. In a note to letter 48, Tony writes: 'I am pretty certain that he [Grieg] was killed in the desert but his name does not appear on the roll of honour'. It seems likely that Shenton was mistaken and that Grieg survived the war. Marsh is pictured with the others in Tony's album.

wish we were nearer the real war as this is all too much like a holiday'.[18]

Unfortunately, Tony offers barely any information that would pin down his whereabouts, and he leaves his parents guessing. He did inform them that he was now serving with Middle Eastern Force, though it covered a vast area and the headquarters were in Cairo. Their friend Major Burke was asked for his opinion, which proved to be 'very wrong indeed'. Tony was emphatically not in Palestine: 'I am sure I have never said so, or in any other country for that matter as it would be against the rules'. All that can be deduced is that he was in a relatively rural district on the coast of Syria, a country where French was widely spoken; photographs of this very pleasant place are captioned 'Syria 1944' in his album, and he reports later that his mail has pursued him there.[19]

At the end of June the Divisional Commander came to stay, followed soon afterwards by the G.O.C.-in-C. himself who was up from Cairo. Much trouble was taken to ensure their domestic comfort. Lieutenant-General Sir Bernard Paget had held the command since January. An officer of considerable talent, Paget was by that time the senior serving general in the British Army. Tony writes that 'in these parts he has very nearly as much power as an Eastern Potentate'. Despite his rank and formidable appearance, Paget was an easy, unpretentious companion, who dined, played bridge and rode with the junior officers. Himself the son of a clergyman (who eventually became Bishop of Oxford), he took a shine to Tony, inviting him to join his staff as an A.D.C. The general's offer was well-meant, but very firmly declined.

There was also 'a lot of excitement of a different kind', on which Tony, of course, is unable to expand, but it seemed that it

---

[18] Letters 117, 118. Referring to Hepper, Tony writes (letter 117) that a 'great friend of mine has recently been given command of a Mountain (mule) Artillery regiment', and had raised the prospect that Tony might be able to join him there.

[19] Letters 122, 124, 136. Syria and Lebanon had both recently received their independence from France, had democratic governments, and had declared their hostility to Germany.

might involve some 'real fighting' at last. This was 'the chance' Tony was waiting for. He asked that his vacancy at the Staff College be postponed, as an opportunity for active service was not to be missed.

A plan had been drawn up for the deployment of the division in Italy, and a programme of intensive training had begun.[20] Tony refers only to increased activity at H.Q.R.A. and to his extensive travels, though he managed a three-day break in Jerusalem, which included visits to Bethlehem and the Dead Sea. He writes of enjoying his stay 'no end', Jerusalem being 'a lovely city with an amazing mixture of races'. The situation, however, was somewhat tense, as the ruthless Irgun, a Zionist paramilitary organisation, had proclaimed in February their revolt against the British mandatory government. On 14 July, Irgun insurgents bombed the Land Registry Office in Jerusalem, killing two Arab constables. Tony wrote nonchalantly that he had been only six hundred yards away at the time. He seems to have rather enjoyed the ensuing drama. 'I spent one very exciting night with a desert police patrol chasing after a gang of gun-runners,' he informed his anxious parents, who can hardly have been reassured. Happily, he was soon back at H.Q. 'Life goes on in a very pleasant way,' he writes, 'but it is getting very hot and sticky.' By 7 August, everyone was 'dripping in the high humidity' and the mosquitoes were 'quite out of hand'.[21]

Tony turned 23 on 17 August, and soon afterwards, as acting G2 Intelligence - a major's job - embarked on a 'great overland "trek" of nearly two thousand miles. The planned deployment to Italy had been cancelled. In spite of themselves, the 6th Indian Division were being reassigned to P.A.I. Force, and were, once

---

[20] See *Persia and Iraq 1941 - 1947: Indian Infantry Divisions* on the British Military History website, https://www.britishmilitaryhistory.co.uk/docs-persia-iraq-1941-1947-indian-infantry-divisions/#:~:text=The%206%20Indian%20infantry%20Division,and%20around%20the%20Kermanshah%20area.

[21] Letters 119, 120, 121, 122, 123, 124.

more, heading east and into the mountains. Their journey took them through 'hundreds of miles' of 'the grimmest desert in the world'. Visibility was much reduced by 'the curtain of heat haze', but Tony's car behaved faultlessly, despite its becoming 'almost red hot' and the pressure of its tyres soaring to over twenty pounds. There was 'one stretch of more than 100 miles through an old lava belt with dozens of extinct volcanoes', an unnerving, blackened landscape. The nights were 'very cold' and the stars 'amazingly bright'. Tony is no doubt describing the Haurun-Druze plateau in south-west Syria, near the border with Jordan.

Towards the end of the journey they fell in with a party of Russians. Tony found them 'an odd crowd and very uncouth'. From a temporary encampment in the mountains, he again writes of feeling 'an awful fraud', as he had only seen about ten days of action (the Battle of Knightsbridge), not counting his 'playing about with Arabs and tribesmen'.[22]

Back to Iraq

No longer with H.Q.R.A., Tony had been transferred to the staff of Divisional Headquarters, as G.S.O. III Intelligence, with an extra £100 a year, making £600 a year in total, untaxed. As a staff captain in the Indian Army he was receiving more than would be paid to a British lieutenant-colonel. He was spending very little and able to send large sums home to his account with Cox's and King's.[23]

Tony was pleased to be back in the mountains. Higher than Ben Nevis, they were wild and barren, 'with huge cliffs and almost vertical up-ended slabs of rock', and were the haunt of the black panther, snow leopard, black bear and wolf, though 'the tribesmen beat them all for sheer animal savagery'.

---

[22] Letter 125.

[23] Letters 126, 130.

Tony occupied a 'very large tent' adjacent to that of the G.S.O. I, the Chief of Staff. It was the highest and best site in the camp, though Tony's office and the mess were about half a mile away in one direction, and the R.A. office about a quarter of a mile away in the other. A varied collection of livestock roamed freely among the tents. These included a magnificent woolly goat that the men of 1/1 King George V's Own Gurkha Rifles had decided not to eat one evening, but to keep as a mascot instead. The Gurkhas were assiduous in keeping the animal clean, washing it once a week in Lux. There were also dozens of turkeys and hens and two cocks, not to mention chuff-chuffs and some fat, but surprisingly agile chukar partridges, which the men were keeping as pets. Most officers on the staff had their own dogs, too, ranging from the Assistant Provost-Marshal's ferocious Alsatian to Stooge, a little sausage dog, of whom the locals, unfamiliar with the breed, were particularly wary, mistaking him for some sort of snake.[24]

Tony immediately impressed 'the Chief' by having a 'clear-out' of his office, putting a match to nearly a ton of old books and files. He worked ten-and-a-half-hour days and, to the disgruntlement of his subordinates - a lieutenant, a sergeant-major and five clerks - banned the practice of the afternoon siesta. The work itself was fascinating, revealing of many secrets and the 'bigger picture'. Tony combed the newspapers and regularly tuned in to the wireless, 'a mass of dials and lights', to pick up fresh news, and one of his clerks would mark up any developments on a map. There was quite a collection of these, each of them eight feet high. Tony was led to conclude that the war was 'drawing to a rapid close'.

'The Chief' was a sympathetic boss and made sure that Tony had the occasional rest. Sent away one weekend, he drove about a hundred miles with a colleague to a clear blue mountain lake, where they spent the whole time fishing and swimming. Tony

---

[24] Letter 130. The Gurkha regiment is identified in *6th Indian Infantry Division,* p.4 and p.6, note 5, https://www.britishmilitaryhistory.co.uk/wp-content/uploads/sites/124/2020/08/6-Indian-Division-1942-44.pdf.

remarks on the enormous, 'quite pre-historic' fish which populated the lake, including 'a kind of carp' that weighed 118 pounds. They also caught brown trout by means of a fly. The pair drove home in Tony's staff car with a net of 64 fish between them.[25]

'Life here is far too pleasant,' wrote Tony, reverting to a familiar theme; 'at times it seems quite wrong to be enjoying it so much while others are going through hell in Holland, Burma and the desert.' He had time to play chess, noting, as many have before, 'how the principles of war apply themselves to the game', and also for some serious reading: Churchill's *My Early Life* more than satisfied his craving for military history, and was followed by a biography of Marshal Murat, and an account of Napoleon's invasion of Russia.[26] There were further fishing expeditions, and long reconnaissance missions that led him far from the beaten track. The day-time temperature was typically about 87 degrees in the shade, but, at night, this would drop to well below freezing. The air at those altitudes was thin and dry, and there were occasional dust storms.

In his home letters he read that the Home Guard had been stood down, and that the sanatorium at Cranleigh had been damaged by a flying bomb. Tony was also in touch with Hepper, who had seen 'real action' in Burma. His regiment, the 29th Indian Light Mountain Regiment, had had to fight its way back up the Tiddim Road. This was the road leading to the border town of Imphal, through which the Japanese had intended to launch their invasion of India. The turning-point had been the 'Battle of the Tennis Court', fought in the grounds of the District Commissioner's bungalow in Kohima. The exhausted Japanese had begun their withdrawal, and Hepper's regiment were helping to hold the road. Tony wrote dispassionately that 'all the Japs seem to have died from starvation, thousands of them, their Q

---

[25] Letter 127.

[26] Letters 130, 134.

work is evidently none too good'. Tony longed to join the regiment as adjutant. Hepper had formally offered him the post, but his fate was not in his own hands. In September, on the advice of the C.R.A., he turned down a vacancy at the Junior Staff College in Palestine. It was a six-month course, but in that time the war would have ended and 'my chances of an active command in battle would be gone for good'.[27]

Meanwhile, the tribesmen were busy moving their flocks to winter pastures, ahead of the coming snow. A certain amount of 'fun and games' ensued, with Tony running on one occasion into an ambush. Their antics coincided with the end of Ramadan (an opportunity for lavish feasting in the camp) and, for the Hindus, with the annual festival of Dussehra, for which 1/1 Gurkhas laid on 'a most ambitious show'. Tony was their guest at a splendid feast. 'We all ate far too much curry, spiced chicken, goat and mutton, sweet rice and cakes.' Then there was dancing and the deft beheading of a goat with a *kukri.* 'They are grand chaps with a very keen sense of humour. I am told that three of them were sent out on patrol in Italy and found three Germans sleeping under a rock. They dealt with the outside ones by removing their heads but left the man in the centre. When asked by their Company Commander why they left the third man unharmed they replied "Ah Sahib - think when he wakes up!"' The local tribesmen would have been ill advised to take them on.[28]

Throughout this period, Tony never once lets on where he is. He was probably in Iraq, somewhere between Mosul and Kirkuk, where the various formations within P.A.I. Force were, by that time, largely concentrated. Tony describes the reddish soil that is

---

[27] Letters 130, 131; *17 Indian Infantry Division (1944 - 45),* p.3, https://www.britishmilitaryhistory.co.uk/wp-content/uploads/sites/124/2020/07/17-Indian-Division-1944-45.pdf. *Cf.* Louis Allen, *Burma: The Longest War* (London 1984), p.638.

[28] Letter 130. Tony's anecdote is in fact very well known and often repeated. See, for example, William Borders, 'Sun that Set on the Empire Casts a Shadow on Gurkhas', *New York Times,* 21 April 1976.

characteristic of that region.[29] But the Germans no longer posed any serious threat to the Persian supply lines; the command had lost its *raison d'être.* By 15 October 1944, it had ceased to exist. The 6th Indian Division was immediately disbanded, its components moving on to new adventures. Tony soon found himself 'stewing down in the southern tip of Iraq', but that is not revealed until later.[30] Come December, he is at least able to offer his parents the name of a country. He is in India.[31]

---

[29] Letter 131.

[30] Letter 135.

[31] Letter 132; https://www.britishmilitaryhistory.co.uk/docs-persia-iraq-1941-1947-indian-infantry-divisions/#:~:text=The%206%20Indian%20infantry%20Division,and%20around%20the%20Kermanshah%20area.

CHAPTER VII

PESHAWAR

East is East

A few days after arriving in India, Tony is sitting under a shady tree in a park, watching a cricket match. He has been struck by the pleasantness of the climate, which has reminded him of the late-summer in England. The scene is of abundant greenery and there is a backdrop of rolling green hills. Colourful birds are singing, or rather squawking, in the trees. It is not only squirrels that crawl up their sides, but also lizards. Tony cannot quite forget that he is 'abroad', but he is surprised by the attractiveness of the country, how 'clean' it is, by the 'general well-kept air about the whole place'. It feels like home.

There had been a frustrating wait in Basra. He had spent his days sun-bathing on the shore, and his nights in a cramped 'E.P.I.P.' (European Private's Indian Pattern military tent), but at last he had embarked, in a 'lovely modern ship', on what had seemed 'like a peace-time cruise'. The sunsets over the Persian Gulf were ravishing. Then, on 3 December 1944, Tony disembarked in Karachi, a city of imposing colonial buildings with a distinctly western feel, which he had not expected. Prosperous, well-dressed people thronged the streets; there were buses and trams, and there was that sense of cleanness that struck him so powerfully, perhaps in contrast to the Middle Eastern cities, like Baghdad and Cairo, to which he had become accustomed. He spent the first night in a 'palatial mess', and then he travelled 'up country' by train. Unlike the 'narrow, swaying railways of Persia and Iraq', this one was 'full gauge … with proper sleeping accommodation and food laid on in a restaurant car'. Tony had settled down to peruse the excellent *Times of India.*

At last he had arrived at the Royal Artillery Base Depot for the India Command. It was less humid in the hills than in Karachi, which was just as well. Tony's temporary quarters were a large tent beneath a tall tree. The site was screened by bushes and agreeably pungent: 'it smells exactly like the garden after a heavy shower'.

Tony had quickly run into old friends, including one from Catterick. He is surprised by their ignorance of Urdu, in which he himself is now highly proficient. He has picked up the habit of many old India hands, peppering his English speech with words and phrases in Urdu, to the great confusion of the uninitiated. He was told months before that his 'English gets worse every day and that it is now about fifty fifty English/Urdu'. James Hepper is worse. The officers of a British unit invited him to dine with them one evening. Asked what they thought of him, they said that they had found him very pleasant, but had barely understand a word he said. After long days conversing with the men, it becomes difficult to switch off. For the moment, however, it makes life easier. Tony now intends to 'have a shot at my Interpreter's exam', knowing that it will stand him in good stead in his future career.[1]

No.11 Mall Road

Ever since Catterick, and perhaps partly inspired by Kipling's poem 'Screw Guns', Tony had dreamed of serving with Mountain Artillery. For someone whose passions in life were mountains, artillery, horses and (above all) fishing, there could hardly be a more suitable destination. He was beside himself with excitement. 'The guns are carried on mules and the officers on horses or else on their own two feet - mostly on the latter. To round off the future I have got the appointment of Adjutant.' The C.O., to whom he owed the appointment, was his

[1] Letters 132, 133, 135. *Cf.* letters 103 (the Hepper anecdote) and 107 (Tony's lapses into Urdu).

old friend, Hepper, 'one of the very best', while the local Brigadier was another old friend and ally, Bob Mansergh, 'so I am not exactly a stranger in the land'.

The 29th Indian Light Mountain Regiment, a Sikh regiment, had been raised at Peshawar as recently as October 1942, combining three pre-existing batteries. The total strength had been 26 officers, 13 V.C.O.s and 787 other ranks, with 48 Horses and 374 Mules. The Mountain Batteries were equipped with 3.7 inch Howitzers, but there was also a Mortar Battery, armed with twelve 3-inch mortars.

The mortars had come into their own on the Tiddim Road, where, from March to July 1944, the regiment had been engaged in a series of fierce battles. One evening, while resting on a hillside at Sekmia, they had suddenly been subjected to a wave of desperate attacks. The slopes in front of them had been too steep for the effective deployment of artillery, or indeed of small arms fire. The mortar battery had taken over, and had been credited with eighty of the 120 kills in a single attack. One of the battery's V.C.O.s, the very courageous Havildar Sher Singh, was subsequently decorated with the Military Medal for his part in the action.

Another ferocious battle had been fought on the night of 25-26 May, at Kha Aimol, near Bishenpur. A Japanese raiding-party had charged the perimeter wire and attacked the nearest gun-pits. The gunners had had to fight them off with their bayonets and the butts of their rifles, losing eight of their men. A further eleven were wounded.

Hepper's leadership throughout the campaign had been exemplary. The regiment had accompanied what remained of 17 Indian Infantry Division to Imphal in July, and there had followed a period of rest at Ranchi. Hepper had busied himself writing recommendations for awards, which were to include Military

Crosses for two of his officers. They had only very recently returned to their regimental headquarters at Peshawar.[2]

All this had happened while Tony was in his 'Paradise' of a camp in Syria, where life had seemed rather too much 'like a holiday'. As he was to discover, the officers in the 29th were all young men like himself, Hepper being the oldest at 35. Three of them were old friends. Pat Langford had been with 1st Indian Anti-Tank Regiment in Iraq.[3] Another man had been in Tony's O.C.T.U. at Catterick. Yet they had all seen 'at least one year's service in action in Burma'. Tony, as ever, had missed out. He never declares his anguish, but he must surely have felt it.

Tony joined the regiment at Peshawar on 21 December 1944. His journey by rail had taken six days, the length of the line from Karachi City Station to Peshawar Cantonment Station being 1,048 miles. There were, moreover, 176 stops *en route.* The train had wound its way through hundreds of miles of 'thickly wooded country', where monkeys darted among the trees, through various plains, some of them cultivated by people who seemed 'well fed and happy', and into the hill country, 'with a wonderful vista of snow-capped mountains away to the north'. He adds: 'For a whole day we wound through gorges and over bridges with rivers racing far below us.'

Tony describes how, on his arrival at Peshawar, 'the dream began. I can still hardly believe that it is all true. I was conducted to a large bungalow standing in a very fine garden with well-kept beautiful green lawns - No.11 Mall Road - where I was told by a

---

[2] Lieutenant-Colonel M. Ranjit Singh, 'A Mountain Artillery Regiment during the Battle of Imphal', *The Sangai Express,* 16 April 2016; *17 Indian Infantry Division (1944-45),* p.6, https://www.britishmilitaryhistory.co.uk/wp-content/uploads/sites/124/2020/07/17-Indian-Division-1944-45.pdf; https://discovery.nationalarchives.gov.uk/results/r?_q=29+Indian+Light+Mountain+Regiment+Indian+Artillery. Ever since the Mutiny, the Indian Army had had no field artillery of its own. Until 1935, this had always been supplied by the British Army. The Mountain regiments had been an exception, although their officers were recruited from the Royal Artillery.

[3] Letter 147 on Langford.

somewhat apologetic bearer that he was sorry not to have the fire lit but he did not know what time I was coming.' Astonishingly, the bungalow was 'all mine'.

For the equivalent of five shillings a week, electricity and the gardener's wages included, Tony was the master of a small estate. He had a comfortably-furnished sitting-room, two bedrooms, a bathroom and a small out-house containing the kitchen and rooms for three of his four live-in servants. A fourth servant, the groom, lived next to the stable, where Tony kept Bishop, his own personal charger. The bungalow looked out onto a broad, tree-lined boulevard, with separate riding- and foot-paths on either side. The traffic on this thoroughfare seemed mostly to be horse-drawn, including, on occasion, Colonel Hepper's superb four-in-hand. This superior vehicle was distinguished by its Gunner badges painted on the doors and by the 'two soldiers in splendid uniforms' who were mounted on the box.

After two years of hardship in a sand-blown tent, Tony was at last experiencing 'all the pre-war way of life of the old Indian Army', as if the war had never intruded. The mess was 'pure luxury with food to match', whilst his office in the regimental lines stood in the midst of another manicured garden. There were polished guns on either side of the door, and a large flag fluttering overhead. An armed orderly, 'dressed as if he had stepped from a Gilbert and Sullivan opera', stiffened to attention whenever Tony passed.

Tony applied himself to his well-paid, but 'not exactly exacting job' at a 'gigantic desk in a large room with a deep piled carpet and brightly burning fire. It could not,' he observed, 'be more different from the E.P.I.P. tent in Iraq.' Best of all, there were stables behind, which housed the horses and mules of the headquarters staff. These were their means of transport whenever they went out 'on column', for 'we are now expected to go into action riding on a horse!' As there were also mounted parades, Tony brushed up on the various manoeuvres in the riding school. He was in need of plain clothes and asked his parents to send them: his old green hacking jacket, a grey woollen polo jersey and his Gunner and Old Cranleighan ties. The old Gurkha *kukri* for which he had previously applied was delivered after Christmas. He hoped for the day that he would be able to carry it into the jungles of Burma.

Unlike Burma, Peshawar seemed peaceful enough. However, the *raison d'être* of the 'cantonment', or military quarter, was its proximity to the romantic Khyber Pass, a British possession since 1849, through which ferocious mountain tribes would launch the occasional raid. In that case the regiment would indeed mount up and proceed against them 'on Column', as if they had all stepped back into the nineteenth century.

The cantonment was vast, covering an area of nearly five square miles. As well as the lines, it contained a church, cinema and shopping centre, and its own native quarter. From its north-western corner, the historic Bala Hissar, or Old Sikh Fort, a concentric castle to rival those in the Holy Land, overlooked the 'Old City' of Peshawar, which, in those days, was set apart from it by some distance. Tony describes the Old City as a 'hot-bed of murders, blood-feuds, thieves and robbers dominated by the old Mogul fort and palace'. To keep these undesirables at bay, there was a barbed-wire fence at the outer perimeter of the cantonment and the gates were firmly shut at dusk. In the hypothetical event of a raid, the British families would take refuge in Bala Hissar, 'while the menfolk take their swords and shields and go forth to repel the invader'. The British in India were, after all, still haunted by memories of the Mutiny of 1857.

Tony was driven out on his first Sunday to view the Pass itself and to get a feel for the regiment's main operational area, a place of which every red-blooded English lad had heard and no doubt dreamed. Tony attended evening classes in Pashtu, or 'Afghani', the main language of the region, and was initiated in the tactical handling of the 'Screw Guns', which bore no relation to the artillery drills he was used to.[4]

Tony was not eligible for leave. Apparently he had been too long overseas (it would be two years in February), and the experienced hands could not be spared. However, he was promised a full 61-days leave, exclusive of all travel, in about eight months time, and should therefore be home in time for the following Christmas, when the war would no doubt be over. Happily, Christmas was a very merry season for the British in Peshawar. On 23 December Tony, Colonel Hepper and George Chapman, the second-in-command, rode with the Peshawar Vale Hunt, which had Whips clad in pink, and a formidable lady Master[5] with a horn, so it felt 'very like England', even if it was the jackal that was pursued. Bishop took the many small ditches 'in fine style', and the gunners finished ahead of the field, just behind the rear Whip. 'I must say it was one of the most thrilling and enjoyable mornings I have ever spent.'

On Christmas Day itself the officers entertained both the V.C.O.s and the British N.C.O.s in the mess, and tucked into their own 'massive' dinner in the evening. All the regimental silver was brought out for the occasion, including giant candlesticks that lined the centre of the table. There was a very English horse show on Boxing Day, including entries for children, and dinner with George Chapman and his young family. This was followed by the Hunt Ball at the club, which involved 'lots of gallops and other wild dances'. On New Year's Eve there was a concert, followed at midnight by another dance, and, on the afternoon of 1 January 1945, the regiment hosted a race meeting, which included a 'stand-up buffet in the mess for as many people as could get in'.

---

[4] Letters 135, 136, 143 (on Peshawar).

[5] Named in letter 147 as Marjory Diamond.

Within the week the regiment had marched out of the cantonment and Tony had found himself back in the wilds. He confessed to feeling quite relieved.[6]

Floating Peaks

The procession must have been a splendid sight. It set out from Peshawar on 10 January. The gunners were going out on exercise, but might as well have been going to war. They slung their leather saddle-bags and rifle-buckets over the backs of the horses, and rolled their blankets across the saddle bows. The battery staff were distinguished by their white head-ropes and shining saddlery. When not riding the horses, they walked or ran with them. Tony's mount was the shy but steely Peter, for Bishop had cut his fore-leg on the hunting field. They had pursued their quarry, a jackal, for three hours before the kill, when Tony had been duly 'blooded'. The creature was the size of a small wolf.

The column covered a distance of about fifty miles.[7] Even for the dependable Peter, the going was wearisome. Eventually, they pitched camp in a little cedar grove, an 'unbelievably beautiful' place. The view for miles around, in every direction, was of towering mountains. It was, however, extremely cold. Soon there was a thin covering of snow.

They began a routine of moving out at first light and not returning till late. On 26 January, Tony rode or, when it was too steep, walked a distance of twenty-five miles 'as the crow flies', which was very much further when measured by the 'man walking'. The horses had to be 'rugged up' in thick, quilted coats. Tony had a close shave when, in the middle of a conference with the Observation Post, he heard an in-coming round. They all

---

[6] Letters 137, 138. Chapman is named in an annotation to letter 105.

[7] Letter 138. Tony says 'we marched for a distance greater than from Barmston to York', which is 42.3 miles. In letter 149 he refers to the white head-ropes.

dived for the nearest cover, the shell exploding a mere twenty paces away. Miraculously, the party of six men and two mules were unscathed; and the mules, far from bolting, as horses would have done, merely waggled their ears, as if only slightly put out by the disturbance. It turned out that the G.P.O. had confused the map reference for the O.P. with that of the target, but, in Tony's sanguine view, he deserved some credit: 'other than for that error he certainly got his sums right'.

Tony was a firm believer in providence. One day, he was sent back to Peshawar in an open truck, reached for the driving gloves that he had last worn in Persia, and discovered his signet ring, long given up for lost, in the tip of the little finger. He had less luck with his father's old valise, which fell from the back of a mule and bounced down a steep rocky slope. Told that it was irreparable, Tony instructed the saddler to make an exact replica, using the straps and other fittings from the original, an outcome that would have pleased his father.

Tony also acquired a pet, a 'rather fine' hound of uncertain breed who, unlike him, had seen action in Burma, having been found as a pup on the Tiddim Road. Tony named him 'Tiger', and he used to travel with the rations in the Quartermaster's truck.[8] The regiment were covering about twenty miles a day, and were becoming extremely fit and brown. As so often, Tony was utterly inspired by the views. At dawn one day, 'when the mist cleared the hills to the south,' he saw 'the most lovely sight I have ever seen'. The snow-clad peaks 'seemed to be floating about a hand's breadth above the horizon; a sea of gold and scarlet completely detached from the earth'.[9]

By 16 February they had moved to a new encampment by a stream, a most secluded spot. At the other end of the valley was a waterfall. Tony was bombarded by telephone and wireless

---

[8] 'Tiger of Tiddim' was said to be 'a Chin … a large black, white and red hound looking very much like a fox hound with the same deep chest'; but this does not sound like a description of the conventional Japanese Chin.

[9] Letters 138, 139, 140.

messages, but the afternoons were quiet. The British amused themselves by hooking tiny fish from the stream; the Indians looked on and made fun of them. The locals, a cheery bunch of ne'er-do-wells, found a ready market for their eggs and walnuts.[10]

Soon afterwards the regiment returned to Peshawar. The days were bright and frosty. Occasionally the wind howled. Tony rode to hounds and competed, on a horse called 'Warrior', in a local race meeting. Warrior was a 'seven-eighter', one of the government-owned horses of which the officers had free use, as long as they paid an indemnity of seven rupees eight annas per month. Tony raced Warrior over 3½ furlongs, and finished third out of nine. With 'hundreds of people all yelling and shouting, the flying turf and the wind whistling round my ears', the experience was utterly exhilarating.

The officers and V.C.O.s posed for an official photograph. Tony had by now received his first campaign medal, the Africa Star. However, the treasured '8th Army' clasp had, owing to an administrative oversight, been omitted. Its value diminished to Tony, he neglected to put it on. He was also photographed on his own for an official pass. Asked to verify the likeness, Hepper scribbled on the back: 'Wanted - may be dangerous'.

On 19 February Tony dined with a dignified Pathan, who was virulent in his disdain for the Congress Party, and for Hindus generally. 'If they try to rob me - me, an honest Muslim - I will see them off, single-handed, any day of the week,' he declared. Such utterances sound ominous in the light of future events.

The Pathan liked to cultivate influential friends among the British. His guests on that occasion included the District Commissioner, the Chief of Police, two Political Agents and Eric Shipton, the Himalayan mountaineer, who had just completed a mysterious assignment as 'Cereal Liaison Officer' in Persia. Tony had encountered both the Political Agents and the 'Cereal Liaison Officer' in Kermanshah. Shipton was a celebrity, having led the

[10] Letter 141.

1935 Mount Everest expedition, of which Tenzing Norgay was a junior member; so he and Tony would have had much to talk about. Shipton produced photographs of the enchanting Kaghan Valley in north Kashmir, near the frontier with Tibet, and persuaded him that he must visit it. Tony conceived a plan of trekking there that summer, with Hepper as his companion.

He also buttered up the 'Military Estate Officer', who presented him with a selection of exotic trees - Syringa Persica, Cedrus Deodara and various hedge plants - with which to improve his garden. He derived much pleasure from his little domain, sometimes referred to as 'the Palace', and, after the rigours of the campaign, liked being able to put his feet up in front of his own fire.[11]

That period was a constant round of races, hunts and hockey matches, though Tony also worked long hours in the office. The country was at its finest in spring, the blossoming flowers and fruit trees giving off a wonderful scent, 'as if someone had upset a bottle of perfume over the whole countryside'. On 9 March, the cantonment was penetrated by 'dacoits' or armed bandits - the bane of the British in India - who helped themselves to the contents of a store. The police and gunners went after them with blood-hounds, as if in pursuit of the jackal. Otherwise, the only incident of note was the prosecution of Lady Cunningham, wife of the provincial Governor, for a minor traffic offence. As usual, Tony felt ashamed at being so far removed from the war, but was confident that his services would yet be required in Burma.[12]

Meanwhile, he explored the 'Old City', apparently for the first time, with a knowledgeable Pathan as his guide. It was like stepping into the pages of Omar Khayyam. The Old City was originally a walled and gated citadel. Parts of the old ramparts, and one spectacular gateway, the Kotla Mohsin Khan, were still intact. Tony and his guide explored the narrow streets, where the

---

[11] Letters 142, 143, 147 (reference to 'the palace'). The Kaghan Valley is named in Letter 149.

[12] Letter 144.

houses were mainly of baked brick. Some had carved wooden balconies; all had flat roofs, on which the occupants kept their goats and chickens. In the streets below, cows and horses seemed to roam freely. They ascended a minaret of the Mahabat Khan Mosque, and viewed the town from its cupola. Tony was fascinated by an old Sikh fort, now used as a police post and prison. Like Omar, they watched 'a potter thumping his wet clay'. They even visited a 'battered caravanserai', 'an old house built round a courtyard with masses of flowers growing in the middle of it', and ordered tea and cakes.

Afterwards they witnessed the arrival of a camel train from Kabul, the backs of the animals being laden with spices, nuts and, inevitably, carpets. Those evenings with the *munshi* had paid off. Tony conversed fluently with one of the camel-drivers, and learned that the beasts typically carried over half a ton in weight, feeding on *boosa,* or chopped straw, as they plodded through the barren passes. Tony negotiated for an 'old and very dirty carpet' that was folded up under one of the saddles, and, after much haggling, bought it for only ten rupees ('about ten bob'). The carpet later cleaned up well and turned out to be a very beautiful specimen. As he roamed their hostile, fly-blown streets, he was conscious of being stared at by the locals, who seemed astonished at his effrontery. He conceded that it was certainly 'not a place to visit at night or even by one's self during the day'.[13]

Another daring excursion was due south, to Kohat, heartland of the Bagash tribe. The Kohat Pass Road, built by the British in 1850, connected it to Peshawar, but the route was through wild, hilly country, where the people, the Adam Khel Afridis, were far from friendly, a stocky breed of warriors and gun-runners with large, hooked noses and shoulder-length hair, each man brandishing a rifle. At the entrance to the pass, the British had built, in 1853, an elaborate, star-shaped fortification to keep these tribes in check. Known as Fort Handyside, it was still manned,

---

[13] Letter 145.

and must have been a lonely posting. It is described by Tony as 'a page from the last century'.

The road beyond the fort was notorious for its hairpin bends. At one point, Tony 'counted the road sticking to the rock in three loops above us and four below'. There was a sheer drop to his left, and not so much as a row of stones to mark the edge. Admittedly, 'the view was simply beyond all description'. Tony nervously nudged the Indian driver aside and took over the driving, 'for, if we were to go over the edge, it was going to be my fault'. Astonishingly, there was a regular bus service along the route, in 'incredibly dilapidated vehicles' that were 'held together with bits of wire and even string. The tyres were patched together with canvas as new ones are very hard to get and would cost anywhere between one hundred to five hundred pounds depending on the blackness of the market.'

The purpose of the outing was for members of the regiment to compete in a point-to-point, a tough, three-mile event, in which Tony came in third on Warrior. The winner was his old friend and rival, Lieutenant-Colonel James Hepper. In the final race of the season, the mile hurdle, Tony managed to come second, despite nearly falling off. The journey to Kohat had been dangerous enough. Reading of his antics on horseback, Tony's parents feared that he would break his neck.

Persia - Principal Communications.

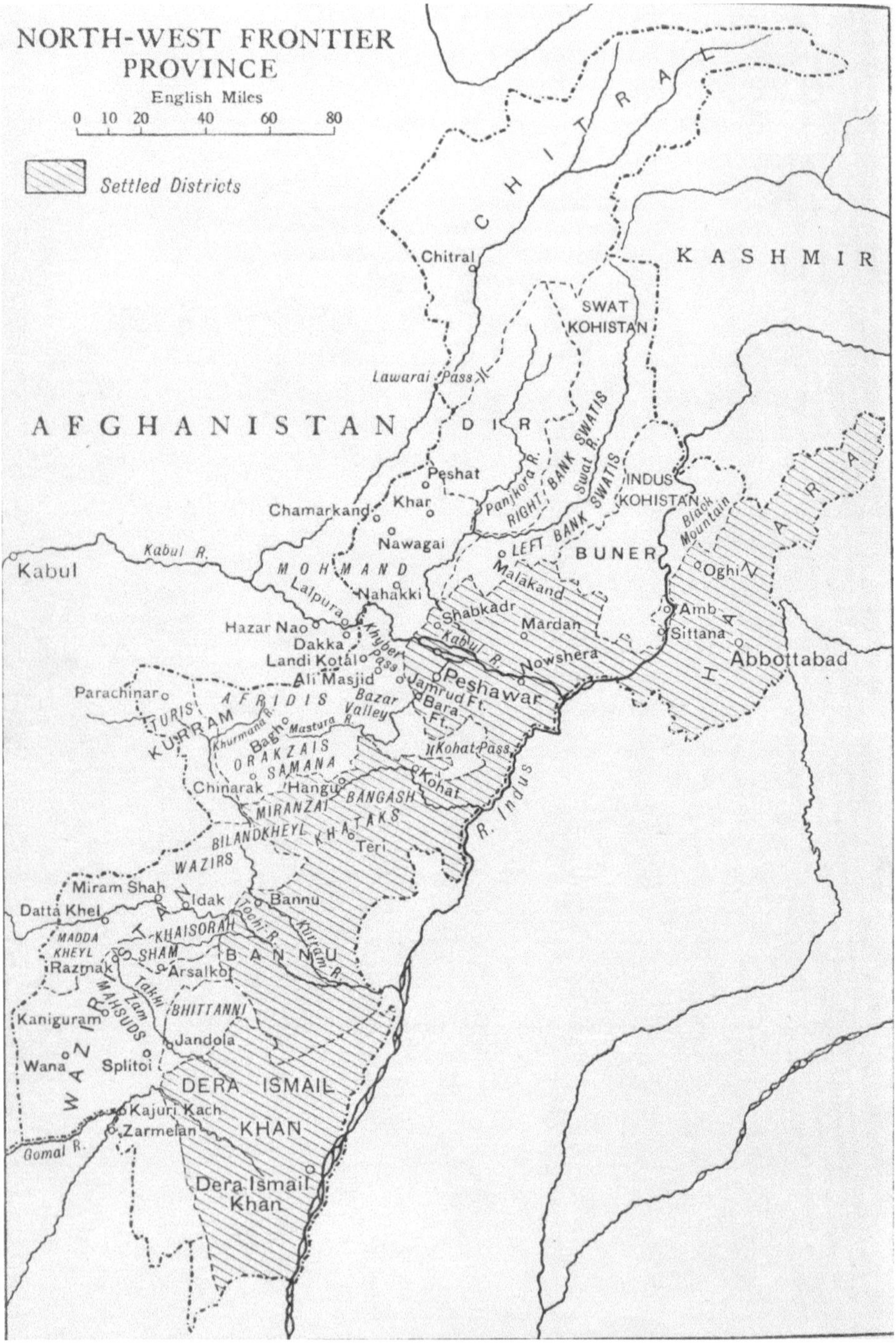
NORTH-WEST FRONTIER PROVINCE
English Miles
0 10 20 40 60 80
Settled Districts
CHITRAL
KASHMIR
Chitral
SWAT KOHISTAN
Lawarai Pass
AFGHANISTAN
DIR
RIGHT BANK SWATIS
LEFT BANK SWATIS
Swat R.
Panjkora R.
INDUS KOHISTAN
Peshat
Khar
Chamarkand
Nawagai
Black Mountain
HAZARA
BUNER
Kabul R.
Kabul
MOHMAND
Malakand
Nahakki
Oghi
Lalpura
Shabkadr
Mardan
Amb
Sittana
Hazar Nao
Khyber Pass
Dakka
Abbottabad
Landi Kotal
Nowshera
Ali Masjid
Peshawar
Jamrud Ft.
Parachinar
AFRIDIS
Bazar Valley
Bara Ft.
TURIS
KURRAM
Khurmana R.
Bagh
Mastura R.
ORAKZAIS
Kohat Pass
SAMANA
Kohat
Chinarak
Hangu
BANGASH
R. Indus
MIRANZAI
BILANDKHEYL
KHATAKS
Teri
WAZIRS
Miram Shah
Idak
Bannu
Datta Khel
Tochi R.
Kurram R.
MADDA KHEYL
KHAISORAH
SHAM
BANNU
Razmak
Arsalkot
WAZIRISTAN
Takki Zam
MAHSUDS
BHITTANNI
Kaniguram
Jandola
Wana
Splitoi
DERA ISMAIL KHAN
Kajuri Kach
Zarmelan
Gomal R.
Dera Ismail Khan

The Snake-Charmer

The regiment spent most of April on exercise, a thousand or more horses and mules marching an average of fifteen miles a day. Sometimes they picked their way by night through the rocks and river beds, alarming the tribesmen by appearing suddenly from the hills. The men slept under bush nets, beside their horses, in the perfect stillness of the night. Tony acknowledged what he had long suspected, that he preferred the life under canvas to that in a house.

According to John Masters, the sight of the Indian mountain batteries in action was 'positively frightening'. Preceded by 'a rhythmic, pounding jingle', they would suddenly appear, 'two abreast, filling the whole road, the huge mules walking out at five miles an hour, the breeches, barrels, recoil mechanisms, wheels, and gun-shields swaying on their backs.[14] Turbans, eyes, and white teeth bobbed up and down amid the flood of tossing steel. No one looked right or left or up or down, only straight ahead.'

Suddenly they would stop, each gun team of eight mules forming a small circle, all but the pivot mule facing out. A subaltern at the flank would bark out a series of orders, and in what seemed like less than a minute the guns would be assembled

---

[14] The 2.75-inch 'screw gun' was so called because its heavy barrel could be unscrewed into two parts. The version then in use was an improvement on that celebrated by Kipling, in that it was a breech- rather than a barrel-loader, and was equipped with recoil buffers and gun shields. The dismantled load could be conveyed by a team of six mules. There were the 'wheel and axle' mule; the 'trail, front part' and 'trail, rear part' mules; the 'recoil trail' mule; the 'breech' mule; and, finally, the 'chase' mule. In addition, there was an 'ammunition' mule, which carried the shells in two ammunition boxes, not to mention the 'pioneer' mule, the 'sub-section store pannier' mule, the 'Artificer's' mules nos.1, 2 and 3 and a 'baggage' mule. A 'relief' mule was specified for each of the seven gun and ammunition mules. In other words, the train of mules for each section was considerable. Tony implies in letter 160 that there were also 25 *horses* per battery. The prescribed pack saddlery and load for each animal is set out in great detail in *The Handbook of the 2.75-inch B.L. Gun: Mule Equipment* (H.M.S.O., 1920), pp.48 *et seq.*

and ready to fire. Masters, an infantryman with a 'proper' sense of his own superiority, 'shuddered and remembered'.[15]

Back at Peshawar on 7 May, Tony sat his gruelling 'Higher Urdu' exam, and was convinced that he had failed. However, he was told at once after the 'oral', which had seemed equally gruelling, that he had passed.

His *munshi,* Sayid Khan, seemed a wise old man and was a great teller of tales. One of his anecdotes seemed incredible, until Tony verified it with the party concerned, who was a brother officer, though even then he had no idea what to make of it.

The officer's wife had gone off to visit friends in Delhi. On the appointed day, she had failed to return. The officer rang up her hosts, and was told that she had left them three days ago, all appearing to be well. The police launched a 'missing person' enquiry but, after three months, had failed to find her.

In desperation, the officer applied to the sagacious *munshi* for help. Sayid Khan led the officer to a neighbouring village and introduced him to an old Pathan, to whom he explained the problem. For some while, the old Pathan seemed lost in thought. Suddenly, he announced that the officer could expect to receive a telegram the following day. It would be from his wife, announcing her return by train that very night. The old man recited the exact wording of the telegram, and specified the exact time of its arrival.

The telegram arrived precisely when he said it would, and was phrased in the manner he had predicted. As it turned out, the woman, having eloped with another man, had since regretted it. Wanting to come home, she begged her husband to forgive her. The most uncanny aspect of the story is that the telegram had been written in the very hour following the interview with the old Pathan. It was as if he had telepathically inspired her to write it. The officer vouched to Tony for every detail of the story.

---

[15] John Masters, *Bugles and a Tiger* (London, 2002), p.214.

Another mysterious happening was the visit of a wandering snake-charmer. While Tony was having breakfast with friends at the bungalow, he heard a strange sound outside. The snake-charmer had appeared from nowhere. He had a King Cobra in a basket before him and was making it dance to the high, thin strains of his *been,* a traditional, flute-like instrument made from a gourd. After a while he put the cobra back in the basket and took out a different instrument. It resembled the chanter from a bagpipe. Within minutes, his playing had drawn an enormous yellow viper from a nearby bush. When it was suggested that he might have planted it there, the man took offence and began to swear at them in Pashtu. He resumed his playing and, half an hour later, had produced no less than eight other snakes, including two King Cobras, all of which he picked up and put into another basket.

To prove that he was not playing tricks, Tony led him to the rose bushes at the end of his garden, from which the charmer produced a further four snakes, and another from the hedge beside the road. None of them was less than three feet in length. The gardener was astonished. In the eight years that he had been working in the garden, he had only ever seen three snakes, all of them tiny.

Just as Sayid Khan knew how to put on a good act, the charmer's exuberant performance depended entirely on trickery. Snakes have a sense of sound, but no ears. Their reaction is rather to the movement of the charmer and his instrument, which they see as potential predators. Hence the cobra may extend its hood. All the snakes are planted beforehand and have usually been disarmed, either by the removal of their fangs or venom glands or even by the stitching up of their mouths. They will all have been starved and dehydrated, and sometimes drugged with paralysing herbs, so that they are barely able to move. Sayid Khan was consulted on the matter, but had no intention of spoiling the illusion. There was no trickery, he insisted, for the snakes are able to travel quickly from a long way off. 'If you were to read the

Bible often enough,' he said, 'you too would be able to do things like that.' Tony had noticed, however, that before being put in the basket, the snakes were 'made to bite on something containing a sedative'. When Sayid Khan assured him that the 'charming fellow' subsequently feasted on his haul, he was being particularly mischievous.[16]

[16] Letters 148, 151. Snake-charming is dying out in India, where it has been banned since 1991, under the *Wildlife Protection Act.*

PESHAWAR

‘A hot-bed of murders, blood-feuds, thieves and robbers dominated by the old Mogul fort and palace’: foreigners ventured into old Peshawar with caution. While roaming the hostile, fly-blown streets of the city, Tony was conscious of being stared at by the locals, who seemed astonished at his effrontery.

Mall Road, Peshawar Cantonment. After two years of hardship in a sand-blown tent, Tony was at last experiencing ‘all the pre-war way of life of the old Indian Army’, as if the war had never intruded.

The traffic on the Mall seemed mostly to be horse-drawn, including, on occasion, Colonel Hepper’s superb four-in-hand.

Tony outside his office. An armed orderly, ‘dressed as if he had stepped from a Gilbert and Sullivan opera’, stiffened to attention whenever he passed.

Tony (front row, second left) with officers of 28 Indian Mountain Regiment at Lake Beale, March 1946; a pair of 2.75-inch ‘screw guns’ to the fore.

16 (Zhob) Battery in the field, and on Battery Drill near Kohat in May 1946, during a sapping heat-wave.

Wireless mules from Zhob Battery, which included a large number of Sikhs. To Tony's regret, they were reassigned ahead of Partition.

The 'insidious siren', Lady B.M., whom Tony met on board the *Capetown Castle;* also posing coyly in front of the Jama Masjid Mosque in Delhi. Their relationship convinced him to break up with Isa.

Raj Wali Khan, the dependable V.C.O. in Zhob Battery, whom Tony sent to the U.K. for Victory Week. Khan had the time of his life.

CHAPTER VIII

FROM LANDI KHOTAL TO KOHAT AND THAL, VIA OGBOURNE

From V.E. to V.J.

Tony considered Peshawar to be easily his best posting to date. The working day for both officers and men began at 6.30 a.m. in the riding school. This was the standard enclosed space for equestrians, about a hundred yards square, with jumps and a soft floor. Horses and riders went through such drills as 'collection', 'half-passage' and 'full-passage'. The subalterns had to be taught from scratch, occasionally under Tony's supervision, and he would wheel out all the classic lines, such as: 'and who gave you permission to dismount, Mr Neal?' or 'Try it with your shirt off, Mr Holt'. Tony went to breakfast at 8 a.m, and to his office by 9, where he would work until 5, with an hour off for lunch. After his lesson with the *munshi* he would ride for another hour, then it was supper and bed, usually by 11 p.m.

In spite of all the advantages of the posting and his serving in the mountain regiment of which he had long dreamed, Tony confessed to being bored, something that he had never experienced before. The local establishment was beginning to get on his nerves. Both civilians and regulars seemed hidebound and artificial. They were cocooned from the war and acted as if nothing would ever upset their *status quo.* Tony predicted that they would soon be in for a nasty shock. Actually, they were in for several.

Thus, when the defeat of Germany was announced on 8 May ('V.E.' or 'Victory in Europe Day'), 'it had very little effect'. Tony and his friends had two days off and celebrated on the first day with a picnic, the men riding ahead and the women following in a trap with the food. With five dogs between them - Tony had recently acquired 'Henry' and 'Rollo'[1] - there were some interesting confrontations with the local pye-dogs or 'pariahs'. Tony had to ward off these ferocious scavengers with a hunting crop. The party settled by the side of a river, and bacon and eggs were cooked on an open fire.

There was optimism that the fall of Japan would soon follow, but Tony had his doubts. He thought it would take 'well over a year as the Japanese do not know the meaning of the word "surrender". Even if the whole Japanese mainland was to be occupied the troops in China and in the odd island in the Pacific will still have to be winkled out by someone.' In that respect, too, his prophecies were accurate. Lieutenant Hiroo Onoda was an extreme case, holding out in the Philippine jungle for 29 years, during which time he killed thirty Filipino civilians. Onodo disbelieved reports of the Japanese defeat, and finally handed over his sword on 9 March 1974, after being coaxed out of hiding by his former commanding officer. He said he had sworn never to surrender and assumed that all his countrymen and women had done the same. Of course, neither Onodo, nor Tony, had yet heard of the Atomic Bomb.[2]

The main cause of Tony's *ennui* was no doubt his being so far removed from the action, and that the opportunities to distinguish himself in the field were slipping away. He was also very unsettled by Hepper's absence on leave in England (the planned trek in the Kaghan Valley had had to be shelved), and by the departure, to the Staff College at Quetta, of his friend George Chapman, the second-in-command, who had taken over from Hepper in his absence. George had been Tony's companion at the visit of the snake-charmer and on the celebratory picnic. He bequeathed his trap to Tony, and custody of the R.H.Q. stables,

---

[1] Tiger of Tiddim had vanished from the scene without explanation.

[2] Letters 148, 149, 150; Rupert Wingfield-Hayes, V.J. Day: A W.W.2 Hero and a Reckoning with Japan's Past', B.B.C. News Online, 15 August 2020, https://www.bbc.co.uk/news/world-asia-53763059.

with their complement of twenty or so very fine and well-fed horses.

It was becoming 'very sticky', with high humidity and temperatures exceeding 110 in the shade. The river banks were like green-houses 'with the furnace at full blast'. All the animals sought shelter from the burning heat, apart from the vultures and jackals and the lizards on which they preyed. There was no respite at night.

The staff horses, however, led a pampered existence. Tony used a 'Coventry Climax' fire pump to water the garden at H.Q. It provided each animal with ten pounds of protein-rich lucerne a day, on which they thrived. The *subedar* was very impressed and announced that he would be investing in such a machine after the war. This man, at least, had learnt something from the British. In the Punjab, the general method of irrigation was still based on the 'Persian wheel', with a blind-folded ox 'walking round in an eternal circle'.

Tony shared his reflections on India with his parents. He argued that the augmented rates of pay for officers serving in the Indian Army were entirely appropriate, in view of the extra responsibilities that it entailed. Most of the men were unable to speak English, so new languages had to be mastered. They were also 'in no way as reliable as the B.O.R.' (British Other Ranks). He adds that 'there are very few Indian sergeants to whom one can give the proverbial order "Carry on sergeant"'.

Tony's men nevertheless felt that they could come to him with their problems, as well as their aspirations. Their main preoccupation seems to have been the supply of water to their home village. Would he write to the local District Commissioner on their behalf? 'The ever pressing shame of India,' wrote Tony, 'is that no one ever thinks of his neighbour, it is only himself who matters so bribes and corruption are the rule of the day. The District Commissioner details a man to investigate a case of theft or of strife concerning the ownership of some land or even who owns a tree, but the man appointed is always a relation of one of the parties involved and you can guess who wins the legal argument. No matter what Mr Bevan or his Labour friends may say the truth is that the country is not yet truly civilised and is certainly in no condition to govern itself. How far this state of affairs is the responsibility of the British government is another question.'[3]

Aneurin ('Nye') Bevan, an ex-miner, was the Labour M.P. for Ebbw Vale, a vociferous opponent of the wartime coalition government under Churchill (who called him 'a squalid nuisance'), and one of the leading advocates for a 'new society' in post-war Britain. This was to include nationalisation, economic planning, a free health service ('pure socialism', as Bevan put it), a 'Welfare State' and the dismantling of the Empire, all of which was subsequently realised. With Germany defeated, campaigning for a General Election, the first since 1935, had begun on 15 June. Tony, who had had no previous opportunities to vote in any sort of election, had already, in August 1944, appointed his parents as proxies. They were charged with disposing of his vote as they thought fit, 'as long as you do not help to raise the red or pink flags - not that there is any fear of your doing that!'[4]

Whatever the outcome of the election, it was firmly understood (and had been since at least 1942) that the independence of India was imminent. It was preferred that this should be a politically united India, without the need for a new, separate state of Pakistan, which would include Tony's predominantly Muslim North-West Frontier Province.[5] A 'Cabinet Mission' had arrived at Delhi in March, but it was for Wavell, as Viceroy, to propose how a united India might be governed, a task that could hardly be achieved in a hurry, if at all. Tony alludes to the Simla Conference that convened on 24 June. Wavell proposed a new Executive

[3] Letters 149, 150, 151.

[4] Letter 126.

[5] Ian Talbot and Guharpal Singh, *The Partition of India* (Cambridge, 2009), p.40.

Council, the entire membership of which was to be nominated by the Indians themselves, apart from the key offices of Viceroy and Commander-in-Chief.

Unfortunately, as both Wavell and Tony Fowle knew perfectly well, the Indians were unable to agree about anything. Wavell wrote in his diary that Gandhi and Jinna, leaders respectively of the Indian National Congress and the All-India Muslim League, behaved from the start like 'very temperamental prima donnas'. Jinnah later told Wavell that 'Indian unity was only a British creation', which was true enough. Gandhi's position was that 'His Majesty King George will sooner or later have to take the Hindu or Muslim point of view as they were irreconcilable'.[6] When both leaders were so intransigent, the tragedy of Partition was a foregone conclusion.

The decidedly left-leaning Army Bureau of Current Affairs, a department of the War Office, was extremely active at this time, promoting compulsory political discussions between officers and other ranks. It was argued that servicemen had a right to be educated in current affairs, but there seems to have been a heavy emphasis on post-war reform and reconstruction. Displays were mounted and bi-weekly pamphlets issued, explaining such topics as Labour's plans for slum clearance and for a free national health service. As far as Tony's own soldiers were concerned, the Simla Conference failed to excite their interest. 'I have often tried to get the V.C.O.s to talk about politics but they just know nothing about it and care even less; all they want is to be left in peace to cultivate their fields. I think all the political agitators are confined to the small town-dwelling part of the population and the so-called "students". The only trouble that ever makes itself felt here, other than that among the tribes, is due to the same old story of people wanting more pay.' He might have added that his Sikhs were preoccupied with the scarcity of cotton. Brightly-coloured

---

6 Stanley Wolpert, *Shameful Flight* (Karachi, 2012), pp.79-82, 242-5.

material for their off-duty turbans, which required 'as many yards of cloth … as in a good kilt', was increasingly hard to come by.

Even the British in Peshawar displayed little enthusiasm for the Conference, knowing that it was bound to fail, but the U.K. Election on 5 July was a matter of profound concern. With votes having to be collected from overseas, the result (including the return for Tony's home constituency of Devizes) was not fully declared until 26 July, but it confirmed a Labour majority of 145, a landslide. The complacent people around Tony were 'all very upset', as no one in Peshawar had voted for them. There had never been a Labour majority before, and there was even some seditious talk of 'staying here until it is all over and of establishing a bulwark of democracy out of reach of Attlee and his pale pink party'. If the service vote had indeed been decisive, as was said at the time, the relentless propagandising of A.B.C.A. had surely played a part. 'Whoever dreamed up A.B.C.A. at the War Office,' wrote Woodrow Wyatt, one of the newly-elected Labour M.P.s, 'was in part responsible for Labour's landslide victory in 1945.'[7]

Unsettled by these events, Tony anxiously awaited orders for home leave, which, ironically, put paid to any chance of his going to Burma. Back in March, he had been promised 61 days, exclusive of all travel, and further time must since have accrued.[8] Hepper, recently returned from a month in England, brought first-hand news of his parents, having very decently made a day-excursion from Savernake in order to meet them. Hepper now offered Tony a new command, that of the 14th (Rajputana) Mountain Battery, which meant promotion to the rank of Major. The 14th was one of the three scattered batteries of which the

---

[7] Quoted in Sal Shuel, *A.B.C.A.*, http://www.jboswell.org.uk/abca.php. See also *The Story of the Army Bureau of Current Affairs,* Imperial War Museum, MGH 56, https://www.iwm.org.uk/collections/item/object/1060009848.

[8] Letter 144. According to John Masters in *Bugles and a Tiger,* p.168, 'An Indian Army officer got two months' "privilege leave" on full pay every year - three months if he was serving on the Frontier or in a non-family station'.

29th Indian Light Mountain Regiment was formed. It was currently stationed at Landi Khotal, about thirty miles from headquarters, so Tony was assured of considerable independence, albeit under Hepper's benevolent oversight.

The 14th was a respectable old unit, formerly the 34th Mountain Battery, which had served very gallantly against the Turks in Mesopotamia in 1918 (picking up a battle honour), in brushes with the Kurds in 1919-20, and more recently, under Hepper's command, in Burma. This was the battery that had been surprised by the Japanese at Kha Aimol, fending them off with bayonets and rifle butts. It was now an all-Sikh unit (since 1944, there had been an official drive to segregate batteries according to religion), so Tony would have felt at home. He writes that it had 'a wonderful collection of plate and a very noble history'.

Having relinquished the adjutancy and his too-comfortable life at Headquarters, much to his relief on both counts, Tony joined the 14th on 31 July. The fort at Landi Khotal was not only the most westerly outpost of the British, but also the highest point on the Khyber Pass. For that reason, as Tony had noted on a previous visit, it was a rather cold and cheerless place; nor was there much traffic along the road, apart from a few 'very dilapidated lorries and busses *[sic]* running between Kabul and Peshawar with loads of carpets, spices and other oriental wares'.[9]

On 6 and 9 August, atomic bombs largely destroyed the cities of Hiroshima and Nagasaki. On 15 August, despite the opposition of his more fanatical subjects, the Japanese Emperor insisted on surrender, the date being commemorated ever since as 'V.J.' or 'Victory over Japan Day'. Although the official instrument was not to be signed for several weeks, the Pacific War was over.

---

[9] Letter 153, and *cf.* letter 149, on Landi Khotal; on the 14th, late 34th Mountain Battery, C.A.L. Graham, *The History of the Indian Mountain Artillery* (Aldershot, 1957), pp.183, 185, 186, 188, 192, 219, 260, 263, 269, 363, 448 (referring to the Gunner Mess as 'famed for its all-concrete billiards table, built by the Sappers in the early 1930s, and which still functions well despite the earthquake shocks to which that area is prone).

Zhob Battery

Tony barely had time to establish himself at Landi Khotal. From 23 August he was on stand-by for leave, which meant being packed and ready to go at a moment's notice. Frustratingly, orders to report to the local Railway Transport Officer were delayed for several weeks. Unable to settle down to any serious work, he idled away the time on horseback. After two false starts, he finally boarded a plane in late September or early October. Whenever there was room in their aircraft, the R.A.F. were flying people back in record time, though, as Tony discovered, it was a far from comfortable experience.[10]

One can only imagine what he made of his battered homeland. He had reported in July: 'All the officers who have gone home have written saying they wished it was a bit warmer'. This was in a season of searing, breathless heat in the North-West Frontier Province. Landi Khotal was, however, considerably cooler, being 'six thousand feet up', so was a 'good toughening up place for England'.[11]

In the event, Tony's preoccupations were not with the weather but of the comforting, domestic kind. He was to evoke them later in Betjeman-esque terms. 'I often think of you all back in Ogbourne,' he wrote on his return, 'and wish I could see how you are getting on. I suppose that by now the wood has all been cut up and the hall repaired and painted De Lux[e], and that there are new bell-ropes hanging in the tower.'[12] This was surely the period when Tony became engaged. The lovely Isa McDonald had

[10] Letters 144, 151 (Hepper's journey home taking seven days and reports of R.A.F. flights achieved in less than 12 hours), 156 (Tony's last letter home before leave, dated 26 September), 157 (discomforts of the flight). It is assumed that Tony had accrued extra leave since March, when he had been allocated 61 days, perhaps nearer three months in total.

[11] Letters 152, 156.

[12] Letter 160. Ogbourne's late-medieval bell tower has a ring of five bells, with an 18-hundredweight tenor tuned to E-flat. They would, of course, have been inactive during the war.

patiently tolerated his absence for two years, but as they were about to endure a further, indefinite separation, the relationship was foredoomed.[13]

At the expiry of his leave on 27 December, Tony had duly reported to the Royal Artillery Depot, Woolwich, probably visiting the historic home of his regiment for the first time. After a night in the mess there, he had boarded an evening train to Southampton, and had embarked on the Union Castle liner *Capetown Castle* for India.[14] No letters survive that describe the voyage. However, the ship's movements are well documented. She entered the Suez Canal on 6 January and arrived at Bombay on 14 January 1946.[15]

On or soon after his arrival in India, Tony was unexpectedly posted to a new regiment, 28 Indian Mountain Regiment, and sent initially to the famous Deolali Camp, which he would have reached by train from Bombay. It was his first foray into the Indian peninsula.[16]

158 miles inland from the port, Deolali had been established in 1861 as a transit camp. The British troops who were drafted there were incessantly drilled or route-marched to acclimatise them to the heat, or they endured long periods of idleness while waiting to be shipped back to England, which had been Tony's recent experience. In either case they were highly susceptible to a condition known as 'camp fever' or, in army slang, 'Doolaly tap'.

By 1946, Deolali Camp was equipped with cinemas, swimming pools, amusement parks and restaurants, though not with a psychiatric unit. The B.B.C. television series *It Ain't Half Hot, Mum,* by the creators of *Dad's Army,* is set in Deolali and features the antics of a Royal Artillery Concert Party. Tony may

---

[13] Tony's notes appended to Letter 38.

[14] Letter 157.

[15] 'Capetown Castle', https://www.bandcstaffregister.com/page188.html.

[16] Letter 158. Pace Tony's annotation to letter 159, '28 Indian Mountain Artillery' is captioned twice in his album.

well have encountered such a troupe during his brief stay, and, if he ever saw the series, would have been struck by its many authentic touches, such as the protagonists' being perpetually bathed in sweat. Attracting up to seventeen million viewers at its height, it ran between 1974 and 1981, making gentle fun of the cowardly 'artistes' and their ineffectual officers, while the Indian characters, including the bearer Rangi Ram and assorted char-, dhobi- and punkah-wallahs (tea-vendors, laundrymen and fan-operators), unfailingly get the better of them. Despite the obvious satire, B.B.C. executives have fretted ever since lest the 'racist', 'homophobic' and 'imperialist' attitudes of the characters, not to mention the 'blacking-up' of the white actor who played the bearer, might cause offence. The series is now considered 'so un-P.C. as to be unrepeatable'.[17] Ironically, the Indian characters themselves are patriotically 'British' and, in the final episode, plan their own repatriation to 'Blighty'. The prescient dhobi-wallah intends to invest in washing-machines and to set up a self-service laundry. He proposes to call this unheard-of enterprise 'a laundry-ette'.

Tony may have languished at Deolali for up to a fortnight. He then travelled about a hundred miles north-west to Lake Beale, arriving on 2 February. High in the mountains, Lake Beale was an enormous reservoir, 43 miles long, which had been created, and named, by the British in 1911. 28 Indian Mountain Regiment was encamped in a 'fine spot' on the water's edge. Tony was introduced to its amiable C.O., Lieutenant-Colonel Birch, and took command of 16 (Zhob) Mountain Battery. Named after a

---

[17] Hannah Furness, 'Banning It Ain't Half Hot Mum from TV is a "shame", creator says, as non-PC moments are just "historical truth"', *The Daily Telegraph,* 20 September 2013; obituary of Windsor Davies, *The Daily Telegraph,* 20 January 2019. The co-writers of the series, Jimmy Perry and David Croft, had both served with E.N.S.A. in India during the war, and its star, Michael Bates, had been born in India, spoke Hindi and Urdu like a native, and had served with the Gurkhas in the war, attaining the rank of major. He certainly had the accent and manner of his character to perfection. It is said that no more suitable Indian actor could be found to fill the role.

wild valley in Baluchistan, the Zhob Battery had also collected a battle honour in the Great War ('Persia 1918'), and, more recently, had served in the operations around Imphal. Tony describes it as 'half Sikh and half P.M.', by which he means 'Punjabi Mohammedans', both types being much to his liking.[18]

The month that Tony spent at Lake Beale seems to have been more of a holiday than a serious exercise. From their 'fine spot' on the edge of the lake, the men had ample time to 'swim in it, boat on it and lie in the sun by it'. They had a sailing boat and two motor-boats at their disposal. Tony tried his hand at water-skiing, or 'aqua-planing', as it was then termed, being a considerable novelty; and accompanied the colonel on a trip to shoot the abundant duck. They took 'some food and bedding, a cook and our orderlies and camped out for the night', rising early to shoot. Their stand was 'by a large but very shallow river about ten miles beyond our lake which is itself about fifty miles from the nearest road and is therefore very wild and deserted'. They returned with a bag of 48 duck and a spur-winged goose, which they ate for dinner.

This was more verdant country than Tony was used to, with its rivers, lakes and trees, but it was still very hot, temperatures reaching about 110 degrees. 'The ground is covered with tall dried-up grass, there are out-crops of rock and a lot of bushes. The hills are about 6,000 feet high but look quite ridiculous as they rise very suddenly out of a level plane just like a child's concept of a volcano. There are quite a number of villages about the place but the people are a very poor type, not in the least like the burly Pathans from the north, they are all Hindus and very pro-Congress.' Apart from Gandhi, the figurehead of the Indian

---

[18] Graham, *History of the Indian Mountain Artillery,* pp.192, 367. Tony describes Zhob Battery as 'independent'; in Sept 1939 it had been attached to the 24th (*ibid.,* p.259). *Cf.* Graham, p.127 on 'Punjabi Mohammedans'. Tony's parents are unlikely to have understood the acronym.

National Congress, the membership of the party struck him as a bunch of hypocrites.[19]

Years later, Tony described the nature of their training on Lake Beale. It 'involved getting in and out of landing craft and getting into action on the "beach" as quickly as possible.' These were not skills that would have any application on the Frontier. According to Tony, the regiment had been assigned to 'Jap Force'. It 'was training for the final assault on the Japanese mainland'.[20]

Was Tony's memory playing tricks? After all, 'Victory over Japan Day' had been declared on 15 August 1945. The Allies' plans for the largest amphibious invasion in history had happily been shelved, for the predicted casualties were enormous. The American General Douglas MacArthur, Supreme Commander of the Allied Powers, had arrived in Tokyo on 30 August and, on 2 September, had witnessed the Japanese instrument of surrender. By the end of 1945, Japan was already swarming with American G.I.s, some 430,000 of them.

However, on 31 January 1946, the long-planned involvement of a British Commonwealth Occupation Force, to be about 40,000-strong, was announced. The initial contingent was to take possession of the port of Kure, near the devastated city of Hiroshima, and to establish its headquarters there. As Kure had been the Imperial Japanese Navy's largest wartime naval base, and as fanatical elements were still at large, it was by no means assumed that their landing would be unopposed - hence the intensive amphibious training. In the event, a Royal Navy shore party and Australian ground forces took peaceful possession of the port and facilities on 21 February, and the support of 28 Indian Mountain Regiment was no longer required.[21]

---

[19] Letter 158. He believes Gandhi to be 'sincere'.

[20] Tony's annotations to letter 159.

[21] Eiji Takemae, *Inside G.H.Q.: The Allied Occupation of Japan and its Legacy* (New York, 2002), pp.65, 94; Greg Swinden, 'The Navy and the British Commonwealth Occupation Force in Japan 1945-1952', *Semaphore,* Issue 2 (Sea Power Centre - Australia, Canberra, 2018).

Tony knew nothing of this at the time, reporting on 7 February that everyone was 'on tenterhooks, as we have just had a warning order to move', presumably to the Frontier. It had never occurred to him that they might be sent to Japan.

Of more immediate concern was a mutiny by naval ratings and communications operators at H.M.S. *Talwar,* the Royal Indian Navy shore base at Bombay, which was only 22 miles from the camp. Erupting on 18 February, the Communist-backed insurrection had spread rapidly. Within two days, it encompassed 88 naval vessels, including 45 warships. The harbour and its shore establishments had been completely overrun.

That evening, the Flag-Officer Commanding, Admiral John Godfrey, flew in from New Delhi. From his previous role as Director of Naval Intelligence, Godfrey was Ian Fleming's model for 'M' in the James Bond novels. In a broadcast on 21 February, he told the mutineers that they must 'surrender or perish'. He was prepared to destroy the entire fleet if necessary. Blockaded by British troops and with the R.A.F. flying menacingly overhead, the last of them had surrendered by 26 February. Had the mutiny not been condemned by Gandhi and other nationalist leaders, it might have had a very different outcome. Confidence in the Royal Indian Navy and Godfrey's own reputation had, however, been shattered. There is no doubt that conditions in the service were dismal and that it had been extremely poorly led. Godfrey retired under a cloud and was denied the knighthood that would otherwise have been his due.[22]

Tony correctly identified the communications staff as the main troublemakers, as they tended to be middle-class people with matriculation or college education,[23] or in his words 'men who

---

[22] See, for example, Chris Madsen, 'The Royal Indian Navy Mutiny, 1946', in Christopher Bell and Bruce Elleman eds., *Naval Mutinies of the Twentieth Century: An International Perspective* (London, 2003).

[23] Daniel Owen Spence, 'Beyond Talwar: A Cultural Reappraisal of the 1946 Royal Indian Navy Mutiny', *Journal of Imperial and Commonwealth History,* 43 (2015), p.493.

have a slight veneer of the so-called education given by Indian universities and high schools and, since their student days, have always relied on strikes or civil disturbance in order to gain their own undisciplined ends'. In recent weeks there had been a series of demonstrations or 'strikes' by British airmen serving at several dozen R.A.F. stations in India. Their main complaint was that they wanted to be demobilised and sent home as soon as possible. Some were communist sympathisers. On instructions from the Labour government, a lenient hand was applied and the issues were soon resolved, with only a few of the airmen facing courts-martial.[24] Tony, who took a dim enough view of the 'unmilitary' R.A.F., was incensed. He thought the response to both mutinies should have been to 'shoot one in ten' of the culprits.[25] In a telegram to the Prime Minister on 24 February, Wavell himself observed that the 'example of the Royal Air Force, who got away with what was really a mutiny, has some responsibility for the present situation'.[26]

Tony had 'little or no fear of a similar occurrence in the army', or at least in his own regiment, where there was proper discipline. The contrast with the whingeing British conscripts, who thought it acceptable to go on 'strike', is stark. 'During the Second World War,' writes its historian, Brigadier Graham, 'the Indian Mountain Artillery maintained the good reputation it had had for close on a hundred years. The units were proud to support British infantry, and as proud to have served through the most strenuous war on record with their comrades-in-arms over many years in the Indian Army. The artilleryman's record was second to none - he was hard and tough, cheerful in hardship and not prone to grumble at

[24] For the view of a participant, who longed for 'the sight of India disappearing over the stern of the ship', see David van Vlymen, 'The R.A.F. Strike - India, 1946', *The John Carpenter Club Gazette: Journal of the City of London Old Boys Association* (2007).

[25] Letter 159.

[26] Quoted in Nicholas Mansergh ed., *The Transfer of Power in India, 1942-47*, Vol. 6 (London, 1976), p.1055.

the lack of amenities. He fought well, the result of the military traditions of a fighting race and the family spirit in the battery, and, last but not least, of his friendship and intimate contact with his British officers. It seems sad that the bond of friendship, grown so firm and strong through generations of soldiering, should be ruthlessly broken a short time later.'[27]

In their isolated valley, 28 Indian Mountain Regiment had therefore been unaffected by these events, apart from a 'single smashed windscreen'. They had, in any case, other things on their mind. By 23 February, a new destination had been confirmed, and their training schedule was adapted accordingly. They would indeed be returning to the frontier, to the troubled region of Waziristan, and to a place with which Tony was already familiar, the little military cantonment of Kohat.[28]

Kohat Cantonment

The transportation of 28 Indian Mountain Regiment, consisting of 'about a thousand men, four hundred animals and a hundred tons of kit', began on 12 March 1946. It was a complicated manoeuvre, involving 'four trains leaving from three different stations on three different days'. There were also 'two parties going by road'. The distance to Kohat was about a thousand miles.

The last days at Lake Beale had been truly like a holiday, with plenty of time for games, swimming, riding and boating. The colonel and Tony had converted one of the kayaks into a sailing boat, in which they had sped across the lake in the evening breeze. Tony was one of the older hands in the camp, and for a while in February, had been acting C.O. Most of the officers had never been to the Frontier. Tony prepared them for the experience with a series of 'sand-table' lectures.

---

[27] Graham, *History of the Indian Mountain Artillery,* p.415.

[28] Letter 159.

Zhob Battery travelled by a specially-requisitioned train from nearby Asvali. Enjoying 'independent' status, it was the only battery that would be taking its own animals, the pick of the regiment's horses and mules. As 'O.C. Train', Tony was the only British officer on board. The train was comprised of nineteen cattle trucks for the men and animals, twelve goods vans for the kit, and a brake van where Tony set up his camp bed. These were rather cramped quarters, however, as they were shared with the *subedar,* with the vet, and with ten *havildars* and *naiks* (the Indian equivalents of sergeants and corporals).

The hundred or so mules walked calmly up the ramps into their carriages and it was only a couple of the horses that gave any trouble. The men seemed quite content to bed down with the animals, except for one, a Sikh driver, who having 'slipped off the pile of hay on which he had been sleeping' was accidentally trodden on. While waiting for an ambulance at their next stop, Tony helped the vet, an Indian, to patch up the man's scalp, which apparently was 'hanging down the back of his neck exposing the bone of the skull'. Using a pair of forceps, Tony pulled the skin and hair back into place while the vet sowed it up. Half a bottle of rum was administered to the patient to keep him calm. He was eventually to re-join the battery, apparently 'none the worse for the experience save for the most horrific scar across his forehead giving testament to our lack of skill with the needle'.

By contrast, Tony was impressed with the efficiency and friendliness of the railway staff, who put themselves completely at his disposal, cheerfully stopping the train for an hour at a time in order to water the animals (this happened at least four times a day) as well as for a further three hours for the cooking of an elaborate meal. 'The guard was a grand fellow and thoroughly entered into the spirit of the journey. "If we go now, Sahib, we shall get in front of the Bombay mail and it will have to slow down for us!"' (Perhaps he was like the character of Gupta, the enthusiastic driver of the 'Empress of India' in the 1959 film *North West Frontier,* starring Kenneth More.) Tony was initiated into some of the arcana of railway management, 'tallies and clearance certificates, loop lines, guard and detention reports all coming in as part of a day's work'. The only incident of note was a 'minor derailment due to a hot axle, but there were no casualties and we were under way again in six hours'.[29]

Zhob Battery arrived at Kohat on 18 March 1946. It was almost exactly a year (less one week) since Tony's last visit. He had approached it then from the opposite direction, to compete in a point-to-point. That journey had been by the hair-raising Kohat Pass Road. This time he pulled in to the town's elegant station, after a rail journey lasting six days and five nights.

A far greater danger than the terrain was the hostility of the locals, the intractable Adam Khel Afridis. A proud and warlike clan, they were known for launching savage attacks on the cantonment, often in revenge for some slight. In 1920 they had killed the garrison surgeon in the course of looting his home, and had attempted to drag away his wife, who later died of her injuries. Three years later, police had searched the house of a bandit chief, Ajab Khan Afridi, who had been one of the instigators of that raid. He, in revenge, had led a second daring incursion, during which he had broken into the bungalow of Major Archibald Ellis, stabbed his wife to death, and kidnapped their seventeen-year-old daughter, Mollie. The terrified girl was eventually released through the intervention of a remarkable missionary sister, Mrs Lilian Starr, whose husband had also been murdered by tribesmen. A lone Englishwoman, she had, at great risk to her own life, led a rescue party into the Tirah hills. Such was her celebrity that, in 1927, Mollie was given a small part by Alfred Hitchcock in one of his films. She was invited back to Kohat in 1983, and was at last able to pay her respects at the grave of her murdered mother.[30] Such atrocities were shocking to

---

29 Letters 160, 161 (with later annotation about the injured Sikh driver).

30 Jayne L. Gifford, '"A Damnable Blaze": John Loader Maffey, the North-West Frontier and the Abduction of Mollie Ellis, 1919 – 1923', *The Journal of Imperial and Commonwealth History,* 10 (2023), pp.1-29.

Europeans, but the older hands knew better than to judge the tribes by Western standards. These were sophisticated guerrilla warriors, with a strong code of honour and hospitality, for whom 'murder, raids and robberies' were not considered to be terrible crimes, but the honourable acts of 'heroes and champions'.[31]

The perimeter defences of Kohat cantonment had since been improved - there was now 'a barbed wire fence with steel gates which are closed at dark'[32] - but British officials and their families could never consider themselves entirely safe. Tony was unconcerned and would no doubt have welcomed a scrap. He describes Kohat as 'a smallish garrison town lying at the foot of the pass guarding the road up to Kazmak and Bannu'. It seemed to him 'a very fine station' with its Victorian architecture, formal gardens, abundant trees and sporting facilities, including grass tennis courts, a polo ground and hockey pitches, and its backdrop of snow-capped mountains. The valley was well-watered and shady, but 'further away in the hills there is not a single blade of grass to be seen'. The Gunner Mess was a recently-converted elephant stable. There was 'also a very medieval looking fort or "keep" into which all the women and children are herded in times of trouble', the only law recognised by the Pathans being that of the rifle. The buildings were of brick, and 'designed for the hot climate', with flat roofs. Tony was assigned a first-floor flat, one of four, in 'Albert Mansions', overlooking a deliciously scented garden.[33]

Despite the heightened tension elsewhere, Kohat seemed remarkably calm. In early March, the 'Victory Week' celebrations in New Delhi had been marred by rampaging mobs. A woman-friend of Tony's had been besieged in the Wavell Canteen, opposite the railway station, and had had to be rescued by the

---

[31] Major George Roos-Keppel, Political Agent in the Khyber, 1901, quoted at https://www.nam.ac.uk/explore/north-west-frontier-india.

[32] Letter 163.

[33] Letters 161, 163; Graham, *History of the Indian Mountain Artillery,* p.448 (on the converted elephant stable and the abundant flowers).

army. A new 'Cabinet Mission' arrived from London on 24 March, the 'mission' being to propose formulae for independence that would preserve the unity of India. It was doomed to fail. Meanwhile, in early April, over 150 horses and riders took part in a gymkhana at Kohat. Tony rode in four events (he came third in the 'Handy Hunter Trials'), and judged two, in the capacity once more of acting C.O. The colonel had taken leave to get married, and Tony hoped he might be absent for a while, in which case he would accede (if only temporarily) to his rank.[34]

By the end of April the regiment had still not found its feet, but was busy 'reorganising and getting back to the peacetime system'. The weather was 'very hot indeed with sudden violent storms'. Tony drove up to Tret, in Kashmir, on business, and there was a trip to Peshawar along the perilous pass road, on which all European travellers, even the women, carried revolvers. A large sign at the entrance to the pass advised: 'Tribal Territory: Go Carefully'.[35] There were various fishing expeditions, one being with the colonel of the infantry battalion at Kohat and his family, and a flurry of dinner invitations, from the wives of both colonels, from the Brigadier and from the District Commissioner, who lived 'in great pomp surrounded by guards and union jacks', but was by no means pompous himself, organising elaborate, light-hearted party games for his guests.[36]

By mid-May, the heat was becoming unbearable, but Tony had 'obtained permission to send three quarters of my men off on three months leave'. Those who remained were excused all duties beyond the care of the animals. The Sikh element might not be

---

34 Letters 161, 162; *Delhi Victory Week Parade and Anti-British Hartals, March, 1946,* https://zikredilli.com/delhi-depository/f/delhi-victory-week-parade-and-anti-british-hartals-march-1946; Talbot and Singh, *The Partition of India,* p.40.

35 There is a photograph at the sign of an R.I.A.S.C. officer, Ronald Osbourne, and his wife Beryl, dated April 1946 - https://www.indianmemoryproject.com/62/. Beryl is armed with a revolver.

36 Letters 162, 163.

returning at all, as it had been decided, in unhappy anticipation of a partitioned India, that 28 Indian Mounted Regiment was to be an all-Muslim regiment. Tony admired the 'P.M.s', but would miss his warlike Sikhs and the 'balance of power' in the regiment that they helped to maintain. He was proud of the fact that half his battery had taken part in the Delhi Victory Week (4 to 9 March 1946), and his senior V.C.O., Subedar Raj Wali Khan, was even then on his way to England. Tony had selected Khan for the June Victory Week, the equivalent celebrations at home, a series of parades to be held in various parts of the country. Khan, 'who looks rather frightening but is a grand man and speaks fairly good English', had firm instructions to call at Ogbourne for tea.[37]

Tony was enraged by the policies of the Labour government, particularly their support for Zionism in Palestine. According to one of the newly-elected Labour M.P.s, Richard Crossman, the establishment of a Jewish homeland was 'an important part of the Socialist creed'. Another, Michael Foot, was to inform the House of Commons in July that, were he a Jew living in Palestine, he would certainly join the Haganah (admittedly the least violent of the Jewish paramilitary organisations), despite having been a non-combatant in the recent war.[38]

The Foreign Secretary, Ernest Bevin, was more cautious than Tony allows. No friend to European Jews, he was decidedly uneasy about their mass settlement in Palestine and the creation of a Jewish state. Unfortunately, he was pledged to support the unanimous findings of the 'Anglo-American Palestine Commission', of which Crossman was a member. Indeed, Bevin felt that Crossman's stance had been as much a 'stab in the back'

---

[37] Letter 163.

[38] 'Israel, Palestine and the Labour party history that has made Keir Starmer's position so difficult', *The Conversation,* 8 Nov 2023 (online). Foot had applied for the army, but been turned down on health grounds.

to him personally as to the Palestinians.[39] 'I am very pro-Arab,' Tony wrote, 'as I believe are all Englishmen who have actually been to Palestine. I can see no reason for the Jews from Poland and Germany to go there, why can they not be given a state in Germany?'

As for his own immediate future, Tony had his eye on the Arab Legion, 'a wonderful body of men who lead a very interesting but somewhat exacting life'. He was already giving up half an hour a day to the study of Arabic. It seemed more likely, however, that he would be staying on in India, as it would 'take ten years to hand over the army and train sufficient Indian officers'. He had already been ear-marked to give a series of lectures (in Urdu) on mountain artillery, at the Mountain Warfare School in Kakul. The last thing he wanted was to 'become some poor regimental officer stationed at Woolwich or some equally grim place'.[40]

In the closing days of June, the region was affected by an unprecedented heat-wave, followed by four days of torrential rain. Tony was quite sapped by the experience, especially as he had had extra responsibilities, running some unspecified course for the benefit of his *bête-noir,* the R.A.F. It involved about thirty hours of air time, sweltering in a cockpit that seemed to catch all the sun. Although they grumbled about the heat and refused to work beyond 11 a.m., Tony was delighted to have R.A.F. officers under his control. 'The first day they turned up looking like a lot of tramps but by the end of the course they looked fairly civilised with the majority of them even shaving every day, something quite unheard of in the R.A.F.!' He also refers jauntily to the kidnapping of the Political Agent, nothing unusual in those parts,

---

[39] Ritchie Ovendale, 'The Palestine Policy of the British Labour Government 1945-1946', *International Affairs,* Vol.55, No.3 (July 1979), pp.409-31; Anthony Howard, 'Crossman, Richard', in *The Oxford Dictionary of National Biography*. Confusing Bevin with his homonym, Bevan, Tony hopes that he will soon return to the coal mine from whence he came. It would have been more accurate to hope for his return to the Bristol docks.

[40] Letter 164, 166 (on the Kakul assignment).

but a cause of 'great excitement as we may have to go out on column to re-capture him'.[41]

Meanwhile, Subedar Khan had been having the time of his life in the United Kingdom. The 'Indian Victory Contingent' had disembarked from the S.S. *Mauretania* at Liverpool and entrained for London, arriving at Euston on 23 May. They had paraded through London on 8 June, in front of huge crowds,[42] and then again in Sheffield, Newcastle and Edinburgh, before returning to their temporary barracks in Victoria. The proposed visit to Ogbourne had taken place, and Tony cherished the letter from Khan that described it.

> 'Dear Sir,' he wrote, 'I went [to] your house I have seen your mother and father and they treated me very kindly and also they gave spoon for you and for me one small plate, and clay too. It means for memorial. I saw your house including the garden, very fine, very lovely, there I saw some nice rose flowers and after I left your house your father, mother and myself went to railway station with your mother car but couldn't remember the station. I never forgot you Sir, because you send to the Victory Contingent, I never seen in my life and also I never seen in my dreams too these places, but I have seen all places in England and Scotland, very beautiful with kindness.'

Tony thanked his parents for 'being so good to him', and enclosed the letter. Perhaps Subedar Khan had not always been understood. 'He does not officially speak English as it is frowned on by the older members of the army, as it discourages officers from learning Urdu.'[43] He and Tony were to meet again in

[41] Letter 166. Before that, bribes will be offered and, if necessary, villages bombed.

[42] Imperial War Museum, D 27672, H 42786. For a photograph of the Nepalese contingent on their arrival at Euston, see the 'Mauritius Images' website.

[43] Letters 165 (the Subedar's), 167.

Kashmir in June 1948.[44] Khan was by then an officer in the Pakistan Army, formed as a result of the partition of India and the British withdrawal on 15 August 1947. Tony would not have been a witness to these events. By that time, he was already at home in England.

Thal

This was an uneasy time in India. On 11 July 1946, Indian postal workers launched an indefinite strike.[45] For the first time since 1939, Tony was denied his morale-boosting letters from home. Some of them arrived, almost miraculously, but after a long delay. Tony had a sense that everything was falling apart. His fate was in the hands of staff officers, who seemed all to be 'lazy and inefficient'. Many key positions, such as those in the personnel sections at G.H.Q., had already been handed over to corrupt Indians. Tony was 'quite sure there will be a plot in the army and civil war on a large scale in a few months if not weeks. We are just being weak minded in clearing out of the country. It is like letting a prep school run itself without any masters'.

On top of it all, officers serving in India were now to be paid at the domestic rate, even though their messing costs were four times higher. Tony, who stood to lose £200 a year, conceded that 'we can do things here that only a very rich man could dream of doing at home. We have for instance started playing polo three days a week,' the ponies being 'fed and maintained at His Majesty's expense'. The problem was finding the time to train them. Tony's officers were all either on leave or in hospital, many having succumbed to heat stroke, whilst he himself was travelling thousands of miles by road on a 'special job'. One mission took

---

44 Letter 179. Khan was then serving in a 25-pounder regiment, and finding it 'a great come-down after being with the mules and the horses'.

45 *The Canberra Times,* 13 July 1946.

him to north Kashmir, where at long last he caught a glimpse, albeit a distant one, of the famed Kaghan Valley. Tony spent a night among the pine trees, and awoke to a view of the snow-covered mountains. 'It was wonderful,' he wrote, 'to feel the cool wind and hear the trees dripping down onto the tent roof'.[46]

There were further frustrations on his return. Tony had been selected for a two-month course at the Senior Tactical School, near Simla. With so many officers in hospital, the Colonel had been obliged to turn it down, a blow for Tony, as a place would never be offered again. By way of consolation, the Colonel had put him down instead for a six-month gunnery instructor's course at Larkhill, beginning next January. 'There is a very good chance of my getting it as the General has recommended me.' He might even be home in time for Christmas.

On 3 September Tony embarked on a month's leave in the mountains, close to the imaginary line, drawn by the British, where India merged with Tibet. Far from any road or post office, he fished where he could and trekked to a base camp at 75 45° E, 30 30° N (as he helpfully informed his parents), the surrounding mountains rising to 24,000 feet. At just over 29,000 feet, Mount Everest was not much taller. Supplies were carried by pack ponies or by bearers from the local villages.

Tony returned to Kohat on 2 October, to be met by three 'accusatory' letters from home. It seems that, some time before, probably after his return to India, Tony had broken up with Isa. Old Major McDonald had taken it badly. There was an embarrassing complication. Isa's mother, a very old-fashioned woman, had recently died, and had bequeathed the family home to Tony by way of a dowry.

McDonald had complained to Tony's parents who were mortified. They had written to him immediately, but the letter, which was as vague as it was censorious, had left him bemused. It

---

[46] Letters 167, 169, 170.

was several days before he heard from McDonald himself about the contents of the will.

It was implied in his parents' letters that Tony had abandoned Isa for the sake of another woman, whom they represented, in colourful Victorian language, as a sort of Jezebel. He was also accused of being over-friendly with the women of Kohat. Tony's response was indignant: 'The "insidious siren" as you call her, happens to be a "lady" in at least three senses of the word; she is on the staff at Viceroy House. Your idea of the "crowds of women and girls" at Kohat is a bit wide of the mark, there are exactly four of them - all married: the Brigadier's wife, the Colonel's wife, the wife of the Chief of Police and that of the Commissioner. The next woman is sixty miles away in Peshawar. The opportunities of "having a good time" are also very strictly limited to the polo field, the hockey ground and the tennis court. The gates are closed at night and anyone going out is likely to be shot at, only last week three people were killed.'

Tony's titled friend at Viceroy House was surely the woman who had been besieged by rioters in the Wavell Canteen during 'Victory Week'. In a photograph of the Viceroy House staff under Mountbatten (about a year later), there are at least fourteen very presentable young women in the group who might have fitted the bill.[47] There are further clues in Tony's own album. A photograph labelled 'B.M. and self on C.C.' reveals that they had met on the *Capetown Castle,* the ship that had conveyed Tony to Bombay in January. The couple are absorbed in a game of chess on the deck of the ship. In other photographs, Lady B.M. poses coyly in front of the Jama Masjid Mosque in Delhi, which must have been during 'Victory Week', when Tony was in the capital for the parade. Unusually, neither the voyage nor Tony's trip to Delhi are documented in any of his home letters, but B.M. was a serious enough love-interest for him to end his engagement. Their

---

[47] See https://www.rct.uk/collection/2517801/their-excellencies-and-staff-viceroys-house.

opportunities to meet would, however, have been extremely limited, and the lady is not heard of again.

As for his unexpected inheritance, it is inconceivable that Tony would have behaved dishonourably in such a situation and, of course, he took immediate steps to transfer the property to Isa, the vagaries of the Indian postal system permitting. As far as his parents were concerned, all was explained and soon forgiven. Knowing that they were being 'starved' by the Labour government - he had access in the mess to four-day-old copies of *The Times,* or rather to its 'air mail' edition - he arranged for regular food parcels to be sent home, containing 'surplus American tinned food, teas, coffee and sweets', which 'may be of some help'. A most attentive son, he later sent a separate parcel that he had assembled himself, containing tinned turkey, bacon and 10lbs of butter, all of which would have been in short supply.[48]

Towards the end of October 1946, Tony took his battery up to a new station at Thal, in the heart of the volatile Kurram Agency. This was said to be 'an unpopular station for mountain artillery, being unhealthy and very restricted from a training point of view, and it was difficult to keep men and animals fit'.[49] Its bazaar was frequented by traders from Afghanistan, or, as Tony puts it, it was 'a well-worn route for the gangs which go down to the settled areas to collect loot and prisoners for ransom'. The British, whose function was to oppose these raids, were holed up in a fort, built in 1909, that overlooked the Kurram river.

The river was, however, too great a temptation for a committed fisherman. Officially requiring an escort of at least twelve rifles, Tony preferred to venture out unarmed, with an elderly local and 'two large setters' in tow. He reckoned that, with no rifles to tempt them, the Afridis would leave him alone. 'Usually after I

---

48 Letter 168 and annotations to letter 38; letter 170 on *The Times;* letters 169 and 171 on food parcels.

49 Graham, *History of the Indian Mountain Artillery,* p.450, with the additional information that 'a peculiarly virulent type of malaria was rife in Thal'.

have been about half an hour on the river six or seven men collect to sit round, with their home-made or stolen rifles on their knees, and offer advice as to the best pools and bait'. At the end of the day they would invite him back to their villages for tea.[50]

There was a decent enough social life at Thal. Tony often dined with Colonel Hamilton and his wife, who was 'very clever', but 'quite mad';[51] and he borrowed freely from the Colonel's library. Sir John Neale's *Queen Elizabeth* and Richard Aldington's *Wellington* were soon devoured. Tony acquired two Afghani officers on attachment to his battery for training, 'quite good chaps but bone idle'. Nehru paid a visit and inspected troops; Tony did not think much of him either.[52]

From mid-November the battery took part in a 'three-week shove', marching through that difficult, bleak but immeasurably grand country, much of it covered in snow, though it was warm enough in the bright sunshine for shorts and shirt-sleeve order. It was disappointing, though, not to fire a single round from the guns, for Tony, as ever, thirsted for 'a bit of real action'.

---

50 Dorothy Ratcliffe, *A Ragbag of Memories* (privately printed, 1992), refers, at p.95, to the 'gipsy-type herdsmen and their families' passing through Thal twice a year. They were a picturesque sight as they drove their animals, 'mostly sheep and goats, down to the plains for the winter and up again into the mountains for the summer. The tiny children were perched on top of camels surrounded by goods and chattels, chickens, puppies, in fact anything unable to walk the enormous distances. The tough little hill ponies carried huge loads and the whole caravan was guarded by very large, fierce dogs, wild and untameable.' The wife of an officer in the R.U.R. who was stationed at Thal from March to November 1944, Mrs Ratcliffe writes (p.97) that anyone venturing out at night was considered fair game, officers being 'looked upon as choice targets'.

51 According to Mrs Ratcliffe (*ibid.,* pp.90 *et seq.*), Thal was unusual among such outposts in that wives were permitted there. She describes the 'little fort' as 'a world of its own', complete with a dairy farm, a poorly-stocked shop and bungalows. 'It was in an enclosed area of several acres surrounded by barbed wire and perimeter lights beyond which it was forbidden to go - exactly like a concentration camp.'

52 Letters 169, 170.

On his return to Thal in early December, Tony found two letters waiting for him. One was an invitation to dine with Sir Olaf and Lady Caroe. A slightly-built Wykehamist, Sir Olaf was the Governor of the North-West Frontier Province. Up from Peshawar on an inspection, accompanied as always by his beloved 'Kitty', he would have been a most interesting man to meet. He was a champion of Tibetan independence, knew the frontier which Tony had recently visited, and was an arch-exponent of the 'Great Game', the historic struggle between Britain and Russia for supreme influence in Central Asia. Sir Olaf was deeply, unenthusiastically embroiled in plans for the British withdrawal, and viewed the impending partition of India as an avoidable tragedy.[53]

The other letter was from the War Office, instructing Tony to report to Larkhill on 29 January. It saddened him that he would imminently be separated from the men and animals whom he had come to know well over the past year. The Larkhill course would, however, be a considerable boost to his career.

The signal finally came on Christmas Eve. Christmas dinners were consumed, crates hurriedly packed (two of which were to be left in store in Peshawar, as a mark of his intention to return), and Zhob Battery was reluctantly handed over to Tony's successor. On New Year's Eve 1946, he arrived at the Homeward Bound Trooping Depot, Deolali. It was almost exactly a year since his previous visit, although on that occasion he had been 'inbound'. The journey had been far from straightforward, involving four days in a train and five hours on the road.[54] The distance between Thal and Deolali was well over two thousand miles.

From Deolali Tony travelled back down to Bombay and, on 4 January 1947, set sail on the S.S. *Cameronia,* bound for

---

[53] Katherine Prior, 'Caroe, Sir Olaf', in *The Oxford Dictionary of National Biography.*

[54] A 'road and a single-track, narrow-gauge railway' connected Thal, at the end of the line, to Kohat, running for 70 miles 'through a wilderness of rock and scrub' (Ratcliffe, *A Ragbag of Memories,* p.91).

Liverpool. A creaking old vessel of the Anchor Line, she had been known for her tendency to pitch heavily, but had had a rather glorious career as a troopship, not least for her part in the evacuation of Crete and in the D-Day landings.[55] This was no pleasure cruise. The 18,000-tonner was crammed with 4,000 people, many of them the wives and children of fellow officers. There was simply nowhere to sit. Even brigadiers' wives slept four to a cabin, whilst Tony shared a state-room with no fewer than 63 other officers. All were of the rank of lieutenant-colonel or major.

The ship chugged into Aden on 12 January, in the middle of an unprecedented downpour. After a rough passage through the Red Sea, they heard that they were being diverted to Greece to 'pick up some sailors', and that they might then be going to Naples. At that rate, Tony would be lucky to be home by 29 January, the start-date of his course, and there would be no time to call at Ogbourne.

He wrote on 17 January from somewhere north of Crete, during a gale of such severity that 'one of the deck houses was washed clean away'. The twelve Indian majors in his charge, bound, like him, for a course at Larkhill, took 'a very dismal view of the whole thing' and, like most of the passengers, had retreated to their cabins. Tony was immune to sea-sickness, enjoyed the extra rations in their absence, and looked forward to their docking at Piraeus that afternoon. If only the weather cleared, he might catch a glimpse of the Akropolis of Athens, and perhaps later of Naples too. Of course, this being no pleasure cruise, the passengers would not be allowed ashore.[56] By land or sea, life was a great and glorious adventure for Tony Fowle.

---

55 https://heritagemachines.com/nostalgia/british-atlantic-intermediate-liner-cameronia/.

56 Letter 172.

CHAPTER IX

NOWSHERA

Partition

The India that Tony left behind was on the brink of an agonising transition. Admiral Lord Louis Mountbatten arrived there in March 1947, with General Lord Ismay as his Chief of Staff. Ismay compared India to 'a ship on fire in mid-ocean with ammunition in her hold'.[1] Attlee's government was determined to withdraw as soon as possible. However, with entrenched divisions between Jinnah's Muslim League and Nehru's predominantly Hindu Congress Party, the country seemed to be heading for civil war.

'The Moslem League,' wrote Ismay, 'would not agree to any plan which did not provide for the creation of Pakistan as an independent sovereign state.'[2] Jinnah, indeed, had declared it to be 'a matter of life and death for us'. The name was a contrivance, invented in 1933 by one Rahmat Ali: 'It is composed of letters taken from the names of our homelands: that is *P*unjab, *A*fghania, *K*ashmir, *I*ran, *S*indh, *T*ukharistan, and Baluchis*tan.* It means the land of the Paks, the spiritually pure and clean.'[3] By April, Mountbatten and all the nationalist leaders (apart from Mahatma Gandhi, who was vehemently opposed) had agreed on the partition of India as the only course.[4]

---

[1] Quoted in Larry Collins and Dominique La Pierre, *Freedom at Midnight* (New York, 1975), p.95.

[2] Hastings Ismay, *The Memoirs of General Lord Ismay* (New York, 1960), p.419.

[3] Jinnah is quoted in Stanley Wolpert, *Jinnah of Pakistan* (New York, 1984), p.251. Rahmat Ali, who had announced the new name in a pamphlet entitled *Now or Never,* is quoted in Karl E. Meyer, 'The Invention of Pakistan: How the British Raj Sundered', *World Policy Journal,* 20, No.1 (Spring 2003), p.79.

[4] V.P. Menon, *The Transfer of Power in India* (London, 1957), p.385.

Lines of demarcation were hastily drawn up by the British, but neat divisions between the Hindu, Sikh and Muslim populations were impossible. Sir Cyril Radcliffe, the London barrister charged with segregating the religious communities whilst also taking account of 'natural boundaries, communications, watercourses and irrigation systems',[5] submitted his hurriedly-prepared partition map on 9 August 1947, the day that Tony received his regular commission. It is as well that Tony was in England. He would have found the lowering of the British flag on 15 August, and the events that followed, most unedifying.

The 'Radcliffe Line' seemed to please no one. For example, Kashmir and the Punjab, with very mixed populations, were crudely split between both countries. Under pressure from Mountbatten, Nehru and Jinnah, Radcliffe had had to complete his work within a matter of weeks. The appointment of a Hindu as Assistant-Secretary in his office was inexplicable. The man was a spy and had reported Radcliffe's every move to Nehru. There is evidence of Radcliffe's being suborned by Mountbatten and Ismay, to alter alignments in India's favour.[6] Mountbatten and Nehru, a smooth Harrovian, were close personal friends. Mountbatten even connived at Nehru's passionate affair with his wife.[7]

The outcome probably cost more in human misery than the feared civil war. Throughout both India and Pakistan, angry mobs turned on the religious minorities in their midst and slaughtered them. It is estimated that about a million people died.[8] Millions

---

[5] Anthony Read and David Fisher, *The Proudest Day: India's Long Road to Independence* (New York, 1998), p.483.

[6] Prem Shankar Jha, *Kashmir, 1947: Rival Versions of History* (Delhi, 1996), pp.141-2; Meyer, 'The Invention of Pakistan', p.82. Notably contentious decisions in India's favour concerned Ferozepore and the Chittagong Hill Tracts.

[7] Philip Ziegler, *Mountbatten: The Official Biography* (London, 1985), p.473.

[8] Haimanti Roy, *The Partition of India* (Oxford India Short Introductions, O.U.P. India, 2018), p.76.

more, finding themselves on the wrong side of the border, were forced to abandon their homes and set out by train, truck, car, boat, ox-cart or on foot in search of safety on the other side. The elderly might have to be carried considerable distances in a makeshift *doli* or palanquin.[9] Many fell by the wayside or were put to death.

In the Pakistani part of the Punjab, where Hindus and Sikhs were subjected to genocidal violence, there was an organised transfer of populations. About fourteen and a half million people crossed the new Pakistan border in both directions, the largest mass migration in history.[10] The cities of both countries were soon thronging with refugees. At Delhi, the squatter settlements of Punjabi Hindus survive to this day.[11]

More than anywhere else, the people of the Punjab seemed to be possessed with a murderous hatred for their neighbours. Modern scholars refer to the process as 'ethnic cleansing'. It was not enough to ship the hapless refugees out of the country. The 'Special' trains laid on for them were systematically attacked. Typically, when they pulled into the frontier city of Lahore, they would be full of dead and dismembered passengers. The message would be scrawled on the side: 'A Present from Pakistan'.

The people of the eastern Punjab responded in kind. On 22 September, a train conveying Muslim refugees from India was attacked by militant Sikhs at Amritsar. The Sikh leader, Tara Singh, had previously incited his people to violence by declaring 'Death to Pakistan'. In a murderous, three-hour rampage through the train, Sikh warriors wielding swords and spears put 3,000 men, women and children to death. A further thousand were wounded, and only a hundred passengers emerged unscathed,

---

[9] One of these was photographed by the American war correspondent, Margaret Bourke-White.

[10] Ian Talbot, 'Partition of India: The Human Dimension', *Cultural and Social History,* 6(4) (2009), pp.403-10.

[11] These are the neighbourhoods of Lajpat Nagar and Patel Nagar.

their clothing soaked with the blood of the dead and dying under whom they had hidden.

A party of Sikh soldiers, the type that Tony so admired, had disembarked from a passing troop train to participate in the massacre. There was a lone British officer on board, commanding a unit from the Jat Regiment that was supposed to defend the train. He had bravely turned a machine gun on the attackers and had kept firing until his ammunition ran out, only to be killed by his own men, who were Hindus.[12] Another British officer, reporting on the aftermath, said that conditions at Amritsar Station were 'beyond description'. A third wrote that 'the results of vicious hatred and communal fury have outdone even Belsen and other bestialities created by the warped Nazi mind'.[13]

There is no end to the chilling statistics. Up to 3.2 million Muslim migrants from western India simply went missing.[14] Women and small children were considered fair game. Around 83,000 women from all sides were abducted and raped during the riots, some picked out of trains or refugee columns. It was 'the most wide-scale kidnapping of modern times'. Many realised that they would never be accepted back by their families and reconciled themselves to miserable new lives among strangers.[15] Tony was fortunate to miss such scenes, especially as he would have been forced to look on helplessly.

As an act of faith, he had left two crates of his possessions in store at Peshawar. With his knowledge of the country and fluent Urdu, and with British expertise much in demand, it was

---

12 '3,000 Dead in Indian Train Massacre', *The Advertiser (Australia),* 27 September 1947.

13 Navdip Kaur, 'Violence and Migration: A Study of Killing in the Trains during the Partition of Punjab in 1947', *Proceedings of the Indian History Congress,* Vol.72(1) (2011), pp.947-54.

14 K. Hill *et al.,* 'The Demographic Impact of Partition in Punjab in 1947', *Population Studies,* 62(2) (2008), pp.155-70.

15 Ritu Menon and Kamla Bhasin, *Borders and Boundaries: Women in India's Partition* (Rutgers, New Jersey, 1998), p.99.

inevitable that he would be sent back there. For over a year, however, he was stationed at the School of Artillery, Larkhill. Situated on the south side of Salisbury Plain, it was within easy reach of Ogbourne St George, on the north side, so there are no letters that document this period.

Tony attended the six-month gunnery course at Larkhill, passing out in July 1947 as a Gunnery Instructor. This entitled him to wear a red band on his hat, and to the post-nominal letters 'I.G.' in the *Army List.* He was to stay on at Larkhill till February 1948, still in the rank of Major, instructing in Maths and Ballistics. While on leave he helped his parents move out of the Vicarage at Ogbourne, his father having retired at the age of 81, and into Queen Elizabeth Cottage at nearby Broadtown, which had a busy duck-pond and an untidy garden, which it was proposed to adorn with fruit trees.[16]

The hoped-for orders finally came. Early in March 1948, Tony embarked at Tilbury on a P. & O. liner that, exasperatingly, is not named, though it may have been one of the 'Strath' class. A very large and swift vessel that had served as a 'trooper' in the war, she was bound for Suez, Aden and Colombo before doubling back to Bombay, where Tony was to disembark.

Though his ultimate destination was a mystery, he surmised (correctly, as it proved) that he would be going to the School of Artillery at Nowshera, in the district of Peshawar.[17] The former North-West Frontier Province was no longer in India but in the Dominion of Pakistan; King George VI was its nominal head of state, the cadaverous Muhammad Ali Jinnah, leader of the Muslim League, his all-powerful Governor-General. A referendum in July had determined that it should be so, though much of the population of N.W.F.P. had had no vote or had chosen not to exercise it. The provincial Chief Minister himself, Dr Khan Sahib, had led the boycott, resentful that the options of

---

[16] Letters 167, 173, and Tony's annotation to letter 175; Ministry of Defence: *A.P.H.B. Fowle, Particulars of Service.*

[17] Letter 173.

independence for his province or of its combining with Afghani territory to form a greater 'Pathanistan' had not been offered to them.

With scant regard for the constitution, Jinnah had simply removed Khan Sahib's elected government on 22 August and had appointed substitutes from his own party. The new Chief Minister had obligingly thrown Khan Sahib and his supporters into gaol. The position of British officials serving the new administration became increasingly awkward. These included Sir George Cunningham, who had been invited to return to N.W.F.P. as Governor, General Sir Frank Messervy, Commander-in-Chief of the newly-formed Pakistan Army, and Lieutenant-General Sir Douglas Gracey, who was Messervy's Chief of Staff and, from February 1948, his successor as C.-in-C. Like all other British officers on attachment, including Tony, they continued to wear the King's uniform and were at least nominally in the King's service, Pakistan being a dominion and George VI its head of state.

The Royal Pakistan School of Artillery

After the calm of the Thames Estuary, Tony's ship soon encountered a 'heavy swell', which 'made a lot of people shy of the excellent lunch'. He had been assigned a place at the First Officer's table, along with a planter and his wife, *en route* to Colombo from home leave, and the wife of an R.A.F. officer who was going out to join him in Aden. The ship's officers and crew were impressive. She had participated in all the major landings of the war, so most of them were festooned with medal ribbons. The 1,500 other passengers were mostly to be avoided, many of them the wives and noisy children of government officials. Tony was one of only fifteen service personnel, a 'very odd' draft indeed, including former members of the S.O.E. He enjoyed the trip immensely.

Tony made the most of his twenty-four hours in Colombo, the easternmost point of his travels to date. Colombo was at that time the political as well as the commercial capital of Ceylon (now Sri Lanka), which had also received independence from Britain, along with dominion status, only weeks before, on 4 February 1948.

With its high rainfall, the place seemed remarkably fresh and green. The planter and his wife treated him to an excellent dinner at their home. In the morning, a party including Tony were again motored ashore and were given the use of a car, in which they toured the surrounding area. This seemed to consist of a 'forest of palm trees right down to the very blue sea where huge rollers cast up mountains of spray'. The scents from the flowering trees were 'wonderful'. They set sail in the small hours during a raging thunderstorm.

On Thursday 1 April the ship made landfall at Bombay, from which he would have to make a separate journey to Karachi. The port seemed chaotic. 'The dockside is one mass of people who have been living there for weeks in the hope of getting onto a ship.' Tony was assured of a place on a vessel, albeit 'a very small one', that would be leaving on Sunday, but was warned that it would be 'very uncomfortable and very crowded with refugees'.

Meanwhile, the British passengers and certainly those in uniform were confined to Colaba, an island that had been transformed (by reclamation work in 1905) into a headland. Part of Catherine of Braganza's dowry for Charles II, Colaba is described by Tony as 'a British stronghold'. Historically it had been the main point of entry for the British and was the location of the famous 'Gateway of India'. Now, however, there was trouble ashore and the British were in 'enemy territory'.

On 30 January, Mahatma Gandhi, the true father of independent India, had died of gunshot wounds in New Delhi. His assassin was a Hindu who believed that Gandhi had been too conciliatory towards the Muslims. No doubt he had. As Gandhi fell to the ground, he put his hand to his forehead in the Hindu gesture of forgiveness. Stalin, unmoved by the tragedy, and viewing both Gandhi and Nehru as capitalist lackeys, had declined to send a message of condolence. The Indian government had taken great offence and, on 29 March, had launched a brutal purge against the communists of India, among whom were active subversives. When Tony arrived in Bombay, the police were busy seizing documents and rounding up the usual suspects. He and his friends were wise to 'keep well clear'.[18]

The voyage to Karachi was 'a real eye-opener. The ship, which was the size of a normal cross-channel steamer, had more passengers on her than are carried by the largest P. & O. liner.' Understandably, train travel through hostile territory was no longer considered safe. The over-loaded vessel chugged along at a snail's pace and arrived at Karachi on 7 April. Disappointingly, somebody broke into Tony's cabin and stole his fishing rod.[19] 'The only bright spot was the hoisting of the Pakistan flag; we had a proper parade with a guard of honour with fixed bayonets and the whole ship went mad, partly with relief at the thought that they were now in safety and partly through real pride in their country.'

Karachi was no less chaotic than Bombay, for 'thousands of Hindus are waiting for passages to India and equal numbers of evacuees are waiting on transport across the desert.' Much to his surprise, he was met at the dock by his former orderly, now out of the army, a man who was 'quite worth his weight in gold'. Tony engaged him as his servant on the spot. 'Quite how he knew I was coming is a question that will never be answered - it is one of the wonders of the east.'

Tony next found himself in a transit camp for British officers and civilians. It was 'just outside the city on the fringes of the Sind desert', with tents dug into the ground and daily sand-storms, all reminding him of Egypt. It was also 'very badly run', though it was a relief to be out of the city, the 'vast influx' of

---

[18] Letters 173, 174; 'India Opens Attack on Communists', *The Daily Mirror,* Tuesday 30 March 1948, p.5.

[19] Tony refers to the theft in letter 178.

refugees having 'wrought havoc with the water supply and with what little sanitation there ever was'.[20]

Tony had guessed correctly that he would be heading to Nowshera, to instruct at the new Royal Pakistan School of Artillery. It was in tribal territory, 27 miles east of Peshawar. The old British cantonment occupied the right bank of the mighty River Kabul, which was crossed here by the ancient highway known as the 'Grand Trunk Road' (built by the Moghul emperors, it stretched all the way from Kabul to Chittagong) and by a railway bridge, Nowshera being an important junction. Tony arrived there on 15 April 1948.

He had had a hot but fairly comfortable journey across the Sind Desert, and had awoken to an exhilarating view of the distant mountains. Nowshera was 'like a different world; there was a cool breeze blowing down from the hills and the countryside was clothed in early spring green which, after the barren sands of the west Punjab and Sind desert, looked really wonderful.' Tony brushed off the coating of white sand that he had acquired on the journey and took up residence at No.3 Club Road, 'one of the best bungalows in the station', a former married quarter. The trees in the garden were covered with deep-red flowers and the roses were out at the front. The views were truly magnificent. Tony could look down from the bungalow to the river, which gushed with melting snow, and beyond the Vale of Peshawar to the snow-capped mountains of the Hindu Kush. These very superior quarters had been reserved for him by a friendly C.O., John Marshall.

The Indian Army School of Artillery had been at Deolali, but that was now in India, so the Pakistanis had had to start one of their own from scratch. According to Tony, the Indians had handed over as little of the old equipment as possible, and none of it in good condition. Discipline in the Pakistan Army was intact, but too many inexperienced officers had been promoted to senior

---

[20] Letter 175.

ranks. Tony was one of only four British officers at the School, whose expertise was desperately needed. The rest of the staff were Pakistanis and 'not a very bright crowd', apart from a couple of men who had been with him at Larkhill. He writes that some of his subordinates were openly resentful, feeling that they 'ought to be holding our ranks', but that the people in general seemed 'very glad indeed' to see them.

Tony wanted nothing more than to resume his old way of life, but so much had changed. The buildings were suitably grand, for the School occupied the old Brigade H.Q., but funds and supplies alike were in short supply. Broken light bulbs and window panes could seldom be replaced. The mess was efficiently run, but the Pakistani officers were mostly married men, who hurried home to their families after the day's work. They therefore missed out on opportunities to bond with their fellow officers in the mess and also with the men by participating in team games. Tony's three British colleagues also had their wives with them, but in spite of that, he insists that the old mess life was to some extent preserved. There were frequent dinner nights, and a high turnover of officers on courses who were not allowed to bring their wives, so the mess was adequately populated and the spirit of conviviality maintained.

The victuals in the mess were good, but not plentiful. Staples including *gee, atta* and sugar (though not rice) were in extremely short supply. Prices had generally doubled and such items as ordinary cotton cloth for shirts were almost unobtainable. Petrol was very strictly rationed and, naturally, there was a thriving black market in all sorts of goods. One delivery to the mess that could always be depended on was the three-day-old, air-mail edition of *The Times* of London, conveniently but 'beautifully printed on very thin paper'. The news on the wireless was 'horribly biased', and the 'local' paper, printed in Lahore, was a 'very odd sort of publication containing nothing but speeches made by very dubious people who no one has ever heard of before making wild accusations against all and sundry but against

India and America in particular. On the other hand there is not a word against Britain, a great change as we used to bear the brunt of every critic. I think our excellent policy in the Middle East has something to do with this change of face.'

Tony and two of his brother officers were keen to get their horses back. The army was eventually prevailed upon to provide six horses and to pay for their stabling and grooms. Often accompanied by the adjutant, Tony also resumed his regular fishing trips. Almost miraculously, his stolen fishing rod turned up one day, still in its steel case. The thief, a *lascar,* had been picked up by the police in Aden; Tony's name and address on the case had given him away.

The daily routine began at 6 a.m. and finished at 12.30 (with a half-hour break for breakfast at 8), which was about all that could be managed in the searing heat. Temperatures were typically rising to 110 in the shade. By mid-June, there were early-afternoon readings of 115. When conducting an exercise on the range, Tony might be out in the open till 3 p.m., in some rocky wilderness devoid of trees, yet had enough energy to play team games in the evening with the men. In the occasional dust-storm the air would become thick with particles of fine clay, which, mixed with one's sweat, left a coating of mud. The consummate professional, Tony addressed a question that seemed never to have come up before: how did such vast changes in temperature and air pressure affect the accuracy of predicted fire?

The courses themselves brought him little intellectual satisfaction, the standard of instruction being 'very low indeed', equivalent to that of the 'very lowest course at Larkhill'. As much as the native officers were 'not a very bright crowd', the men were barely educated 'and find it impossible to follow a drawing or diagram'. Tony ran a three-week course for them which was conducted entirely in Urdu. This was not the native language of the men but was a *lingua franca* that had been instilled in them when they joined.[21] Most of them would have spoken Punjabi, some Pashtu. Tony had recourse to his dictionary for words like 'detonation wave' and 'fin stabilisation', the concepts being hard to explain in any language.

The other British officers were not Urdu-speakers. They instructed the Pakistani officers only, and in English. As a result, the civilian workers at the school would flock to Tony with their petitions. There were minor quarrels and disputes to be settled. Some needed help with their applications for leave or with the purchase of rations. 'They will never go to the Pakistani officers,' wrote Tony, 'as they say they take no notice. The problem is that the Pakistani officers and officials lack the slightest sense of responsibility and usually award the result of any case in favour of the man who offers the highest bribe.'[22]

In spite of that, Tony was surprisingly optimistic about the future of Pakistan. His initial impression had been that 'things are getting on very well indeed'. The new nation had the enthusiasm of the populace in its favour, 'except of course for the tribes who are a real menace in the north and in the remoter parts of the country'. As for the army, he was 'sure that it will sort itself out in ten or fifteen years'. The country was in Tony's blood and he was naturally well disposed towards it. Whether his optimism was justified remained to be seen.

Skullduggery in Kashmir

Tony had had a long fascination with Kashmir, although he appears to have visited it only once, in July 1946. Little did he know that he was to become embroiled in a murky war there, one that, owing to its clandestine nature, is poorly

[21] Urdu is still the official language of Pakistan, though it is the mother tongue of only 8 per cent of the population: Meyer, 'The Invention of Pakistan', p.83.

[22] Letters 175, 176, 177, 178.

documented. Tony's home letters from 1948 are therefore a primary source of some importance.

There were 175 princely states in India, and that of Jammu and Kashmir (the territories were combined in 1780) was the largest. Its existence had been guaranteed under treaty by the British in 1846, in return for the service in arms of its people. The Dogras of the Jammu had been remarkable for their loyalty, not least in the Mutiny of 1857, and the territory had a key role in the 'Great Game', being 'part of a complex political buffer zone interposed by the British between their Indian empire and the empires of Russia and China to the north'.[23]

The inauguration of the current Maharajah, Hari Singh of the Dogra dynasty, had taken place in Srinagar in 1926, and had been quite the spectacle. He had arrived in a golden howdah on the back of an elephant, fanned by an attendant. On the third elephant behind him, a watchful British official had lurched his own way to the ceremony in a cloying suit and solar topee. Weighed down by jewels said to be worth twenty million dollars, the youthful Maharajah had sat, cross-legged, in public court, receiving the tribute of a gold coin from each of his chiefs.[24] Since then he had been further encumbered with the Grand Crosses of three British orders of chivalry and of the French Légion d'Honneur.

In some ways, he was a remarkably benevolent and enlightened potentate. In 1939 he had subjected himself to a written constitution and had since ruled through an elected government. He had made primary education compulsory in the state, had introduced laws prohibiting child marriage, and had opened places of worship to low-caste subjects.[25] Since the

---

[23] See https://www.britannica.com/place/Kashmir-region-Indian-subcontinent/The-Kashmir-problem.

[24] See https://en.wikipedia.org/wiki/Hari_Singh, which includes a link to footage of the inauguration, *An Indian Durbar,* photographed by Herford Tynes Cowling (Eastman Kodak 1927).

[25] Raghubir Lal Anand, *Is God Dead? The Truth About Jammu and Kashmir* (Partridge, India, 2014), p.25.

British withdrawal in August 1947, the princely states had been free to decide their own fate. Observing the violence of Partition with dismay, the Maharajah had decided that his country should remain independent of both Pakistan and India, at least for the time being. Some sort of equal federated status was his ultimate goal. If not, as a Hindu himself he would be more inclined to accede to India than to Pakistan.[26]

Unfortunately, the Maharajah's reforms had failed to address the ethnic imbalance. The population of Kashmir included Hindus, Sikhs and Tibetan Buddhists, but a clear majority of his subjects, with huge concentrations in western regions such as Gilgit and Poonch, were Muslims. Impoverished, uneducated peasants, they were an oppressed majority, heavily taxed for their exiguous holdings, ruled and often cheated by a Hindu elite.[27]

Notwithstanding Kashmir's strategic significance and that its 'economic, cultural, and geographic contiguity with the Muslim-majority area of the Punjab could be convincingly demonstrated', Radcliffe had conceded only an insignificant portion of the country to Pakistan. The relevant department of Attlee's government, the Commonwealth Relations Office, had anxiously awaited developments. Staffed, it is said, by 'a disproportionate number of I.C.S. [Indian Civil Service] men from the Punjab cadre', the C.R.O. had a grand strategic vision for Pakistan as a friendly buffer state, for these officials, now based in London, were playing the final chukka of the Great Game. Kashmir's not falling into Indian hands was vital to their plan.[28]

Nor would that have been remotely tolerable to Pakistan. 'Kashmir's accession to Pakistan was not simply a matter of desirability but of absolute necessity for our separate existence,' wrote Major (later Brigadier, and later still, the founder of the

---

[26] Jha, 'Response', *Commonwealth and Comparative Politics,* 36(1) (March, 1998), pp.113-23.

[27] Sumantra Bose, *Kashmir: Roots to Conflict, Paths to Peace* (Harvard, 2005), pp.16-17.

[28] Jha, *Kashmir,* pp.92-3.

Shangrila Resort in Skardu) Aslam Khan, M.C., of the Royal Pakistan Army. With reports of Muslims being killed in Bagh (western Kashmir) even as the flag of independence was being raised (15 August), the Pakistanis were spurred into action. They planned nothing less than the annexation of Kashmir by force.

From 31 August, they began to send bus-loads of bloodthirsty Pathans into Poonch, and unleashed them on the local Hindus and Sikhs.[29] Their Muslim neighbours obligingly pointed out where they lived, and looked on as they were murdered or raped. The Pakistani government pretended that it was not involved and that these outrages were the spontaneous acts of irregulars. It was important that British officers in the Pakistani service, including General Messervy, who were aware of these operations and even actively involved, were kept officially 'in the dark'. The second-in-command in the field was a regular officer, the aforementioned Major Aslam Khan, who was officially on leave. 'You can describe me as a deserter,' he told the reporter for the *Daily Express.*[30]

The Kashmiri government responded to the attacks with equal viciousness. On 14 October, extreme violence against the Muslims erupted in Jammu. The Maharajah's government and army not only bussed in the rioters, but supplied them with arms and ammunition. The Prime Minister himself was on hand to witness the ensuing massacres and, in effect, to oversee the 'ethnic cleansing' of the province. The total number of deaths may have been as high as 100,000.[31] Countless others, including women who were abducted and raped, simply disappeared.

On 22 October, vast numbers of Pathans were bussed into Kashmir from two directions, swelling the invasion force to

---

[29] The tribesmen were motivated by the promise of unlimited loot and, even while crossing Pakistan, helped themselves to whatever they wanted. See https://www.brownpundits.com/2018/02/26/the-north-west-frontier-in-1947/.

[30] Jha, *Kashmir,* pp.22-31.

[31] Christopher Snedden, *Understanding Kashmir and Kashmiris* (Oxford, 2015), p.167.

60,000. It was reported - and can hardly be doubted - that they 'had had connivance from the local Pakistan authorities in obtaining artillery and transport'.[32] In a well-planned military operation, the garrison at Muzaffarabad was wiped out, with hundreds more women being abducted and raped.[33] The intention behind the 'Great Raid' was to frighten the dithering Maharajah into submission. His improbable dream of independence was indeed shattered, but it was of course to India that he turned. Mountbatten, in his new role as Governor-General, agreed to send troops, but in return demanded Kashmir's immediate accession. The Maharajah was compliant, and the instrument was signed on 26 October 1947.

The supposed 'liberators of the oppressed Muslims of Jammu and Kashmir' were by now only a few miles from Srinagar. On 27 October they stormed into Baramula, a prosperous town nearby. An orgy of killing ensued. Of its population of 14,000, only 3,000 were left alive. Father Shank, of the town's Catholic cathedral, described the tribesmen (who were mainly Mahsuds, not the Afridis with whom Tony was familiar) as 'great, wild, black beasts', and their killing as indiscriminate. One man, a National Conference worker, shouted 'Long Live Hindu-Muslim Unity' as he was done to death. The adjacent hospital was totally destroyed, and European nuns, patients and a luckless British colonel and his wife, who happened to be on holiday in the town, were wantonly murdered. The survivors were lined up before a firing squad, until a young officer intervened. One nun described how a raider had come in later for medical treatment, his hands covered in rings. 'I killed fifteen men to get them,' he told her grimly.

---

32 Jha, *Kashmir,* p.112.

33 Following the massacre at Mirpur on 27 November, abducted Hindu women are said to have been sold in the brothels of Rawalpindi. Others committed suicide or were put to death by their own menfolk. See Col. Tej K. Tikoo, 'Genesis of the Kashmir Problem and how it got Complicated: Events between 1931 and 1947 AD', in *Kashmir: Its Aborigines and their Exodus* (New Delhi, 2013).

Mindful of British interests, the C.R.O. in London turned a blind eye to these atrocities. It also advised Attlee to ignore all appeals from the Maharajah. Messervy, however, had cold feet. Neither he, nor Sir George Cunningham, had been told the full extent of the plan. The Pakistanis had already sent in a skeleton administration, ready to take over in Srinagar. Having advised strongly against this, Messervy returned to London, leaving his Chief of Staff, Sir Douglas Gracey, in charge.

According to Mountbatten's account, Jinnah was champing at the bit, poised in Abbottabad 'to ride in triumph' into Kashmir. On 27 October, the day of the Baramula massacre, Jinnah ordered Gracey to send in two brigades of regular troops. These appeared to be standing by in readiness on the border. But Gracey felt that the deployment of regular units was a step too far. He refused to comply.[34]

Gracey's disobedience to a direct order was reported, no doubt by Jinnah himself, to Sir Francis Mudie, the eminent former Governor of Sindh, whom Jinnah had invited to stay on as Governor of the newly-divided (West) Punjab. Enraged by Gracey's obstinacy, Mudie picked up the telephone and harangued him. For Mudie, the propriety of Pakistan's support for the Pathan raiders was not in question. It was also entirely appropriate that its army should now be entering Kashmir in support of the local insurgents. Mudie writes of India at the time as a 'powerful, truculent and unscrupulous neighbour'. Her only interest in predominantly-Muslim Kashmir, 'which would be a very difficult province to hold', was as a springboard for future attacks on Pakistan, as it is 'easy to attack the plains from the hills'. Later he writes: 'Kashmir goes right to the root of the matter. It is a negation of the two nation theory - a negation of Pakistan's right to independence. It would outflank the West Punjab - should it ever come to the one-nation theory [being] enforced by war … The possession of Kashmir is as important to

[34] Sisir Gupta, *Kashmir: A Study in India-Pakistan Relations* (London, 1966), pp.110-15, 127.

any power wanting to attack Pakistan as the possession of Austria was to Hitler when he attacked Czechoslovakia.' His personal sympathies apart, Mudie saw the preservation of Pakistan as vital to British interests, as 'the barrier to Communism spreading south of the Himalayas'.[35]

According to Gracey, Mudie's invective was 'of undiplomatic tone and imperiousness'. Ironically, he was personally no less fervent than Mudie in his support for Pakistan. The difficulty for Gracey was that his superior, Field Marshal Sir Claude Auchinleck, was Supreme Commander of both the Indian and Pakistan armies. Anticipating a possible conflict between the two countries, Auchinleck had recently issued a General Order called the 'Stand Down Order'. The tenor of it was that, in such an eventuality, all the British officers on both sides should immediately stand down. As Auchinleck was in Lahore at that time, Gracey had an opportunity to consult him in person. The 'Auk' informed Gracey that he had acted correctly.

The 'Auk' may thus have averted a full-scale inter-Dominion war, for 'India would have immediately counter-attacked Pakistan at Lahore and Partition would have been undone in the bloodiest possible way'. Such a war might also have provoked the intervention of Russia which, as Mudie himself foresaw, would have been a disastrous outcome. It was inconceivable for the 'Auk' to be Supreme Commander of two warring armies, or for British officers on attachment to have to fight each other on opposing sides. Gracey was instructed to tell Jinnah that if Pakistani regulars were sent into Kashmir, Auchinleck would invoke the 'Stand Down Order' that he had previously issued. This meant that all British officers would have to resign from the Pakistan Army. Jinnah had no choice but to give in.[36]

---

35 Rakesh Ankit, 'Kashmir to be?', *Epilogue: J. & K.'s Monthly Magazine* (Oct 2010), pp.45-7, citing letters in the India Office Records, British Library MSS Eur F164/48 and F164/12.

36 Jha, *Kashmir*, pp.96-108; Alastair Lamb, *Crisis in Kashmir, 1947 to 1966* (London, 1966), p.49; Ankit, 'Kashmir to be?', p.46.

Further Subterfuge

The fighting, however, was by no means over. By the time Tony arrived at Nowshera in April 1948, Pakistani-backed separatist forces, those of the so-called 'Government of Azad Kashmir', had established a line in Poonch, which they were holding against determined Indian attacks. The 'state' of Azad ('Free') Kashmir claimed independence from both India and the Maharajah, and Muzaffarabad was its capital.

The situation had been very different since the end of November, when Supreme Headquarters had been wound up. Auchinleck, that wise overseer of the sub-continent's military affairs, had left India for the last time on 1 December 1947.[37] Gracey and his British subordinates had since felt themselves to have a freer hand. On 23 January 1948, Gracey had told Sir Laurence Grafftey-Smith, the British High Commissioner to Pakistan, that 'he and other British officers cannot be expected to obey "stand-down" orders that would have grave consequences for British-Pakistan relations'. He warned that defiant British officers losing their pensions could expect to be compensated for their losses by the Pakistan government.[38]

Thus it was that, even while he was in the transit camp at Karachi, Tony had been approached by 'the representatives of the Azad forces in Kashmir'. They had invited him and other new arrivals 'to join them at a salary of Rs 2,000 a month, about two thousand [pounds] a year'. Tony had previously written (2 April) that he was 'very glad to be going to the School as the job will be purely instructional and there will be no call to take part in security drives or operations in Kashmir where a full scale war is now in progress'. He was therefore unsurprised by these representations, but declined to 'sign up'. 'I have spoken to some

---

[37] Lamb, *Crisis in Kashmir,* pp.51-2; Philip Warner, *Auchinleck: The Lonely Soldier* (London, 1981), p.289.

[38] Ankit, 'The Defiant Douglas', *Epilogue* (Jan 2010), p.47.

people who have been up there,' he writes, 'and they all say that it is not worth it.'[39]

At that time it was volunteers who were called for, subject to the permission of their superiors. By May, however, British officers were being sent up under orders. On 19 May, Gracey reported to C.B. Duke, Grafftey-Smith's deputy, that there were now 'three brigades in position on the west Punjab side. Three battalions had so far gone in with two mountain guns.' Gracey claimed they were not there for offensive purposes, but to protect the countryside and infrastructure and to control the potential mass exodus of Muslim refugees. On 26 May, in an ill-tempered exchange with his Indian counterpart, General Sir Roy Bucher, Gracey further lied through his teeth, dismissing rumours of the three battalions as 'nonsense'. He was less than honest, too, with Grafftey-Smith, confirming on 13 July that only 'three British officers had at times been into Poonch', one of whom, Major Alan Macfarlane Sloan, R.E., had been killed.[40] Sloan is now considered a 'forgotten hero' and even a 'martyr' in Pakistan.[41] In his letter of 2 April, Tony implies darkly that there had been other casualties: 'when any British officers are killed they are reported at home as "having committed suicide in a fit of depression"'.[42] One suspects he was not joking.

The involvement of even three officers was concerning news to the Attlee government. On 17 July, it extracted a pledge from Pakistan that it would withdraw all British officers from Kashmir. It is clear that, by now, Gracey was fully embroiled in the subterfuge. Not only were no British officers withdrawn, but more were being sent up. Within days of his arrival at Nowshera, it fell upon Tony to stand in for his C.O. on his being posted to the

---

39 Letters 174, 175.

40 Ankit, 'The Defiant Douglas', p.47.

41 See https://www.scribd.com/document/636094335/Major-A-M-Sloan-Martyr-in-Kashmir-1948-War.

42 Letter 174.

front, 'officially on sick leave'. As acting 'Chief Instructor in Gunnery, Pakistan', during Colonel John's prolonged absence, an unwilling Tony found himself responsible for all artillery training and for decisions affecting the future policy of the regiment. 'We are all very much concerned with events in Kashmir,' he writes. 'I cannot say much about it as there is a great security drive on. Nearly every night the convoys go through with men going up to the front[. T]hey fire their rifles off into the air and shout and sing but are most interesting to talk to. The men coming back on leave are even more interesting to talk to and have very strange stories to tell.'[43]

Meanwhile, Tony had been shopping at the 'thieves' market' in Peshawar. He had bought a 'camel back' (a type of carpet that fits under a saddle) from an Afghani tribesman, and had bargained (unsuccessfully) for one of his Saluki puppies. Turkeys could be bought for next to nothing, so Tony invested in a dozen for the mess. His bearer informed him that they had belonged to Hindus (probably now dead) and were considered 'unclean' by the more ignorant Muslims, owing to 'a little bristle somewhere on the neck which reminds them of the pig'. Tony writes chillingly of 'whole streets in the old city selling stuff that has been looted from the Hindus and stuff that has been brought down from Kashmir by the Azad forces. There was one small stall which had hundreds of rolls of film but, not knowing what they were, the shop keeper had opened them and I should think they were all spoilt. My friend who is a keen photographer bought a complete enlarging machine for only three shillings, the seller had no idea what it was. Another place was piled high with brand new books which had come from a Hindu book shop, all going at a flat rate of nine pence each. I came away with six.' One can only imagine how these items might have been obtained; no doubt Tony had yet to hear of the atrocities in Kashmir.[44]

---

43 Letters 177, 178.

44 Letter 177.

Before long he was, in spite of himself, directly involved in the campaign. His first foray into Kashmir, a brief one, was in June. Although the country was 'very lovely' and he took his fishing rod, 'most of the "game" was of a very different nature. I do not know how much is common knowledge but you most likely know that our "Free" brothers [*i.e.* the Muslims of Kashmir] are not quite as free as they are made out to be.' His language is rather self-consciously opaque. 'The people from the South [*i.e.* the Indians] are going about things in the wrong way as they are trying to use armoured columns in country which is very wooded and mountainous where all the mobile people have to do is to dodge behind a rock or a tree and then shoot up the unarmoured vehicles coming up in the rear. The motorised columns make the most wonderful targets for the artillery as they cannot get off the road. I expect you are going to hear a lot more about this part of the world in the very near future.'

It is reasonable to infer from his account that Tony had personally trained a gun on such a column. He adds that 'my old regiment [*i.e.* the former 28 Indian Mountain Regiment] is up there giving a very good account of themselves', and that he had been reunited with Raj Wali Khan, the ex-V.C.O. whom he had sent to England - and Ogbourne - for the Victory celebrations. Khan, who asked to be remembered to Tony's parents, was serving 'up there' in a 25-pounder regiment, and missing his horses and mules.[45] It would have been enlightening for Grafftey-Smith if he had seen Tony's letter. According to the information passed on to him on 28 June, only 'eight to twelve British officers were serving in Kashmir - in the Signals regiment'.[46]

At about that time Tony ventured into the Swat valley, the beautiful but untamed tribal district in the north. It was to the same country that the Malakand Field Force, also based at Nowshera, had set out in 1897 to quell a tribal insurrection, as

---

45 Letter 179.

46 Ankit, 'The Defiant Douglas', p.47.

chronicled by the young Churchill, who was a participant. Like Jammu and Kashmir, Swat was an autonomous princely state, but its picturesque ruler, the Wali of Swat, had already acceded to Pakistan (3 November 1947). The 'wilder' inhabitants of Swat were currently on deployment in Kashmir 'as part of the cover plan', so British officers were receiving a friendly welcome. Indeed, 'by a policy that will be well known to you', the 'tribal question' had been temporarily solved. Tony reported 'only one minor incident during our trip.'

In the same letter, he anticipates a further foray into the war zone, though he makes it sound more like a pleasure-trip: 'Next month I shall be going up round the west border of Kashmir and shall be away for about five weeks. It is wonderful country up there but there are no roads, no telephones and no post offices. The hills can really be called mountains as they go up to sixteen thousand feet, there are even a few glaciers. With any luck there will also be some good fishing.'

Unfortunately, that trip, if it came about, is undocumented. The mail had become increasingly unreliable and, in any case, was now heavily censored. News was more efficiently communicated by word of mouth: 'an event happening at Balakot on the Kashmir border miles from mail or telephone is common knowledge in a few hours down here hundreds of miles away'. Similarly a certain colonel of a Mountain Regiment, known to Tony, had achieved mythic status on the frontier, even in the smallest villages. 'He has a very forceful manner and a wonderful command of Pashtu, which of course is more than half the battle with the Pathan.'[47]

Tony was in Nowshera throughout a very dry July, but with Ramadan (locally 'Ramzan') strictly observed, at least by the men, little work was achieved. Tony wrote that they 'get up at

---

[47] Letters 179, 180. In letter 182 he writes: 'The War Office says that no letters written during June or early July had arrived in the U.K, is this correct? I have written about once every ten days and would be interested to know how many have arrived.'

half past two to eat a huge meal', and 'then have nothing to eat or drink until nine at night.' Any breaches would incur the severe disapproval of the N.C.O.s and of 'general opinion'. He adds that 'in the bazaar if anyone is seen drinking water he is set on by the mob, rather on the sour grapes principle'.

For his part, Tony claimed to be busier than ever and to be putting in fourteen hours a day on average. In his quieter moments, he wondered how he might inveigle himself into Nowshera's 'very large' Masonic Lodge, the Cabul River Lodge. He had a couple of new pets to distract him. A brother officer, on a long course in England, had left him in charge of 'Gunner's Dilemma', an enormous bull mastiff. Said to weigh 72 pounds, the dog, better known as Don, now kept a ferocious watch on Tony's bungalow. He assumes a most aristocratic posture for a photograph and, as it later transpired, came from a long line of champions, but no cat or burglar was safe from him; he also consumed two pounds of underdone beef a day.[48] The other new arrival was a gargantuan bull 'with a hump and horns two feet and eight inches long', whose job was to irrigate the garden by means of a Persian wheel. Later in the month, two days of torrential rain did wonders for the lawn, also transforming the nearby river into a 'swirling mass of dark chocolate with trees and all kinds of debris sweeping down'. Further unprecedented rainfall in the ensuing weeks caused damaging floods, but at least it kept the temperatures down.

Although the home letters of British officers had ceased to be censored (after they had made 'a great fuss' about it), Tony is remarkably reticent about his next excursion into Kashmir, which probably took place at the end of that month. He was by now a confirmed partisan, railing against the distortions of the Delhi press, in spite of which he reported satisfactory progress, their gains for the Azad government amounting to an 'area about the size of Wales'. He seems oblivious to the atrocities of his own

---

48 Letter 188 for details of Don.

side, reserving his censure for the 'so-called "army of liberation" from the Indian Union'.[49]

The British officers regretted that the war, being *sub rosa,* was 'not a "real" one', so there would therefore be no awards for their services. This was particularly galling for Tony in the light of 'a very interesting little incident', for which, 'if I may be allowed to boast, the Director [of Artillery] told me that if the show had been "real" I should now be wearing a little ribbon in white and magenta'. Tony would have to wait for an officially-declared war before he would receive the coveted Military Cross.

By 3 August, when *The Times* reported it, the Kashmir operations had 'at last come into the open', and Tony wondered how the 'cover plan', by which he means the deployment of the Pathan hordes, could ever be unravelled. The campaign had been a very effective outlet for their warlike proclivities, but Peshawar was already infested with lawless tribesmen, and was 'like the film idea of Chicago', with almost daily gun-battles in its narrow streets. How could they ever be returned peacefully to their homes?[50]

On 22 August the Indians captured a soldier of the 1/1 Punjab Regiment. This was one of the battalions which, by Gracey's own admission, was on Kashmiri soil in support of the Azad militia. The soldier obligingly told his captors that fifteen officers of the Pakistan Army were directing the entire operation, and that twelve of those fifteen officers were British. The names of Lieutenant-Colonel Williams, Major Jorie (Durie?), Major Frier, Major Jones and Captain Ripps are not entirely convincing, some of them perhaps mispronounced.[51] If nothing else, the involvement of all these officers was doing wonders for British prestige.

---

[49] Letters 180, 181.

[50] Letter 182.

[51] Ankit, 'The Defiant Douglas', p.48.

NOWSHERA

Tony (seated, second left) with fellow instructors at the Royal Pakistan School of Artillery.

(Above) The Kaghan Valley was a place of enchantment for Tony. It was also the gateway to disputed Kashmir, to which Tony travelled on several secretive missions.

(Centre right) The English church at Abbottabad. The town was founded in the 1850s by an English officer. Tony recovered here in the autumn of 1948, from injuries sustained in an Indian bombing raid.

(Bottom right) Don, Tony's faithful guard-dog, terror of cats and burglars.

While instructing at the Royal Pakistan School of Artillery, Tony spent much time on the ranges, here firing old 4.5-inch Howitzers.

No.3 Club Road: in fine colonial style, Tony entertains the C.O., John Marshall, and his wife, with their infant child and dog Panda, to tea.

General Gracey on his annual inspection of the School, June 1950. Commanding the Royal Pakistan Army, Gracey consistently misled his own government as to the extent of British involvement in Kashmir.

Fort Malakand, gateway to the untamed Swat Valley. Unclear from Tony's photograph is its extraordinary hill-top position. He first visited in June 1948.

The Jeep which transported Tony on one of his trips through the Kaghan Valley. The mountain roads were so steep and narrow as to be positively terrifying.

A pleasant and recurring feature of Tony's life: travel by passenger liner; in this case the S.S. *Caledonia,* pictured from the wharf at Port Sudan in August 1950.

On a 'quick trip' from the *Caledonia,* Tony visited the Great Pyramids, and posed for the obligatory photograph.

The splendid Suez Canal Building at Port Said, familiar to all Oriental travellers.

The Rev. John Sydney Fowle in later life, with his grandson Charles.

CHAPTER X

SHIKAR STORIES

Gilgit

On or around 21 August 1948, as the war in Kashmir rumbled on, Tony set off for Kohistan, the far north-easterly district of Pakistan, ostensibly to 'fish'. However, he was bristling with official passes and his leave was combined with 'a job of work', about which he is teasingly reticent. It was probably no more (nor less) than the delivery of guns to Kashmir.[1]

For the first hundred miles of his journey, Tony boarded a rickety bus. It was crammed with passengers and their voluminous luggage, whilst the roof was piled high with precious sacks of sugar and *atta.* The vehicle regularly broke down; on two occasions it had to be extricated from river beds that it was attempting to ford. At Balakot, Tony transferred to an army truck, 'my kit and several Pathans filling up most of the space'. Ahead of them was a hair-raising, 92-mile drive through the awesome Kaghan Valley, along an ancient, but now reconstituted caravan route that led through the Karakoram mountains and eventually all the way to China.

'Towards evening we arrived at the base camp,' he writes, 'a most wonderful spot set in pine-clad mountains with the glint of snow to the north and east. We stayed there for a whole day, a bridge behind us being destroyed in the meantime - and not by natural causes! Then the fun really started.'

The road, which followed the course of the River Kaghan, amounted to no more than a rocky track, but it was one of the main routes into disputed Kashmir. Tony refers to its 'huge military importance; judging by the number of times the Indian

[1] Letters 181, 182, 183.

air force has bombed it they fully realise what an important link it is in our war effort'.[2] It was considerably more frightening than the 'Paitak' Pass into Persia, which Tony had crossed in 1944, or the equally-twisty Peshawar-Kohat road. '8 ft at the widest and a mere 5 ft at the narrowest', it hugged the steep side of the valley at heights of up to 1,500 feet. 'In several places the track is built out on tree trunks set into the rock face'. It was so winding that 'there are "S" bends where even a Jeep has to "tack" to get round; imagine reversing on a slope of 1 in 4 while towing a loaded trailer with only an eight foot road between you and a thousand foot drop. Nothing would induce me to drive over that track yet convoys drive up, have a day's rest and then drive back. The Jeeps are driven by ordinary Pakistan Army drivers and so far, only one vehicle has gone over the edge.'

Amazingly, the driver on that occasion survived, being 'caught by his webbing cross belts on a scrub oak' as he fell. Leading his own convoy of two Jeeps and trailers, at a top speed of ten miles per hour, Tony sat apprehensively on the side furthest from the drop, ready to bale out in a hurry.

The river below was a wonderful sight: 'it hurls itself down waterfalls and flows into large lakes of the most brilliant blue. It is of course quite unfordable as it is very deep and never less than two hundred yards wide save where it rushes through narrow gorges with cliffs rising sheer from the water.' They camped for the night at the top of the pass and encountered some wild, cave-dwelling locals who had never seen a motor vehicle. The troglodytes ran away from the leading Jeep in terror, and when 'finally induced to return they brought grass and threw it down in front of the vehicle for it to eat'.

Tony relished the Alpine climate, the warm sunshine and the cooling breezes. He observed that there were several foot- or mule-bridges across the foaming river, always where it was narrowest and therefore at such a height that they could not be

[2] Letter 186.

washed away. The bridges were impressively engineered, but challenging in a strong wind. 'The trick is not to take long strides as this starts the centre tree bouncing up and down forcing one to walk in time with the bounce.' The slopes on either side were thickly forested with Deodar and Caucasian Pine, and swarmed with colourful birds, including white and pale-blue wagtails and 'a little finch which is royal blue with a minute scarlet crest'. Waders, ducks and all kinds of snipe clustered at the water's edge.

Tony befriended the locals and had an opportunity to inspect the huts and caves in which they lived. Their dwellings were surprisingly clean, though the tribesmen themselves were filthy. They wore heavy goat's-hair costumes, with baskets slung over them, and 'rough leggings made from uncut and unsewn skins', which were 'bound round the feet and leg with grass rope'. Tony's Pathans openly despised them for being an inferior, Mongoloid race and for not washing properly or saying their prayers. 'There was very nearly an incident.'

Tony broke bread with the local chief and 'a funny little man' who had come down with a caravan from China. His conversation was unguarded and, afterwards, Tony sent one of his men down to the police post, reporting him as a Russian spy.

His account is vivid, but it is difficult to trace his movements. Describing his ascent of the region's highest peak, Saiful Muluk, he speaks of being caught in a snow-storm and of having to shelter for three hours in a cave. He visits Lake Chitta Katha, high in the valley, with its pale blue or even silver water (caused by the mica in the rocks), and its wall of snow-capped mountains which rise 'almost sheer from the very edge of the water'. The lake is shunned by the locals, who believe it to be haunted, and by most wildlife, apart from a few wild geese. Tony and his party have a few basic supplies; otherwise they live off the land. There are 'plenty of Ibex about and my body guard goes out every third day to bag one'. The river is full of 'real live snow trout': Tony catches six a day and tussles with one gigantic specimen, a 28-inch monster weighing five pounds, for forty minutes. The fish are cooked over a wood fire and taste remarkably good. By now they have crossed the border into Gilgit, a contested region of Kashmir.[3]

The former Gilgit Agency had been handed over to Jammu and Kashmir at the time of Partition, despite its Muslim majority. The Maharajah's decision to accede to India had been met there with incomprehension and dismay. What was Pakistan for, if not as a homeland for regions with Muslim majorities? It was at this point that a remarkable, 24-year-old British officer had taken decisive action. Major William Brown, late of the Argyll and Sutherland Highlanders, had arrived in Gilgit in 1943. Fluent in the local languages, he had recently been appointed acting commandant of the local defence force, the Gilgit Scouts. A man of the highest principle, Brown was moved by the entreaties of his men, who 'despised and hated Kashmir and everything connected with it'. They told him 'how happy and content they had been under the British rule, and how they considered they had been betrayed by the British in the unconditional handing over of their country to Kashmir'.[4]

Brown had warned the governor, Brigadier Ghansar Singh, that, for the avoidance of bloodshed, he should comply with the wishes of the majority. On 31 October, his Scouts having surrounded the residency in Gilgit City, he had taken Singh and his staff into protective custody and, at some risk to himself, had organised the protection of the Hindu minority. Brown's *coup* was determinedly bloodless. He wrote later that 'my actions appeared to possess all the elements of high treason. Yet I knew in my own mind that what I had done was right.'[5] On 2 November, he had announced Gilgit's accession to Pakistan and, with Sir George

---

3 Letter 183.

4 Yaqoob Khan Bangash, 'Three Forgotten Accessions: Gilgit, Hunza and Nagar,' *The Journal of Imperial and Commonwealth History,* 38:1 (2010), pp.125-126.

5 See Victoria Schofield, *Kashmir in Conflict: India, Pakistan and the Unending War* (London, 2003).

Cunningham's blessing, had stayed on in Gilgit City as Chief Military Adviser. In the subsequent distribution of Birthday Honours he was discreetly awarded an M.B.E. for his services, no doubt on Cunningham's recommendation. He is described in the *London Gazette* as an officer on the 'Special List (ex-Indian Army)'.[6]

Brown had been relieved on 10 January by the redoubtable Aslam Khan, M.C. Himself an Afridi from Jammu, Khan had taken personal command of the Scouts, raised an additional force of 600 Azad rebels, and led them in an attack on the fort at Skardu (location of his future Shangrila resort), where a Kashmiri garrison held out. It had finally fallen on 14 August 1948, after a six-month siege. The defenders had run out of ammunition and the only men left alive were the brave officer in command, a Gurkha, and his Sikh orderly.

The Indian government had effectively given up Gilgit for lost, but not the neighbouring region of Ladakh. A major offensive was mounted that autumn. This was the 'main front' to which Tony refers. 'At the top of the [Kaghan Valley] road I first went east, that is round the north of the main front, where I met my old battery.' He would have liked to stay with them, as he would always 'much rather be with the men at the business end of the guns', but he was too useful in his now permanent 'back seat' role as 'Chief Gunnery Instructor'. He asked his parents not to address him as such on any envelope. Nor should they share extracts from his letters (as they had jokingly threatened they might) with Mr Perkins, the editor of *The Marlborough Times,* 'as the whole of the area described lies in the war zone where British officers are not officially supposed to set foot'. After all, that journal was taken in the mess at Larkhill. One of the many Indian officers on courses there might see it and pass it on to Indian intelligence, 'who could use it as a lever to get the British officers out of the Pakistan army'.

---

6 *London Gazette,* 4 June 1948.

Tony ends the fourth instalment of his adventures on 10 September, at Babusar Top, gateway to Gilgit. Here he plans his return to Nowshera in a train of three mules, obligingly provided by the local chief. His party will cross the pass into Kohistan 'and then through Swat and so down to the Indus'. He refers to visitations by the Royal Indian Air Force and implies that he may himself have been caught in the bombardment. The next his parents hear from him, he is in hospital.[7]

Shock Waves

Tony had arrived on 13 September at Abbottabad, a delightful city near the southern end of the Kaghan Valley. Founded in the 1850s by Major James Abbott, it was notable for its cantonment, sanatorium and very English-looking church, of which Tony took a photograph. Despite increasing giddiness and loss of appetite, he carried on as normal and was even seen swimming in the club pool. That evening, the General's A.D.C. turned up in a staff car and handed over a note. Would Tony please report to the M.O. at the hospital at once? The A.D.C. would see to his kit.

Standards had certainly slipped at the hospital. It was squalid. There were no British doctors and no nursing staff other than orderlies. Tony's doctor was 'quite a reasonable sort of fellow', but had nearly 200 surgical cases in his wards. Tony enlisted 'his own fellows' to provide for him. His cook provided palatable meals, while his orderly cleaned the place up. Don, the bull mastiff, lay under the bed and growled at anyone attempting to take Tony's temperature. Eventually they stopped coming.

However, the wives of the British officers would visit daily, bringing 'piles of fresh fruit, papers and books which are most welcome'. Tony's preferred reading was a volume that had been sent in a package from Foyle's. It was Bertrand Russell's

[7] Letters 183, 184, 186.

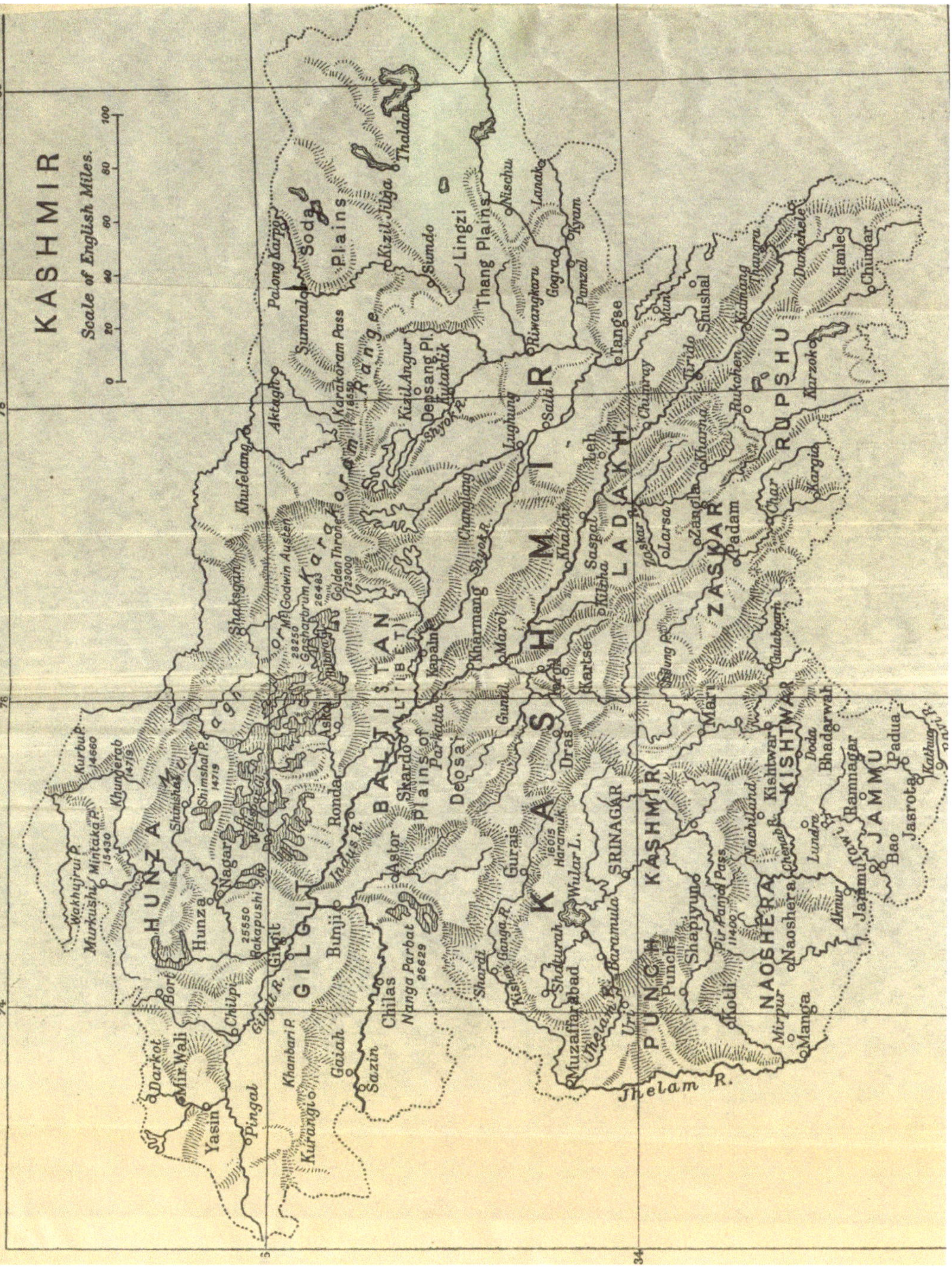
KASHMIR
Scale of English Miles.
HUNZA
GILGIT
BALTISTAN
LADAKH
ZASKAR
RUPSHU
PUNCH
KASHMIR
SRINAGAR
JAMMU
KISHTWAR
NAOSHERA
Jhelam R.
Indus R.

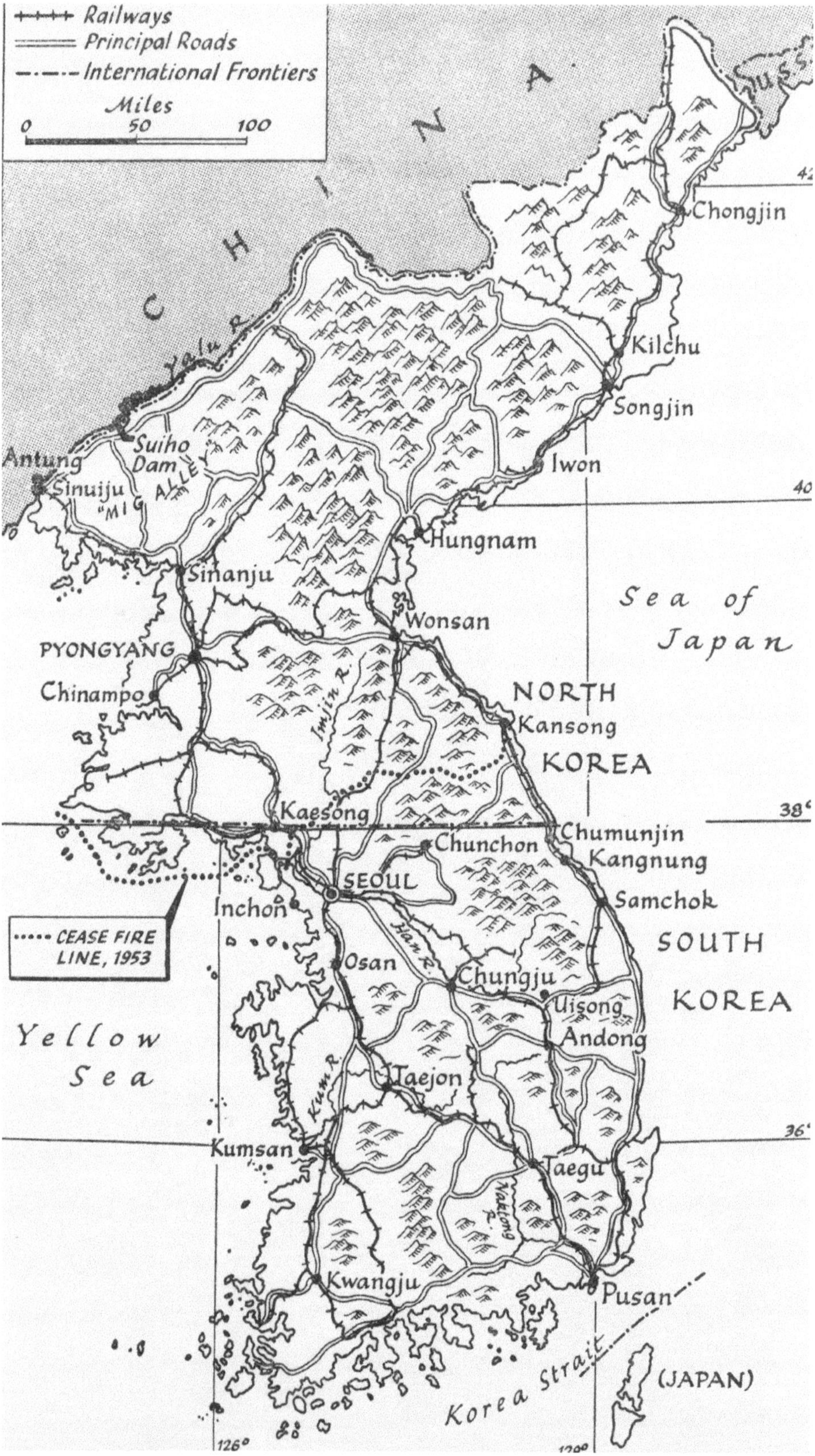
Railways
Principal Roads
International Frontiers
Miles
0
50
100
CHINA
Yalu R.
Chongjin
Kilchu
Songjin
Iwon
Antung
Suiho Dam
Sinuiju
"MIG ALLEY"
Hungnam
Sinanju
Wonsan
Sea of Japan
PYONGYANG
Chinampo
Imjin R.
NORTH KOREA
Kansong
Kaesong
Chumunjin
Chunchon
Kangnung
SEOUL
Inchon
Samchok
CEASE FIRE LINE, 1953
Han R.
SOUTH KOREA
Osan
Chungju
Uisong
Andong
Yellow Sea
Kum R.
Taejon
Kumsan
Taegu
Naktong R.
Kwangju
Pusan
Korea Strait
(JAPAN)
38°
36°
40°
126°

Mathematical Philosophy. A batch of about twenty officers' wives had recently come out, on War Office instructions, via Bombay, but the Indian Police had immediately arrested them as 'enemy aliens'. One of Tony's visitors described a hellish week in a detention camp, locked in a tiny room with her three small children and denied access to her luggage. Apparently the British High Commissioner had done nothing to secure their release. Tony railed against a country 'riddled with communism and corruption' and the daily anti-British tirades of its press. He predicted an all-out India-Pakistan war in the near future; 'the Kashmir show does not seem to count'.[8]

Tony does not seem to have been hit by shrapnel but to have been affected in some way by the blast from an Indian bomb. He was told that 'something inside got strained and that I have to rest and take things quietly'. After about six weeks laid up in hospital he could expect to be on sick leave for a further month. Initially his intake of food was strictly controlled. His injuries were clearly quite serious, though he barely refers to them.

Other wounded officers came down from the front. Like Tony, they all seem to have lacked immediate medical attention. One man, riddled by shell splinters, had had to wait three days before his wounds were dressed, and 'when he was finally sewn up the M.O. failed to clean the wound properly so that some of the little ticks which abound in that area got sewn up inside'. Three-hourly injections of penicillin were doing little to assuage the pain.

Tony, who claimed to be quite fit, was deeply frustrated by the mass of work that was piling up, with 'no one else to do it'. Following his transfer, by mid-October, to the hospital at Nowshera, his orderly was able to bring him daily tasks from the School - 'working out gunnery problems sent down from the front, writing training pamphlets and working out sums' - to which Tony applied himself for about five hours, sitting at a small

---

[8] Letter 184.

table on the lawn, before handing them back to the orderly in the evening.

Among the other patients were a Pakistani officer from the School, laid low with malaria, and 'a gunner captain with a rather unpleasant gun shot wound in the back', no doubt picked up in Kashmir. The weather was 'really lovely'. Tony was allowed out for exercise, taking gentle daily walks and even dips in the pool. He strolled down to the bungalow and was relieved to find the gardens and stables in good order, the house re-painted and the paths re-gravelled. He was no longer at risk of starvation, for he could now order anything he liked from his own cook, whose offerings were excellent. He even went out for late dinners with the Station Commander, Colonel Stroud, who was 'very good fun', as was his delightful Austrian wife, who told how her family's *schloss* had been wantonly sacked by the Americans. A keen cook, she visited him in hospital every day and plied him with delicacies, ranging from 'fresh trout cooked in white wine to chocolate cake covered with thick frozen cream'. Together they planned a fishing and shooting trip down the Indus in the colonel's own boat, as he had private means and seemed to live rather well.[9]

Tony reveals in his letters a growing disenchantment with Pakistan, where the Strouds were soon his only friends, the other two British officers having left for home. The commandant of the school was an ex-ranker with limited expertise in the field of gunnery, no 'gent', in short, who 'never thinks of going out into the wilds'. When a new Gunnery Instructor turns up at Nowshera with his family, having turned down a posting in East Africa, Tony is astonished. 'Why anyone with a family should choose Pakistan in preference to East Africa is beyond me.'

It was not only the medical services that were falling apart, but every other institution, from the army, with its office-bound 'chiefs' and grafting, over-promoted officers, to public services

---

[9] Letters 185, 186, 188 (on the Strouds).

such as the Post Office. No fewer than three provincial governors, several police chiefs and the Chief Customs Officer had all been suspended for corruption in recent weeks.

A model of efficiency during the war, the postal service had become a national embarrassment. Mail deliveries were completely unreliable and subject to inexplicable delays. On one occasion, eleven letters from Tony's parents were delivered at once. He also reports that 'every parcel that arrives here shows signs of having been opened'. In some cases they were reduced to 'a piece of wrapping paper with a label stuck on it', having been systematically robbed of their contents. The National Book League, to which Tony subscribed, informed its members that sixty per cent of its books were being stolen in transit. Recognisable by the Book League stamp, Tony knew exactly where they were going - into 'every book shop one goes into', where they were being sold at fifty per cent above the cover price.[10]

Tony's official release from hospital, on 22 October, put an end to such gloomy reflections. He had had to fight for his freedom: the Commandant would have had him stay another week. A month's sick leave beckoned. Tony headed straight for the office, where the work was mounting up, but on about 1 November, in obedience to the 'medic', embarked on a fishing holiday in Swat, though he took his work with him. Travelling into that territory could only be done by prior arrangement and with special permission, but the Political Agent of Malakand was extremely obliging. Tony was given the use of the sumptuous Durbar Bungalow in Fort Amandarra, which was romantically perched atop a rocky hill, above a bend in the Swat river. Tony's arrival after dark, with his bearer, created a stir among the guard, who insisted on being inspected. For the rest of the time Tony was undisturbed and able to finish off his work. Every day he would go down to the river to fish, netting some enormous *mahseer*

[10] Letters 182, 185, 186, 187, 189, 190.

(somewhere between a salmon and a pike), which he shared with the bearer and the men of the guard.

He had intended to stay for ten days but was called back after a week. On the night of 6-7 November, a division of the Indian Army, with supporting field artillery and two troops of Sherman tanks, had advanced into the Poonch district of Kashmir. The Kashmiri garrison at Poonch town had withstood a year-long Azadi siege. The brave and resourceful defenders had constructed a makeshift air strip, so the R.I.A.F. had been able to keep them fully supplied and to evacuate many of the refugees who had assembled there. They had also flown in a section of 25-pounder guns, to counter the guns of the Pakistan Mountain Artillery that were constantly trained on them.

Tony had full confidence in the three Pakistani divisions that were in action, not to mention the 100,000 Azadi militiamen. 'It looks as though things are coming to a head,' he wrote. '[O]ur armour has moved down together with a very considerable gunner supporting element. I think that in a month's time we will see Punch [*sic*] cleared of the enemy.' The British-built aircraft of the R.I.A.F., under the overall command of Air-Marshal Sir Thomas Elmhirst, were 'making things very unpleasant for our gunners[,] but at night we have it all our own way'.

Tony's optimism was misplaced. On 20 November, a string of Azadi outposts having fallen to the Indian relief force, the garrison at Poonch town was able to break through the investment and link up with them. The siege of Poonch town, as epic as any medieval siege, was over.

Pakistani forces were now concentrating for a counter-attack; hence the urgency with which Tony was summoned home. He remained in Nowshera, where he gave an exhausting round of lectures at the School, and tested fuses and shells at the ammunition depot, as they were affected in some way by the conditions in Kashmir. Slit trenches had been dug everywhere, even in Tony's own garden, in case of a sudden air attack. 'It seems very odd that although we are as much members of the

Pakistan army as anyone else, we are not *officially* allowed forward, and to give advice and work out answers to situations that are reported second hand is very hard indeed.' When the Director General of the Royal Artillery flew in for a visit, he hinted that the British element might soon be separated into a 'military mission', with a purely advisory role. That was not Tony's idea of soldiering. His notion of an army officer was that he 'should give orders and expect them to be carried out without question. Some people here have already found out my ideas on that subject.'[11]

A few weeks later, the Pakistani and Azad forces had managed to reverse some of the Indian gains, but the newly-formed United Nations Organisation was now actively brokering a cease-fire. The rival British generals, Gracey and Bucher, are said to have been powerful advocates of moderation; the alternative was mutual destruction.[12] The U.N. Security Council Resolution 47 was adopted on 5 January 1949. It required the withdrawal of forces on both sides, and effectively marked the end of the war, at least for the time being.

Tony planned to spend Christmas with the Stroud family, cruising down the river on their boat, fishing and shooting duck, but his next letter home is dated 4 March 1949. It seems that, during a hard winter, he had been fully occupied on the cease-fire line in Kashmir, living in a dug-out. Owing to the heavy snowfall overnight, each pit, whether for men or guns, had had to be freshly excavated in the morning. 'The cease fire seems to be working very well, but very few people have any real faith in the ability of the U.N.O. commission to solve the question. We are holding on to the positions that we have won, only evacuating the really high features as they are impossible to hold in this weather.'

Tony had been earmarked as a consultant to the Commission, but that would be 'a rather tricky sort of job as for the last months

---

[11] Letter 188.

[12] Lamb, *Crisis in Kashmir,* pp.52-3.

I have been trying to avoid them[. T]hey have been told that no British officer has ever been near Kashmir: Mr Attlee also said as much in the House - little he knows about it.' The Pakistan government had renewed its promise to compensate any British officer 'who gets into trouble for partaking in the scrap', and, indeed, Tony had already received a bounty of £300 for 'services rendered'.

Tony had re-entered Pakistan through the romantic city of Attock, otherwise known as Campbellpore, at about the point where Alexander had crossed the Indus. The 'wonderful old Mughal fort' of the Emperor Akbar, completed in 1583, hung on a cliff overlooking the river. It was now the sole place of detention for Indian P.O.W.s; apparently they were well treated.[13] Tony spent a day and a night there, investigated the fishing, and shot some duck.

The British population of Nowshera seemed to have expanded rapidly in his absence, including three new officers at the School, with their families. Tony, who was now the only unmarried British officer on the station, put up one of the new arrivals in his bungalow, a thoughtful, chess-playing lieutenant-colonel who, in his pre-war life, had been a Classics master at Harrow. Mainly they were 'ex-rankers who appear not to know the form. Their wives are the worst part of it; an ex-ranker gets knocked into some sort of shape in the mess where he is taught how to behave but his wife gets no such "education" and so always betrays her origin.'[14]

Tony coolly composed his letter in the aftermath of an earthquake. For two minutes he was 'really frightened', with his pictures in the bungalow crashing down around him and the fan above suddenly going 'mad'. A building opposite collapsed 'like a pile of cards', two trees were brought down and the 'electric light

---

[13] Catherine Rey-Schyrr, 'The ICRC's Activities on the Indian Subcontinent following Partition (1947-1949)', *International Review of the Red Cross,* No.323 (30 June 1998).

[14] Letters 189, 190.

cable snapped between two poles like a piece of cotton but with a report like a gun'. With the rumble of a final shock wave, Tony's chimney came tumbling down. The terrified locals threw themselves on the ground with imprecations to Allah.[15] Tony learnt later that there had been terrible damage in Lahore, though the epicentre of the earthquake was in Badakhshan Province, Afghanistan. With a magnitude of 7.5 it is classed as 'severe'. Perhaps it was the arbitrariness of nature that had prompted Tony to resume contact with his parents, after an unusually long interval.

Adventures on the Frontier

In March 1949, Tony was sent up to Chitral. Exceedingly remote, romantic and mountainous, Chitral was a princely state that had acceded in 1947 to Pakistan. Chitral is in the far north of the country, close to the borders of both Russia and China, and had been of vital strategic significance in the 'Great Game'. The name is resonant in British military annals. In 1895, 400 British soldiers under Captain (later Major-General Sir Charles) Townshend, an Old Cranleighan, had been besieged for a month and a half in Chitral Fort. To the astonishment of the Chitralis, a small relief force from Peshawar had arrived before the end of winter. It had crossed 150 miles of mountains, including the 12,000-foot Shandur Pass, through waist-deep snow, dragging a couple of mountain guns on sledges. The campaign was a celebrated instance of British gallantry and endurance.

There is still no road to speak of and, like his predecessors, and at exactly the same time of year, Tony had crossed the Shandur Pass on foot, with a train of mules to carry the kit. He describes the country as 'too wonderful for words, mile upon mile of unbroken snow clad mountains and the lower slopes covered with

[15] Letters 188, 189.

flowers and bright green shrubs'. He does not state the purpose of his visit.

From Chitral, he headed south-east to the border city of Jhelum. It was here, on the banks of the Hydaspes or Jhelum River, that Alexander had defeated the Indian king Porus in 326 B.C. Tony then crossed into Kashmir near the small, now 'liberated' town of Nowshera, which is not to be confused with the Nowshera in Pakistan. Again, he says nothing of his activities there; only that it was 'rather cold at night'. His visit was brief and soon he was in a dusty, fly-blown camp near Rawalpindi for a large-scale exercise. He writes that 'living in a tent or sleeping in the truck … is just the sort of life I like'.[16]

Around the middle of May he was sent off again 'to the northern front to visit the forward positions and have a look at the "enemy" lines'. Besides the faithful Don, who was as glad as he to escape the heat of the plains, he was accompanied by a newly-appointed instructor at the School. Lieutenant-Colonel Roddy Keelan[17] was an old friend from Larkhill and had been a very welcome new arrival in March, among an influx of generally lacklustre British officers and their families ('the majority seem to be ex-rankers who appear not to know the form').

Their first stop was at Bagh, a city well inside Kashmir, but now under Azad control. Tony was in for an unpleasant shock when, lured into the civilian hospital by 'an enthusiastic Red Cross doctor', he encountered the victims of recent atrocities - 'civilians suffering from sword cuts and other Sikh unpleasantries' - whose wounds had 'mostly gone very bad'. Tony was so sickened that he 'nearly had to call it off'. The hospital itself was spotlessly clean and efficiently run by its dedicated staff, but half of it had been flattened by the R.I.A.F., who in October 1948 had targeted it on three occasions, killing patients, despite its being marked with the Red Cross emblem. This

---

16 Letter 191.

17 Roderick Esmond Thomas Keelan had been commissioned from Sandhurst in Sept 1932 (*London Gazette*).

appeared to be a breach of the Geneva Convention. Responding to a complaint by the I.C.R.C., the Indian government stated that under no circumstances would its pilots have deliberately attacked a medical facility; it could only assume that the marking of the hospital had been inadequate.[18]

From Bagh they proceeded to the front. Keelan was content to leave the scaling of the higher mountains to Tony. These were the haunt of the black bear, the musk deer and the ilex; panther and red leopard lurked among the lower slopes. Some fifty miles from Srinagar, Tony inspected 'the very forward unit on the highest peak'. It was a mere eighty yards from the Indian lines, where the 'enemy' were dug into 'bunkers constructed of pine logs about three feet thick … with only two feet showing above the surface'. Tony's role was to help position the guns, 'which often have to be carried by hand for miles to the tops of mountains', so that they could achieve direct hits on these bunkers. One night he 'went on a patrol with the Dyad forces to a place well behind the so-called line'. He also spent three nights with the men of his old battery at the top of an 11,000-foot mountain. It is astonishing to think that the guns, each weighing a ton, had had to be carried up from the jeep track at 5,000 feet, without even the benefit of a foot path. For Tony, it was worth it for the view. He and Keelan had a shared interest in ornithology and the variety of colourful birds at these heights left them both entranced.

Tony comments on the warm welcome and hospitality that he received. A cup of tea was offered at every outpost and to refuse it would have caused offence. He would be expected to dine with every unit he visited. He was surprised to encounter a Pakistani brigadier and two lieutenant-colonels who had served with him in H.Q. 6 Division in Iraq, junior to him then, who 'gave me a very good time and a great deal of help in collecting the data I was after'. The local Dyad irregulars were particularly attentive.[19]

---

[18] Rey-Schyrr, 'The ICRC's Activities on the Indian Subcontinent following Partition'.

[19] Letter 192.

Back in Nowshera, the weather was very peculiar, either boiling hot or abnormally cold. There was a week of solid rain, and other strange happenings. A party of thieving tribesmen, said to be from the other side of Peshawar, had worked out how to infiltrate the heavily-guarded cantonment and, during the past month, no fewer than thirty-two bungalows had been broken into. These truly slippery individuals normally wore only a loin cloth and were said to grease themselves with panther fat to deter dogs. Returning from the club one night, Tony surprised one of the thieves in his back garden. The man ran off, but Don 'brought him down before he had gone fifty yards'. Tony arrested him and handed him over to armed police who were patrolling the area. On another occasion he and Don noticed the suspicious flashing of a torch in the neighbouring bungalow. On entering the bungalow Tony saw three men bolting out of the back window, but was just in time to catch one of them by the leg. He, too, was consigned to the 'cooler'.

On 1 June, Tony welcomed a new intake of twenty-three newly-commissioned officers on a five-month course, on which he was to teach them technical subjects and theoretical gunnery. He had set his own sights on the Technical Staff Officers' course at the Military College of Science, Shrivenham. Graduates of the two-year course were credited with a B.Sc. in Engineering, so many doors would be opened. Tony already had the recommendation of his old chief at Larkhill, but would have to pass a 'really stiff entrance exam in maths, chemistry and physics', which he would sit in Pakistan in October.[20]

Roddy Keelan was not only an ornithologist but also a passionate fisherman, and had brought out his car from home. It was a Vanguard, the latest model from the Standard Motor Company of Coventry, a vehicle specifically designed for the overseas market. Every weekend the pair would drive off together with their rods, as far as the resort of Murree, near Abbottabad, on

[20] Letters 188, 189, 190, 192, 193.

one occasion. Tony dreaded the imminent arrival of Keelan's wife.

Meanwhile, he paid court to the daughter of Brigadier Davis of Peshawar,[21] whose love of horses and expertise with the fly-rod made her a particularly appealing female. She had 'a rather half-hearted job as private secretary to the wife of the Governor, Lady Dundas', but not for long. Sir Ambrose Flux Dundas was to retire in September, the last British Governor of North-West Frontier Province. Mudie, the Governor of West Punjab, was also poised to resign, the staunchest advocate for Pakistan, yet defeated by the endemic corruption of the Muslim League and its keenness to put Pakistanis in top positions. There was even talk of Pakistan's leaving the Commonwealth and of her combining with other states to form a Muslim league. 'The British government is in great disfavour over the Kashmir show,' wrote Tony, 'as it is supplying arms to both sides and refuses to arbitrate. All we want is a free plebiscite as 90 per cent of the population is Muslim and wants to join Pakistan.'[22]

If all went as planned it was on or around 14 July that Tony flew back to England on leave, returning to Pakistan in late September. His next letter is dated 12 December. The entrance exam for Shrivenham had been put off till the spring of 1951. Tony was preparing a specialist ten-day course for senior officers to begin on 2 January, but had enough leisure time to take up golf. His regular partners were the solitary British civilian in Nowshera (he was manager of the local branch of Grindlay's, bankers to the army and business community in India since 1828, now owned by the National Bank of India), and Colonel Tommy Wainwright

---

[21] Brig. A.L. Davis is listed as President of the Cantonment Board, Peshawar, from Dec 1948 to Sept 1949: https://peshawar.cantonment.gov.pk/en//list-of-presidents. Tony describes him as 'a bit of a three-bottle man but a real soldier'.

[22] Letter 193. There was to be no plebiscite, and, as there had been no conclusive military outcome, the stalemate of 1948 'has persisted more or less to the present day': Alastair Lamb, *Incomplete Partition: The Genesis of the Kashmir Dispute, 1947 - 1948* (London, 1997), p.181.

who commanded the Cadet Wing. The 'ex-ranker' Commandant of the School had been promoted to full Colonel and, being now also Station Commander, seemed 'very much more human'. His vulgar wife, however, was more insufferable than ever.[23]

With ten days leave over Christmas, Tony went off on another frontier adventure. He first took a train to Campbellpore, which he had scouted out in March. A car from the gunner depot there conveyed him by a steep hill road to Chhoi (usually spelt with two aitches), where he had arranged to stay in an official bungalow. There was a fine view up the Indus to Attock (Campbellpore), which was about twelve miles away, and in the other direction one looked over the densely-forested Kala Chitta range (meaning literally 'black and white'). Water was drawn from a distant well, and heating was by logs on an open hearth. It was a very remote and unfrequented spot.

With the help of the local headman, Tony hired a *shikari* or guide and, early the next morning, clad in a cotton shirt and pullover and carrying his rifle and telescope, set off in pursuit of his goals, which were some particularly exotic game. Looking like 'an escaped desperado', the guide was an expert tracker. 'From a square yard of sand at the bottom of a dried up river bed he could point out the foot marks of a fox, gazelle, ibex, urial and panther.' For four days they ranged through the mountains, covering about fifteen miles a day.

Tony decided that he would move further into the hills. He organised alternative accommodation, a hut at Pug-Jahhi (as Tony spells it), and sent his bearer ahead with a team of camels. Meanwhile, he and the *shikari*, 'armed with a blanket each and some *chapatis,* dried milk, tea and sugar set off to get there round the top of the hills, a distance of fifty miles. We did it in two days,[24] spending the night in the open by a fire built by a sort of

---

[23] Letters 193, 194.

[24] These seem astonishing distances to cover in a day, in mountainous country. However, Tony makes the same claim after a second visit to Chhoi (letter 198).

cave near a spring. We slept rolled in a blanket and dined and breakfasted off tea and chapati.'

On the second day they were able to pursue a herd of urial, 'and after a long stalk I bagged a lovely beast with huge horns'. The urial is a species of wild sheep, native to Central and South Asia, that is now sadly endangered. With their long legs and large, curling horns they are particularly beautiful animals. 'The thug then sat down and called and in about ten minutes he got an answer from some people cutting wood three miles away. After an hour they came up and we arranged for them to take the urial down to the track where we would send a camel to pick it up the next day.'

That afternoon, while climbing down a steep cliff, Tony spotted a leopard on a ledge, but it quickly ran off. Over the next few days he bagged a further three urial and two gazelle. Tony shot his final urial on Christmas Eve. The oldest of the herd, it stood at the top of a cliff against the sky-line, offering a perfect shot. A local goatherd helped them carry it down, 'slung on a pole between us', and told them that a *chittar,* a leopard or panther,[25] had been preying on his flock. A crowd of about ten concerned people miraculously collected around them. Tony and the *shikari,* with half a dozen locals, set off in pursuit.

They came at length to a 'very narrow gorge with tall grass at the bottom of it and low bushes at the edges'. The locals backed away in terror. The place had an evil reputation. Tony and the *shikari* fearlessly descended into the gorge. Rounding a bend, they suddenly came upon a leopard, 'no more than twenty yards away, facing us and crouched over the half-eaten goat. It was a lovely sight, the ridge was just in the sun and the sandstone frame with the green trees in the evening sun and the deep yellow and black of the leopard and the red of its prey made the most wonderful picture.' The animal lashed its tail, snarled menacingly,

---

25 The Urdu word *chittar* ('cheetah') means 'variegated', but was applied indiscriminately. The word 'panther' in English tends to refer to the black variety.

and prepared to spring. 'The bullet got there first: its skin is now over the back of my sofa and measures eight foot from nose to tip of tail. Anyway, that is one way to spend Christmas!'[26]

Final Days

A new Gunnery Staff Course commenced on 16 January 1950, so Tony was preoccupied for the next three months with his usual technical stock in trade, including mathematics, ballistics and the manufacture of guns and ammunition.[27] His work was certainly appreciated, even by the undemonstrative Director of the Royal Pakistan Artillery, up from Rawalpindi, who unexpectedly summoned him to his presence and gave him 'a terrific pat on the back'.

Tony knew that his time with the Pakistan Army was drawing to a close. Nearly all the 400 attached officers were to be sent home by the end of the year. He would be very sorry to leave, but by August there would be only one other British officer at the school, the dreaded Commandant. He deplored the inertia that had set in, 'as it does in every place over which the Jack is finally brought low'. No one seems willing to make the smallest decision without consulting either the 'regulations' or 'the next highest authority', so 'nothing is ever decided and nothing gets *done.*'[28]

He resolved to make the most of his remaining time, and in particular to fish, ride, shoot and visit places of interest. One of these was the ruined city of Ranigat, ten miles north of Swabi, which Tony and a colleague had come across while on an exercise. Dating from the second century A.D., Ranigat is an extraordinary monument to the Gandhara civilisation, the ruins spread over a wide area at the top of a great hill. The more outlandish structures are the remains of Buddhist monasteries, but

---

[26] Letter 195.

[27] Letter 194.

[28] Letters 196, 200.

Tony's curiosity was piqued by the 'great caves and grottos in the hillside all full of great idols with carved pictures around the walls'. The entrances to the larger caves were blocked, apart from a small opening, pointed out to him by a shepherd.

Tony determined to mount a proper expedition, 'ten men with picks and shovels, ropes and blasting equipment and tents for the night … to see if there is anything to be found'. Nothing came of this, but the pair returned in early February for 'a bit of digging'. Tony fearlessly wriggled through a tiny gap into 'a long tunnel which ran into the side of the hill from a ruined building'. It was pitch-black inside, but after about twenty yards the tunnel suddenly opened out into a great, bottomless pit. He had no choice but to turn around (which he achieved with some difficulty) and wriggle back to the entrance, where his companion, who was considerably less 'gung-ho' than he, was waiting anxiously. On their way back, the friend's Austin A90 got stuck four times and they had to be helped out by the locals. 'They told us that it was the first time a motor vehicle had ever ventured along that track!'[29]

As the episode shows, Tony had developed a deep interest in antiquities. He had already formed a collection of old Greek coins, mostly the small change of Alexander's soldiers, but also some silver ones which a friendly villager had unearthed with his plough. The prize of the collection was a coin from what he calls 'the period of Ashura' (though he is probably referring to Ashoka the Great, who reigned in that country from *c.*268 to 233 B.C.) which was of pure gold. In the interests of science, Tony had had a plaster cast made of it and had sent it to the curator of coins at the British Museum.[30]

As an indefatigable traveller and explorer, as a linguist and antiquary, Tony was an ideal candidate for election to the Royal Central Asian Society (founded in 1901), of which His Majesty

---

29 Letters 197, 198.

30 Letters 196, 198.

the King was Patron. Tony was put up for the society without his knowledge and duly elected, in May or June 1950. In Korea that December, he would learn that he had been promoted to a full fellowship. In retirement, by which time it was known as the Royal Society for Asian Affairs, he would serve for many years as Honorary Secretary, also lecturing and leading tours to exotic locations, including some of the haunts of his youth.[31]

On 2 March he was lured back to Chhoi for a long weekend, bagging a couple of gazelle, though the urial eluded him. He had stalked a magnificent specimen for an entire day and was poised to shoot it, when his *shikari* 'missed his footing and shot down a twenty foot drop'. Luckily the fellow caught hold of a bush on the way down. For Tony, the beauty of the place was in the contrasting colours. There were the white, snow-capped mountains in the distance, the blue Indus snaking through the green plain below and, all around him, the sandstone cliffs, all yellow and red but for the pink-flowering bushes that grew on them. As a final touch, multi-coloured flowers crowded the spaces between the rocks.[32]

It was an anxious time in Pakistan. In April he writes: 'Things out here have been going rapidly down-hill for the last month and the situation is now very tense indeed'. Indian forces were massing on the border, and war seemed imminent. It was sincerely believed that India would join forces with Russia to carve up the region. Yet the British officers on attachment, the 'main-stay' of the Pakistan Army, were under orders not to fight. Few were at ease with the prospect of abandoning either the country or their men, or indeed of yielding to a communist plot. 'With them,' wrote Tony, 'I feel that I should not be able to act on any order recalling me to the U.K. if the Pakistan Army was engaged in a life or death struggle with India, or any other

---

[31] Letters 202, 211; Norman Cameron, 'Obituary: Lieutenant-Colonel Tony Fowle, M.C.', in *Asian Affairs,* XLVIII, no.1, pp.133-4.

[32] Letter 198.

aggressor'. 'Please remember,' he added ominously, 'that though you may hear nothing of me I am among true friends.'

Happily, the emergency was over within the week. Soon afterwards, Tony received a mysterious letter from the War Office, instructing him to hand in his notice. It seemed to be an order and, on the advice of the Commandant, he did as he was instructed. He would be back in England by August.[33]

The Pakistani government had been courting allies elsewhere, including neighbouring Iran. When the young Shah came to Nowshera on an official visit in March, Tony was detailed to meet him. A grandstand was built on the ranges, and the army and air force laid on an impressive demonstration of their fire-power, bombs and rockets raining all around him.

Tony further consorted with royalty in May. The Nawabzada of Mardan, heir apparent to Nawab Akbar Khan Hoti, invited him to an old-fashioned shooting party. 'The whole thing was done in truly oriental splendour. The Nawab has three sons and built them "a little shack" where they can live and invite their friends. The "shack" has no less than 450 bedrooms.' It was built around 'a massive courtyard lined with flowering trees and vines', and had 'a single small gate, this being guarded by fifty armed retainers'. The old Nawab was a philosopher, 'very pro-British' (indeed, a veteran of the Great War), and had amassed an enormous library, including priceless manuscripts. The Nawabzada, a captain in the Pakistan Engineers, was interested in fishing, and asked Tony to give him lessons. In the 1980s he was to be briefly governor of Khyber-Pakhtunkhwa, formerly N.W.F.P., resigning on a point of honour.[34]

With temperatures soaring, Tony was free to fish or shoot duck in the afternoons, but soon 'the only thing to do … would be to lie

---

33 Letter 200.

34 Letter 201; Amineh Hoti, 'Wealth Beyond Measure', *The Friday Times* (Pakistan), 10 Feb 2017; 'What a Democracy!', *Dawn* (Pakistan), 21 July 2017.

and drip under a fan'.[35] A sweltering June was spent with Divisional H.Q. in Peshawar, although he briefly flew in and out of Skardu (in remote Gilgit) on some mission. He describes it as 'the most wonderful flight in the world', as one passes over 'a tangled mass of peaks and glaciers stretching away as far as the eye can see'.

At the end of the month he met the amiable General Gracey on his annual inspection of the School,[36] but on 1 July embarked on three weeks' 'casual leave' in the cooler north. From Abbottabad he travelled up in a jeep, followed by a train of mules, to Naran, at the head of the Kaghan Valley. The locals had occasionally to help pull the jeep out of deep snow. 'While up there I walked an average of sixteen miles a day and on one "ghust" went up as high as fourteen thousand. We had one small scrap which was rather exciting and luckily got out without casualties to the party.' A terrifying storm hit their camp at Batakundi, fifteen miles east of Naran, sending 'avalanches of rocks crashing through the trees into the river and the screaming locals was in the very best Hollywood style'.

Nowshera was even hotter on his return, but, apart from some activity on the ranges,[37] there was nothing left for him to do other than pack. Curtains, carpets, pictures and some crockery went into crates. Other furniture would be sold. Tony wondered where the crates would be unpacked. Malaya was his preferred option, but Germany seemed more likely. Of course, he would have to resume his old rank of captain.

A great sadness, one faced by many departing officers, was having to leave poor Don behind. Tony was not prepared to put him through six months' quarantine, nor to expose him to English canine diseases. It would also be a struggle in England to satisfy his voracious appetite. One hopes he found him a good home.

---

35 Letter 200.

36 Recorded in Tony's photograph album.

37 Recorded in Tony's photograph album.

On 9 August 1950, Tony boarded the S.S. *Caledonia* at Karachi. Since his previous trip, she had resumed her pre-war levels of comfort. The food was outstanding, the fellow passengers delightful. The liner steamed off through the usual rough seas in the direction of Port Sudan, arriving there on 17 August. Tony intended to leave the *Caledonia* at Port Suez, motor with a party to Cairo, explore the archaeological museum and the Pyramids, and then motor on to Port Said where they would rejoin the ship. (The 'quick trip' went as scheduled and is duly documented in Tony's album, including the obligatory photograph of him on a camel in front of the Sphinx.) There would then be no further stops and she was expected to dock at Liverpool on 28 August. Tony planned to dine with his parents the following evening. Beyond that, he had no idea.[38]

Why had Tony so willingly risked his life in the cause of Pakistan? It was not only that he had made a home there. British officers in India had always been partial to what they called 'the martial races' - the frontier Pashtuns, the Nepalese Gurkhas, the Punjabi Sikhs and the highland Rajputs among others. The lands that made up Pakistan had become the main recruiting ground for the Indian Army. The North-West Frontier is where most Indian Army officers had cut their military teeth and built up comradeship with the men. Tony had often pointed out his preference for Sikhs and 'Punjab Mohammedans', scorning other 'types'. As for the blue-eyed Pashtuns, it was easy to believe that they were the actual descendants of Alexander's Greeks, brave, high-spirited and sports-loving frontiersmen that they were, like Tony himself. The Hindus of the plains seemed, by contrast, to be effeminate shopkeepers, pen-pushers and crypto-Communists. Tony never has a good word to say for them.[39]

With his involvement in Kashmir, Tony helped to shape the future of Pakistan, yet would deplore the chaotically divided,

---

[38] Letters 201, 202, 203, 204.

[39] Meyer, 'The Invention of Pakistan', p.88.

extremist, undemocratic country that it has become. Its chief claim to unity is an ever-more fanatical brand of Islam, on which its authoritarian leaders have increasingly relied. This was the land that sheltered Osama bin Laden, in Abbottabad of all places. Three wars later, there has been no peace with India; Kashmir is still disputed territory. Alarmingly, Pakistan believes that its survival depends on the possession of nuclear weapons, but its arsenals are felt to be far from secure.

It has often happened that a newly-liberated state has fallen apart after the death of a gifted founder. The key event was no doubt the premature death from cancer, on 11 September 1948, of Mohammed Ali Jinnah, an ardent secularist. 'It is hard to believe that Pakistan's *quaid-i-azam* ('great leader') would have approved his offspring's glum clerical cast, its support for Islamic zealots in Afghanistan and Kashmir, its oligarchic rule by generals or feudal landlords - and yet all these things were byproducts of Pakistan's violent birth and synthetic nationhood.' In the unravelling of the British Empire, Pakistan surely ranks as 'the greatest failure'.[40]

---

[40] *Ibid.*, pp.77, 83.

KOREA

Men of 'B' Troop, 170 Mortar Battery, under Tony's command.

A corral of vehicles and guns. The mortars, with their heavy base plates, would be towed to the front line, but might then have to be hauled manually up a mountainside.

Tony encountered thousands of retreating civilians, and found them 'too pitiful for words … Small children and old men just plodding on through the snow to an unknown destination and an uncertain future'.

Friendly soldiers of the Republic of Korea Army.

British soldiers apparently playing football with their porters. These conscripted Koreans, considered unfit for fighting units, were extraordinarily hardy and uncomplaining.

Scenes from the bitterly cold winter of 1950 -1.

A single, 15-foot wide pontoon bridge, 'already surrounded by Chinese', was Tony's means of escape from the Battle of Imjin, 23 April 1951.

Out of the line with 1 R.U.R., including pipers. Tony had a great affinity with the Ulstermen, with whom his father had served as a padre in the Great War.

Tony visited this pleasant resort, possibly Chiba, while on short leave in Japan. He found the country unexpectedly modern, 'a far cry from the Japan of the picture books'.

Tony at Buckingham Palace for his Investiture, 27 Feb 1952, with his proud mother and sister.

CHAPTER XI

IN THE LAND OF THE MORNING CALM

Hill 283

On Monday 25 September 1950, Tony was sitting comfortably by the fire at Queen Elizabeth Cottage, perusing the evening paper. British troops had been in action in Korea, and the news was dire. Two days before, the 1st Battalion the Argyll and Sutherland Highlanders, serving in the far south of the peninsula, had ascended the so-called Hill 283 near Songju, surprising a force of the invaders at breakfast. Enemy troops on a neighbouring hill had promptly launched a counter-attack, raining intense artillery and mortar fire on the British.

Having requested U.S. air support, the Argylls had laid out fluorescent recognition panels in anticipation of a strike. Meanwhile, radio contact had been lost, so they were unable to communicate with the three American P-51 Mustangs when they appeared overhead. The confused pilots had deployed cannon fire and napalm with deadly effect, but had targeted the wrong hill. A distant ground controller had instructed them to ignore the panels. Some sixty men of the Argylls had been killed or wounded; others had hurled themselves down the steep slopes to escape the hellish inferno.

With survivors holding out on the summit, the fantastically brave second-in-command, Major Kenneth Muir, had rallied his men for a counter-attack, for which he was to be posthumously awarded the Victoria Cross. Muir was personally firing a two-inch mortar when he was struck down, exclaiming with his last breath that 'Neither the Gooks nor the U.S. Air Force will drive the Argylls off this hill'. Like Tony, he was a veteran of the North-West Frontier, where he had learnt the importance of occupying the higher ground. Another lesson was that one should never leave the wounded behind.[1] As he read the first account of the battle, Tony may well have shifted in his chair, the comforts of home suddenly irksome to him. At least there could be no doubt as to his next posting.

Until very recently, the Korean peninsula had been far beyond the sphere of British interest or indeed knowledge. An impoverished, rural backwater, it had been annexed by the Japanese in 1910 and its culture suppressed. It had been a major source of rice and minerals during the Second World War, and thousands of its people had been conscripted into the army, to serve not as front line troops but as industrial slave labour, or as guards in the prisoner-of-war camps. Notoriously, thousands of Korean women had been forced into sexual slavery as 'comfort girls'.[2]

In 1945, the peninsula had been arbitrarily divided by the Great Powers at the so-called 38th Parallel. The north and south zones were occupied by the Soviets and the Americans respectively, who were to be the joint 'trustees' during Korea's long recovery. Each had set up puppet regimes that were favourable to their own interests. The 'Supreme Leader' in the North was Kim Il-Sung, an Orwellian dictator. His counterpart in the South was the equally odious Dr Syngman Rhee.

Claiming sovereignty over the entire peninsula, Kim had, on 25 June 1950, launched a full-scale invasion of the South. Two days later, the Korean People's Army had swept into the capital, Seoul, in quest of 'the bandit traitor Syngman Rhee'.[3] He had escaped in the nick of time, after blowing up the connecting

---

[1] Letter 210; 'U.S. Planes Bomb British Units by Mistake', *The Canberra Times,* 25 Sept 1950, citing Reuters of Tokyo; Michael Hickey, *The Korean War: The West Confronts Communism, 1950 - 1953* (London, 1999), pp.79-81; Mark Adkin, 'Muir, Kenneth', in *Oxford Dictionary of National Biography.* Napalm, or jellied-petrol incendiary bombs, were an horrific but very effective U.S. invention that had first been deployed in 1944.

[2] Hickey, *The Korean War,* pp.5-6.

[3] Roy E. Appleman, *South to the Naktong, North to the Yalu* (United States Army Center of Military History, 1998), p.21.

bridge from the north. 4,000 refugees happened to be crossing it at the time; hundreds were killed, whilst units of his own army had found themselves trapped on the other side.

The following day, Rhee had ordered the brutal massacre of suspected political opponents. Between 60,000 and 200,000 men, women and children are said to have been murdered in various parts of the country, these atrocities being witnessed and indeed photographed by American officers.

The U.S. President, Harry S. Truman, and his trusted Secretary of State, John Foster Dulles, were prepared to put up with the embarrassing Rhee, for he was ardently pro-American and anti-communist, and they were seeking 'a battleground on which to challenge communist expansion'. The Soviets at that time constituted a very real menace, and it is clear that, through the surrogacy of North Korea, they were testing the West's resolve. The battleground could just as easily have been Berlin, Greece, Turkey or Iran. Even France and Italy seemed close to falling under communist rule. The Americans had learnt the lesson of pre-war appeasement. As Dulles put it in a cable, 'To sit by while Korea is overrun by unprovoked armed attack would start a disastrous chain of events leading most probably to world war'.

The United Nations Security Council (in the convenient absence of the Soviet representative, who was boycotting proceedings at the time) had, at Truman and Dulles's prompting, unanimously condemned the invasion, and had authorised collective military action under U.S. command. It was proper that all member nations should play a part, though few were in a position to do so. The Americans had pledged immediate air and naval support, but the under-funded British armed forces were severely over-stretched. They were already locked in a struggle against communism, in Malaya. British participation was nevertheless a matter of principle. 'I favoured countering the North Korean invasion,' wrote the British ambassador in Washington, Sir Oliver Franks, 'because I thought that if any army could cross any frontier when it chose, then chaos had come.' He advised the Labour Prime Minister, Clement Attlee, that the continuance of the 'special relationship', which at that time included the payment of vast sums in aid, was contingent on British cooperation. Himself scarred by pre-war appeasement, Attlee unhesitatingly offered his support. In fulfilling what Churchill called his 'inescapable duty', he received the full backing of Parliament. Despite the rantings of the *Daily Worker,* even Michael Foot, on the left-wing of the Labour Party, declared the 'aggression of the North Koreans' to be 'an international crime of the first order'.

Yet even the mobilising of Britain's modest 'Strategic Reserve', the 29th Independent Infantry Brigade Group, came at an enormous cost. Severe cuts in government spending would have to be made elsewhere. As for manpower, the period of compulsory National Service had hurriedly been extended from eighteen months to two years, but no conscripts under the age of 19 could be sent to Korea. It was therefore necessary to recall several thousand reservists to the colours. These 'veterans' alone (typically they were in their late twenties) were to make up three quarters of the strength of the brigade, which had only three months to bring itself up to strength and to prepare for war.

For men with young families to support, mortgages to pay and businesses to run, the arrival of call-up papers was a nasty shock. Some were within days of the expiry of their reserve obligation, having been settled into civilian life for almost the full five years. Almost all of them came back unwillingly, many with 'chips on their shoulders' and 'Bolshie' attitudes. Some, indeed, were 'almost mutinous', soon setting a very bad example to the young conscripts in their platoon.

The core of 29 Brigade, which was based at Colchester, were the first battalions of the Royal Ulster Rifles, the Royal Northumberland Fusiliers and the Gloucestershire Regiment. These were historic regiments, each with a sufficient body of long-service regulars, some of them 'born to the colours', to pass on a sense of pride to the newcomers. Reservists posted to the

'Glosters', who were mainly from London, may have been truculent at first, while those in the R.U.R. baited their superiors by singing *The Red Flag*. According to the B.B.C.'s War Correspondent, René Cutforth, they all grumbled constantly. Yet the British sense of duty, a feature of the age, soon came to the surface, for the men 'kept their fighting spirit ... in another compartment in their minds, and looked upon their job as soldiers with a professional eye. They soldiered well, no matter what.'

Further components of 29 Brigade were tank squadrons of the 8th King's Royal Irish Hussars; crews of 45 Field Regiment, 170 Mortar Battery and 11 (Sphinx) Light Anti-Aircraft Battery, Royal Artillery; and supporting signallers, sappers, Royal Army Ordnance Corps (equipped with morale-boosting mobile laundry and bath units), Royal Army Service Corps (with abundant transport resources), Royal Electrical and Mechanical Engineers (providing field workshops and recovery sections), Royal Army Veterinary Corps and Intelligence Corps personnel. The Brigadier in command was the estimable Tom Brodie.[4]

While these troops were assembling that summer, the North Korean People's Army had overrun the entire peninsula, apart from an enclave in the far south-east, around the port of Pusan. The Republic of Korea Army had rapidly disintegrated, and American ground forces, hastily embarked from Japan, had been driven back, in humiliating disorder, to the Naktong river. Softened by occupation duties, the Americans were physically unfit, dangerously under-trained, pampered and poorly led. The enemy were brutal, fanatical, apt to charge in suicidal human waves, and took no prisoners. The U.N. troops dug themselves into a strong defensive perimeter, 140 miles long, around Pusan.

---

[4] S.P. Mackenzie, *The Imjin and Kapyong Battles, Korea, 1951* (Bloomington and Indianapolis, 2013), pp.15-23; Hickey, *The Korean War*, pp.94-5, 153. Max Hastings, *The Korean War* (London, 1987), pp.43, 51-60, 68-75.

Much of it ran along the line of the Naktong. They were told that there could be no further retreat.[5]

In these desperate circumstances the U.N. Commander-in-Chief, General Douglas MacArthur, had requested an immediate British contribution. Thus it was that the 1st Argylls, along with the 1st Middlesex Regiment, had been urgently dispatched to Korea from the garrison at Hong Kong. The 'bearing and evident discipline' of the new arrivals, who disembarked at Pusan on 28 August, had done wonders for American morale. 'The sight of the Argylls on the march, each rifle company headed by its piper, never failed to excite comment, as did the way in which even junior N.C.O.s were able to control the fire of their rifle sections, in contrast to the prodigal expenditure of ammunition by their allies.'[6]

These reinforcements had, of course, been thrown into action on the Perimeter. On 21 September they had crossed the Naktong and had advanced on Songju, in the course of which the tragedy of Hill 283 had taken place. Meanwhile MacArthur, with absolute command of both the air and the sea, had planned a 'decisive, war-winning counterstroke', with a view to recapturing Seoul. Operation Chromite, launched on 15 September, was a daring, World War II-style amphibious assault on the north-western port of Inchon, 180 miles behind the North Korean lines. The landing was virtually unopposed; Inchon had been bombarded into a smoking ruin. On 27 September, U.S. Marines had indeed hoisted the U.N. flag over Seoul, and MacArthur had entered the city in triumph, to be told by a tearful Rhee that he was 'the saviour of our race'. On both fronts, the defeated North Korean People's

---

[5] *Ibid.*, pp.81-96; Hickey, *The Korean War,* pp.45-53. Hickey refers (p.48) to the American soldiers' 'alarming resemblance in many ways to the venal rabble portrayed in the Phil Silvers "Sergeant Bilko" TV comedies. The disciplinary powers of commanding officers and NCOs had been undermined by strenuous efforts to "democratize" the army since 1945.'

[6] Hickey, *The Korean War,* pp.66, 81.

Army was soon melting away into the interior, with MacArthur itching to pursue them to the Parallel and beyond.

The 'liberation' of North Korea was indeed launched on 9 October. The capital, Pyongyang, fell to U.S. and R.O.K. forces on 19 October. Rhee immediately took control and was given free rein to commit further atrocities. 150,000 executions are thought to have taken place, sometimes in full view of the American Civil authorities and of the horrified men of the Argylls and Middlesex, who had been ordered to join the Americans in their pursuit of the N.K.P.A. The enemy was by no means broken, however, having merely withdrawn to mountain fastnesses. Yet MacArthur had no qualms about advancing to the Yalu, the river that marked the border with communist China. It was a foolish and unnecessary act of provocation. Undetected by the complacent Americans, 'fanatical hordes' of so-called 'volunteers' were soon massing on the border, poised to force the U.S. Army into another humiliating retreat.[7]

A Miserable Start

Tony's entirely predictable posting to 29 Brigade was dated 27 September 1950, the day of the liberation of Seoul. While other parts of the brigade were being intensively trained in the Stamford Training Area or on Salisbury Plain, he was assigned as a captain to 45 Field Regiment, at Woolwich.[8] On 10 October, with other members of 'K' Reinforcement Unit (intended to bolster the units that had already gone ahead), he embarked on the S.S. *Lancashire,* one of the many requisitioned troopships bound for Pusan.

---

[7] *Ibid.,* pp.70-5, 78, 81-9; Hastings, *The Korean War,* pp.116-33, 142-9, 153-61.

[8] Letter 210, referring to Woolwich.

This was to be no pleasure cruise. The *Lancashire* was severely overcrowded and, in heavy seas, the troop deck would be reduced - in the words of an eye-witness - to 'a malodorous shambles in which vomit, disinfectant, and the ever-present smell of sweaty feet greeted the troop deck officers - normally junior subalterns, for senior officers stayed away from such distressing scenes - when they made their daily inspections and night rounds'. There would be Physical Training before breakfast, then a round of lectures on various subjects, followed by target practice at crates thrown over the stern of the ship. There were film shows, a library and a ration of beer to keep the men cheerful in the evening. The presence of twenty Queen Alexandra nurses would have helped to lighten the mood.[1]

One night, while the *Lancashire* was steaming along the North African coast, an unhappy reservist in the Royal Ulster Rifles attempted to kill himself by leaping overboard. He was spotted in the moonlight, picked up, and earmarked for repatriation. It was made known that there were plenty of sharks in those waters, in case anyone else was tempted to follow suit.

The following day, the *Lancashire* anchored off Port Said. All seven hundred soldiers on board, in dire need of exercise, were taken off by landing craft, put ashore on the east side of the canal, and sent off on a seven-mile route march through the shifting sand. Remarkably, not a single man fell out. Having completed the march, they were allowed to strip off and bathe in the cool Mediterranean.

In their subsequent passage through the Red Sea, 'usually the worst part of the trip', a cooling wind blew sea spray right up to the top decks, a relief from the intense heat. The men had to be

---

[1] Hickey, *The Korean War,* pp.97-8; the author describes his own experience as a junior subaltern. The *Lancashire* is not named in Tony's letters. However, he refers to her arrival at Singapore on 9 November, an event that is reported in *The Straits Times* of the following day, at p.5. The report refers to the ship as 'crowded' and it mentions the presence of the Q.A.s. See *The Private Papers of 2nd Lt J.J. Potter, R.A.,* Imperial War Museum, Documents.6882, for further descriptions of the voyage.

discouraged from sunbathing. ‘For some reason,’ Tony observed, ‘everyone wants to get black as soon as possible.’

The training timetable intensified, with Tony having to lecture for hours at a time. A typical subject was ‘Infantry-Artillery Co-operation’. Tony was clearly very good at it, his fellow officers referring to him as ‘the Professor’. Pamphlets were provided on Korea, which can hardly have encouraged the men. They read of its cold, dry winters, when the rivers routinely froze; and of its hot, dusty, fly-blown summers. The whole country seemed to be a wilderness of mountains and forests. As for the people, Tony gathered that they were ‘a very dirty and backward race with few good points in their favour, though the Americans say they are very brave and fight like the Japs’, which was true enough.

The *Lancashire* pulled into the port of Aden, then a British crown colony, where there was a morale-boosting delivery of mail. It was too hot for another route march. A fellow officer, who had served there before the war, took Tony to a good swimming spot (though he found the water too warm to be refreshing) and to a ‘native’ hotel, where the fare was cheaper and more interesting than that served at the club.

The *Lancashire* set off again after a few hours and, cruising through the Gulf of Aden, the soldiers watched in awe as schools of dolphins played around in her wash, or as shoals of flying fish darted out from the bow-wave and, after some impressive moments in full flight, splashed back into the sea. Soon there were frequent sightings of whales, often at close quarters. Meanwhile, training was ‘reaching a really fast tempo’.

On 4 November the *Lancashire* docked at Colombo (which Tony was now visiting for the second time) and, on the afternoon of 9 November, she slipped into the berth at Singapore vacated by the *Empire Halladale.* It was reported in the local press that they were the fifth and sixth large, Korea-bound troopships to pass that way in the past fortnight.[2]

---

2 *The Straits Times,* 10 Nov 1950, p.5.

'The last stage of the voyage out was pretty grim,' writes Tony. 'Work reached a fantastic pitch and there was hardly a minute to spare.' Off the Philippines, they caught the tail end of Typhoon Clara. 'It suddenly got very cold and the wind got up.' The ship was buffeted for six hours by powerful gusts of wind which blew the waves even over the upper deck, a frightening experience for men who had never been to sea in their lives. Tony says it was 'quite indescribable'.[3]

A 'very heavy swell' continued to blight their voyage as they made their way up the China Sea. The ship had to be blacked out, her anti-aircraft guns manned. Her arrival at Pusan, on 21 November, failed to lift the spirits of the passengers. Their first sight was of a range of low sheds and cranes; behind it, a sprawling, ramshackle town, and in the background, some bleak hills. The men lined the ship's rails and watched in silence. The wind blowing down from Manchuria was razor-sharp, 'searing the lungs with every breath'. It carried with it 'a dreadful stench of decay, excrement, polluting smoke, and the noises of a dockland waterfront. Nameless debris floated past on the oily water as the ship steered past a group of anchored cargo ships waiting to unload.'

Suddenly and unexpectedly, led by a strutting drum-major, the all-black 56th U.S. Army Port Band marched into sight, playing a Sousa march. When this was followed by the 'St Louis Blues March', the spirits of the men were raised after all and they gave a mighty cheer.

Rapidly entrained at the station behind the docks, Tony's unit was glad to be shot of Pusan, 'a very dirty place even by Pakistani standards[. T]he people are very wretched and poor with a mixture of Japs and real Mongols in padded clothes and fur caps. The whole place is seething with Americans who are very friendly and helpful and willing to give us anything we want.'

---

[3] Letters 205, 206, 207; memories and photographs of Roger Bentley, one of the soldiers on board, https://www.shipsnostalgia.com/media/troopship-lancashire-in-heavy-weather.27903/.

'K' Reinforcement Unit embarked on a six-hour journey in filthy carriages, arriving at Taegu that same night. South Korea's third city was close to the Naktong river and to recent battlefields, having been just inside the Pusan Perimeter. It was a quaint, primitive place, unrecognisable from the high-rise metropolis of today, being then a tinderbox of wooden houses 'with steep tiled roofs and pointed eaves'. The people were unkempt, but there were no food queues. On the contrary, the market stalls were groaning with produce. Little black pigs ran about in the streets. There seemed also to be swarms of magpies, and a lot of plump and docile dogs, which the Koreans were known to regard as a delicacy. However, 'We are not allowed to buy anything in the food line from the locals as they have curious habits over sanitation.'

The weather at Taegu was positively 'arctic', and the men were suddenly very appreciative of their issue of winter clothes, including unattractive string vests and 'jerseys, heavy wool', the garment known affectionately ever since as 'the woolly pully'. Their mood dipped, however, when they were shown to their quarters, the unheated, rat-infested Pong Sang Primary School, wooden of course, with its broken windows and 'piles of revolting filth covering the ground outside and in every room inside'. 'It will be first class' when cleaned out, Tony reflected buoyantly.

Drains were re-laid, showers installed, and the place made generally tidy. The ground outside was cleared for football. A nightly curfew was imposed, for communist guerrillas were still popping off their rifles in the town. Tony went off to explore, but he found no shops other than those selling food or pots and pans, nor any evidence of local crafts. He discovered, however, that there were sixteen churches in Taegu, for both North and South Korea had large populations of Christians. Tony and a friend were to attend one of them on their first Sunday, sitting on chairs while 'everyone else sat on the floor'. They were fascinated observers, not understanding a word.

Tony soon encountered that 'most odd crowd of men', the U.S. Army C.I.D., whose job was to root out the fifth columnists and the black-marketeers. He was welcomed into their headquarters by the larger-than-life 'Lootenant James Zishetti', with whom Tony, not a known admirer of the Americans, was instantly the best of friends. That same afternoon, he had a seat at a crowded dinner table in their mess and was tucking into a sumptuous 'Thanksgiving' dinner of roast turkey and all the trimmings, courtesy of the U.S. Army.

Tony had typically to make do in his own mess with 'bully-beef' from a tin, for the local fare was still considered 'dangerous'. However, a nearby British Army bakery kept them supplied with fresh bread, and they had soon recruited a skilled Chinese cook, 'who has a vast imagination and turns our Bully Beef and tinned hash into very fine concoctions'. The company was congenial enough, though Tony's fellow officers were mostly reservists who 'have not really got their hearts in the fight; they want to get back to their wives and families'. Among the regulars were two newly-married subalterns who were also pining for home. 'I think it is so very wrong of them to get married so young,' said Tony, who had no intention of making that mistake.

The evenings were initially pretty wretched for the officers. The lighting was too dim to read by; it was too cold to sit and play bridge. The grossly-overheated American cinema became their constant refuge, despite the truly 'awful' films that were shown there (probably those extolling the Americans' single-handed victory in World War II). Thankfully, the sapper officer soon found and installed efficient stoves in every room, though one of them later caught fire, reminding them all of the extreme combustibility of the building. It was Tony who raised the alarm and kicked the stove outside, as others arrived with buckets of sand to douse the inferno.

It seemed an odd sort of war. Had it already been won? No one had the faintest idea what was going on. 'It all seems quite fantastic,' wrote Tony on 25 November; 'they say there is a war on somewhere but there is very little sign of it here.'

In truth, a disaster was already unfolding in the north. The Peking government had inevitably unleashed its massing troops, the misleadingly-named 'Chinese People's Volunteer Army', who had crossed the Yalu in strength and lain up in the mountains, preparing to attack. The first indication of this, on 31 October, had been the capture by a patrol of the Middlesex of a uniformed Chinese soldier; and when the People's Liberation Army attacked the U.S. 1st Cavalry Division on 1 November - there was no longer any pretence that they were 'volunteers' - it seemed like World War III had started.

By 15 November, 250,000 regulars of the P.L.A. had crossed into North Korea. On 25 November, even as Tony was composing his letter, they were scattering the R.O.K. forces, having identified them as the weakest link in the U.N. line. That night, they poured through the gap, outflanking the Americans. 'There is very little news from the front,' wrote Tony. 'We hear nothing but the most alarmist rumours, the Chinese are definitely coming down in swarms ... We shall have to pull back and, maybe, pull right out.'

Naturally, he longed to be sent forward to the regiment, currently headquartered at Suwon, twenty miles south of Seoul, and 'to have a real scrap', but was thwarted by a shortage of transport. In the meantime, he held a 'stop-gap' appointment, as Gunnery Instructor with No.1 Battle Training Team. There were daily three-mile runs before breakfast, followed by Tony's 'holding forth' for an hour and a half; perhaps a further three hours of grenade throwing and bayonet drill and, after lunch, an exercise or perhaps another route march over the hills, in full battle order, for distances up to fifteen miles. The necessity of such drills was all too obvious, but the 'Americans think us quite mad'. 'Why walk when you have trucks?' they enquired.[4]

[4] Letters 207, 208, 209, 210, 211; Hickey, *The Korean War,* pp.1, 96, 147-9; Hastings, *The Korean War,* pp.167-72.

Tony was soon aware that there were 'over a million Chinese coming through the centre and there seems to be nothing to stop them as far as we can see'. On 30 November, the retreating American 2nd Division attempted to drive, hell-for-leather, through the narrow, six-mile pass below Kunu-ri. The Chinese had already occupied the surrounding hills and were lying in wait. The nose-to-tail American convoy hit a storm of mortar- and machine-gun fire which left a mass of blazing wreckage, and numerous dead. That day ended with 'desperate close-quarter fighting among the shambles of vehicles and casualties on the road'. It was now 'Every man for himself'. Betrayed by its officers, who were often the first to 'bug out', the 2nd Division had ceased to exist as an effective fighting unit.

Meanwhile, on the road to Pyongyang, the U.S. Eighth Army was similarly gripped by panic and was retreating in great disorder, having abandoned most of its equipment. Only the British seemed to be keeping their nerve and holding their heads high, the Argylls a model of good discipline as they marched south, each company led by its piper. The Americans struck Tony as demoralised, inept, even cowardly. 'If we could only have three British Infantry Divisions here we would see the whole of this affair finished in a month.' Lieutenant-General Matthew Ridgway, hurriedly appointed to the command of Eighth Army, might well have agreed with him. As much appalled by the defeatism at headquarters as by the sight of his men in full retreat, he ordered the mass culling of inefficient and cowardly officers. It had never occurred to them to get out of their vehicles, take to the hills on foot and defend the high ground.[5]

Tony nevertheless admitted on 4 December that 'I am quite honestly enjoying myself'. He claimed not to mind the cold, and the landscape would have reminded him of Kashmir, were it not for the battle-scorched shrub and undergrowth. Scouring the countryside for defensive positions, he found himself at the foot

---

[5] Letters 210, 211; Hickey, *The Korean War,* pp.167-72; Hastings, *The Korean War,* pp.159-93, 226-9.

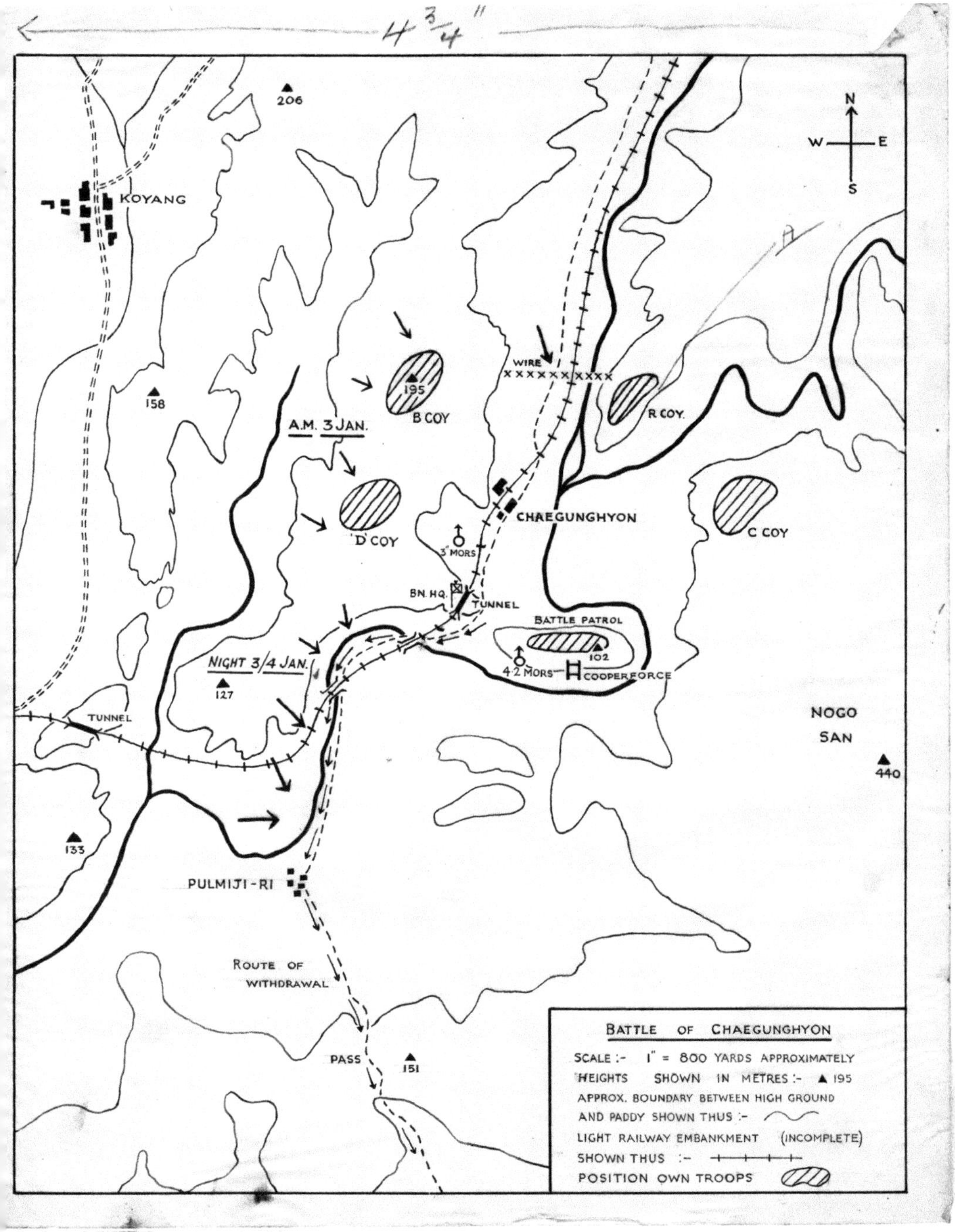

The Battle of Chaegunghyon, better known as 'Happy Valley'. Tony described his personal experience of the withdrawal as 'hell'.

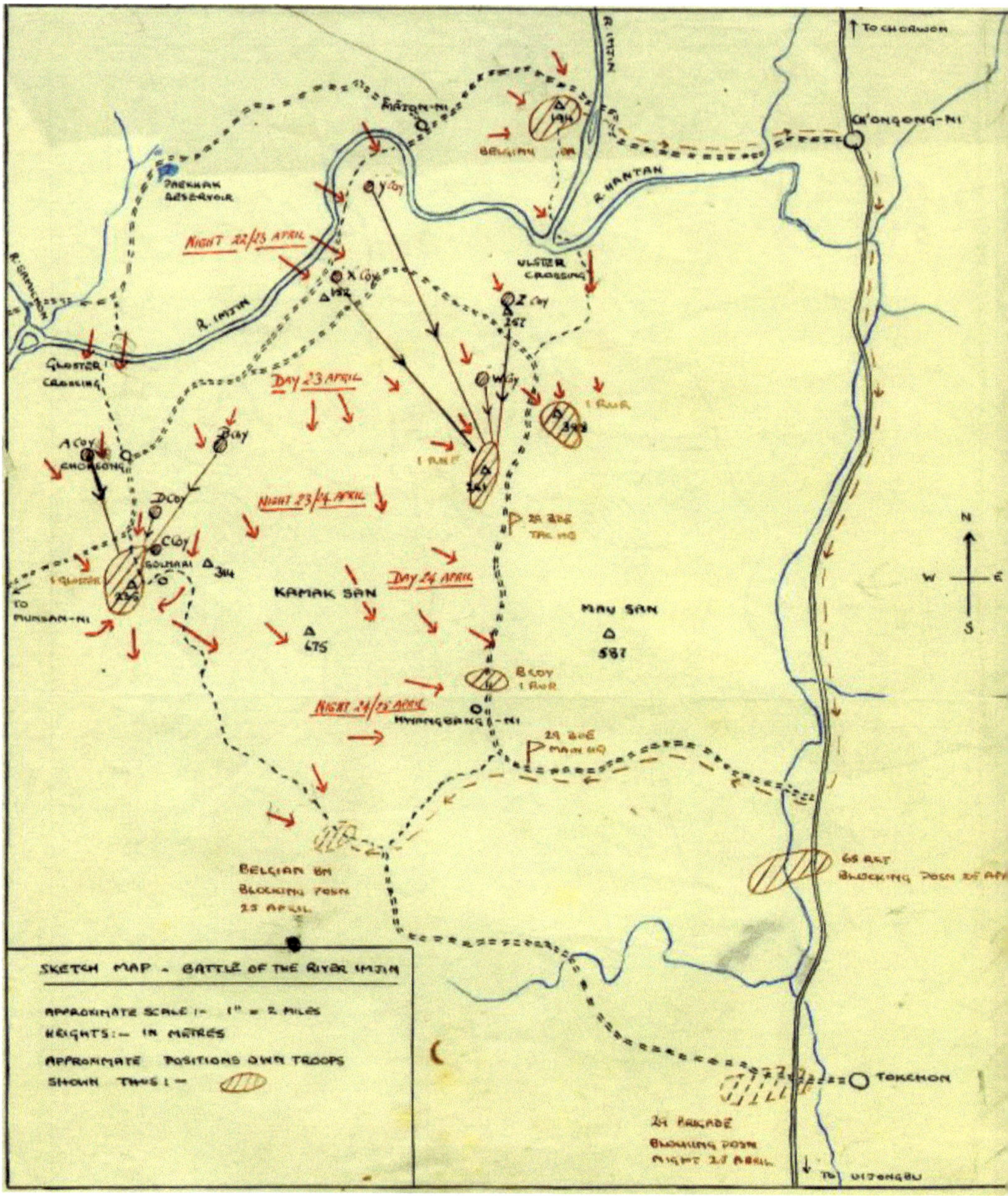

This map of the Royal Ulster Rifles' movements at the Battle of Imjin shows the isolated position of the Belgian battalion (top centre) and also 'Ulster Crossing', by which they, and Tony, made their heroic escape. Their blocking position from 24 April is bottom left.

of Hill 283, where 'the Argylls were shot up by the American air force'; and he remembered reading of it while sitting comfortably by the fire at home.

At last, Tony was detailed to accompany the Colonel on a trip to Seoul. When he went to bed on 23 December, he had already half-packed his bags in readiness to go forward the next day. In the middle of the night he was awoken by a commotion. The tinder-dry Pong Sang Primary School had, almost inevitably, caught fire. The lights quickly went out and the whole building was soon pervaded by thick black smoke. Tony seized his half-packed bags and threw them out of the window, but his room-mate was struggling to breathe; Tony had to drag him out of the room and down the outside stair. Unthinkingly, he went back to collect his carbine, pistol and pipe from the bedside table, but as he groped his way into the room 'a sheet of flame came through the ceiling'. Without hesitating, Tony dived for safety through the first-floor window, falling twenty-five feet to the ground. 'By the Grace of Almighty God I fell on a tent top and slid off onto the ground just as the roof caved in.'

The building was consumed within minutes. Most had escaped in a similar fashion, but many had broken legs or ribs in the fall. Few had managed to salvage any of their possessions. Tony was not only intact, but had lost only his heavy kit, along with such useful items as his driving licence and his watch, which he had placed under the pillow. (The Goldsmiths and Silversmiths of London were generously to send a replacement watch, which arrived within the month.) Two charred bodies were recovered the next day. The dilapidated building itself was no great loss.[6]

[6] Letters 210, 211, 212, 216 (on the watch) and 231 (the driving licence).

Battling Baker

Tony joined his regiment (45 Field Artillery) on 27 December 1950, just as it was about to launch a counter-attack across the Imjin river. For a 'wonderful three days', he was in his element as temporary adjutant, 'sitting on the wireless set controlling the fire from our own guns and those from two American artillery units'. They were then 'pulled back to support 29 British B[riga]de in the mountains off to our right where they were holding the line between the 24th and 25th U.S. Divisions … We dug in and laid a minefield to our front. For two days nothing happened; then, at 6.30 a.m. on 3 January, all hell let loose.'

This was 29 Brigade's first real taste of action. At least two divisions of Chinese, often advancing under a white flag and claiming to be South Korean, had attacked the U.N. positions in Chaegunghyon, otherwise known as 'Happy Valley', north of Seoul. 'The regiment fired solidly all day,' wrote Tony, 'with the guns of the U.S. artillery units under our command; it was almost unbelievable. We put down thousands of rounds of shells into solid masses of the enemy but they still came on, singing and shouting. One of the Troop Commanders of 45 F[iel]d Reg[imen]t R.A. was wounded and I was sent up to take his place in the forward O.P. with the R.U.R. [Royal Ulster Rifles]. The Irish blood was up and they fought like tigers. Then it happened. Our "friends" the Americans on our left and right suddenly pulled out leaving us with completely open flanks. We got the order to pull back to Seoul the other side of the river.'

Whilst the Americans and the 1st R.O.K. Division, visibly headed by their commander, were retreating briskly to the rear, the R.U.R. and the Northumberlands stoutly held the line. Their orders from Brigadier Brodie were to start thinning out at 6 p.m. The R.U.R. and their supporting gunners were the last to disengage, and their retreat 'in the dark, in tumbled country with virtually no motorable tracks', was inevitably a most hazardous operation, the more so when an American aircraft carelessly dropped flares that illuminated their columns. Directed by bugle calls and whistles, the Chinese had already formed up in strength on both sides of the road and had occupied a village through which the riflemen had to pass. The village was soon well ablaze, as were many of the abandoned vehicles on the road.

Tony describes his personal experience of the withdrawal as 'hell'. Under heavy rifle and mortar fire, he negotiated his way, in pitch darkness, along a narrow mountain track. His was one of the many vehicles that were hit and knocked off the road. Tony gathered a party of men and together, wearing berets and armed with bolt-action Lee Enfield rifles,[1] they fought their way out of the valley. They had only a short distance to march, but 'fires were raging everywhere and the odd sniper kept the excitement alive'. The R.U.R. lost 208 officers and men, including their temporary C.O., Major Blake (with 157 later confirmed dead), but 45 Field got all their guns out intact at the cost of only seven killed. It seemed not to be a 'Happy Valley' at all.

Many thousands of Korean refugees followed the retreating U.N. forces across the frozen Han, some of them falling through gaps in the ice. Tony described them as 'too pitiful for words … Small children and old men just plodding on through the snow to an unknown destination and an uncertain future.'[2]

He was in Seoul with his troop on 5 January; in spite of newspaper reports to the contrary, it had not been taken by the Chinese.[3] When Tony next wrote on 7 January, he was 'sitting in a hole in a snow covered bank overlooking a river. The hole is my O.P., the Chinese are about two miles across the other side of the river. All is quiet before the storm.' Having made it back to 45 Field R.H.Q., he had been given command of 'B' or 'Battling

---

[1] Mackenzie, *The Imjin and Kapyong Battles,* pp.13-14, pointing out that steel helmets had been 'almost universally abandoned'.

[2] Letters 213, 214.

[3] Letter 216.

Baker' Troop, 170 Independent Mortar Battery R.A. 'I have sixty men and four heavy mortars which are at the moment deployed about a mile behind me waiting for my orders to fire.' It was six days since he had his boots off, but he professed to be 'quite enjoying life', and asked his parents not to worry about him.[4]

Tony alludes in his next letter to the 'quite fantastically cold' weather. On the night of Friday 12 January, a temperature of -38ºC was recorded. A freezing wind howled down from Mongolia. 'Not a single living thing moves other than humans, the whole countryside is a blanket of frozen snow under a leaden sky softened by a slight mist. The cold gets into everything, even the oil in the gun buffers freezes making it impossible to fire. At night half our strength stands-to in our slit-trenches with eyes probing the freezing mist for any sign of movement.' The command from on high that the defences must be permanently manned seemed utterly pointless and left Brigadier Brodie fuming. When the snow squalls came, visibility might be reduced to a few yards at best.

Tony somewhat understates the discomfort. The area now occupied by 29 Brigade was 'a wide expanse of paddy fields with little shelter. Trenches soon filled with water and clothing froze during the sub-zero nights. The Ulstermen took much comfort in the supporting firepower now available from the Centurions of The Irish Hussars',[5] the turrets of which would have been reasonably warm. The infantrymen were quite numb with cold and could barely bring themselves to speak, yet they were warned not to zip up their sleeping bags in case there was a sudden attack. Engines had to be kept running, or would take hours to unthaw. It was said that the lucky ones were those who could feel the pain in their feet. If their feet were numb it meant that they were probably already suffering from frostbite. Tony writes: 'More than forty

---

[4] Letters 213, 214, 215; Hastings, *The Korean War,* pp.199-202; Hickey, *The Korean War,* pp.154-7.

[5] Major Roy Walker, 'Bravery in the Thick of Battle', *Belfast Telegraph,* 27 April 2001.

men from one B[attalio]n alone have gone down with frost bite or exposure.'

If it was any consolation, the hardships of the Chinese were considerably greater. In fact, they had been fought to a temporary stand-still and the U.N. forces were to have a long wait for something to happen. Equipped only with small arms, mortars and a few other support weapons, the P.L.A. had no heavy artillery of their own, and the pounding that they had received from Tony and his fellow gunners had had its effect. They had no vehicles either, and went only as far, and as fast, as their own legs could carry them. Despite the lack of equipment, this determined, highly mobile guerrilla army had moved at great speed and won an astonishing series of victories. These were men who wore canvas shoes and had no luxuries such as sleeping bags or overcoats, except what they had picked up from abandoned American stockpiles on the drive south. Moreover, their supply lines were so stretched that they were critically short of ammunition and, above all, of food. It has been estimated that as many as ninety per cent of them were suffering from some form of frostbite. They were in no condition to resume the fray.[6]

29 Brigade stood in readiness until 16 January, by which time the Chinese were said to have withdrawn to Suwon. As soon as they realised this the U.S. 3rd Division took over and tentatively pushed the front forward, 'a real Red Letter day', according to Tony. 'The fact of the matter,' he writes, 'is that the 8th U.S. Army, of which we have the doubtful honour of being a part, ran so far and so fast from our little battle above Seoul that the poor Chinese just have not had the walking power to catch them up.'

With the Brigadier's permission, Tony stuck with the battle-weary 1 R.U.R., whom he had supported thus far, and withdrew his troop to a position at Chonan, 'about thirty miles south of

---

[6] Letters 213, 214; Hastings, *The Korean War,* pp.179-81, 192-3, 203-7; Hickey, *The Korean War,* pp.169-71. There is a neat description of the Chinese soldier in Anthony Farrar-Hockley, *The Edge of the Sword* (London, 1954), p.23.

Osan', so that they could clean themselves up and recuperate. The R.E.M.E. pitched up at their primitive camp to set up a field workshop, as did the R.A.O.C. with one of their mobile laundry and bath units, an unimagined luxury. Tony had his first bath and change of clothes since Christmas. The bath is described as 'primitive', but 'fairly warm'. The simple joy of being able to put on a pair of pyjamas was beyond words.

The officers slept in the hut that was Company H.Q., which had an ingenious form of underfloor heating (traditional in Korea), a charcoal fire being lit in a hollow space beneath the floor. 'Stoke it up,' said 1 R.U.R.'s temporary C.O., the larger-than-life Major Ikey May, to a rifleman; 'a man could freeze to death in here even with a drop of rum inside him.' The men enjoyed comparative comfort, too, 'in a couple of fairly modern and almost undamaged houses' that Tony had found for them. (They were 'Japanese-style', with paper walls and sliding doors.) A single bottle of rum bought him a few petrol stoves from the Americans, 'so my gunners sleep warm and dry'. The British soldiers were evidently not short of reviving spirits, though all alcohol was prohibited in the U.S. Army, a hangover from the days of Prohibition.

Ikey May was a seasoned professional and a 'true Irishman', much admired by Tony. Among other eccentricities, he accoutered himself in a very dirty goat-skin coat that 'now smells worse than any goat alive', though, until his recent bath, the same could no doubt have been said of Tony. Both men would sleep, rolled up in blankets, on rush matting spread over the heated floor. One night, Tony was awoken by a sharp jab in the ribs. 'There is a powerful smell of burning in here,' said Ikey. 'By God, it's me on fire'. The flames were dampened down and the pair went nonchalantly back to sleep, the charred goat-skin coat now smelling even worse than before.

The men could hardly believe their good fortune but, after the strain of the past few weeks, many succumbed to sickness. Tony writes of the reservists that they 'fight well enough, putting their backs into it when the enemy is close but, in a rear area, they lose interest and only think about getting home'. A subaltern in the Northumberlands had had a succinct answer to the 'belly-aching' in his platoon: 'It's going to be no good sitting on top of some mountain saying "I shouldn't be here" while some bugger blows the top of your head off.'[7] Tony himself was 'as fit as a fiddle', experienced in the field and had the necessary will-power to carry on. A tot of service rum in a mug of tea or coffee always did him the power of good. He yearned only for a face flannel and for any sort of reading matter, especially that which would fit easily into one's pocket.

The chaos of Korea seemed to Tony 'like a bad dream: it is all so fantastic'. This was a country 'quite remote from civilisation or reality ... money means nothing as all that is wanted is heat, food and clothing'. He writes very movingly of a Sunday church parade, presided over by the R.U.R.'s Protestant padre, which had a congregation of about two hundred. Tony had ordered his troop to turn out. All were armed, even the padre, the Rev. James Kelly,[8] 'who had a large pistol stuck in his belt. He started off by strapping himself into a large piano accordion on which he played the hymns and very well too. The Irish gave full vent with their voices. There was a remarkable feeling about that half hour service which I shall not forget for a long time. The B[attalio]n had lost a lot of men killed and there was a most wonderful spirit of real sincerity and worship among all those who were present.'

The two other officers in Tony's troop were an 'oldish' schoolmaster who had been recalled to the colours, and a Second Lieutenant fresh from Sandhurst. The Second Lieutenant, like Tony, was the son of an army chaplain. 'Both are very steady,' he

---

[7] Hickey, *The Korean War,* p.199.

[8] 'Ulster Rifles sail from the Princess Dock, Liverpool, on their way to Korean War', *The Belfast Newsletter,* 1 Nov 1950, in which 'the Rev. J.G.M. Kelly, of the Church of Ireland', is described as 'the only chaplain going with the battalion'.

writes. 'We all three read a chapter of the Bible before turning in at night. I am glad to say that many of the men do the same.'

On 23 January, Tony's troop, still supporting 1 R.U.R., was ordered to move about ten miles further north. 'Battling Baker' spent the night in a vast, leaky warehouse, quickly making themselves comfortable. The Americans then tasked them with hunting down suspected Chinese infiltrators in the surrounding villages. They spent the next ten days in the open, often operating at night, but found 'very few' insurgents and certainly met with no resistance. Tony organised and led a mixed force of Ulstermen and gunners on one of the night patrols, marching them over the hills for about four miles to a suspect village, surrounding it and searching it 'with a fine-toothed comb'. The men thoroughly enjoyed the outing and so did Tony.

By 4 February 1951, the three troops of which 170 Independent Mortar Battery was comprised had assembled in a 'Rest Area' near Osan, where 29 Brigade had set up its H.Q. A corral of vehicles and guns, 'surrounded by lines of very home-made huts made from tarpaulins and mats slung over poles', it had been pitched 'on a sandy patch in the bed of a river' and resembled 'a gypsy encampment'. Although the snow was gradually melting away, it was still bitterly cold at night and in the early morning. 'Anything liquid freezes solid, including shaving soap and toothpaste.' Thankfully, they were allowed to light fires here and to cook. Fresh meat, and butter, were plentiful. But the skies were depressingly grey. With the snow turning to slush, the drivers had a hard job towing the guns into action, both on and off the road. Tony's was very skilled, however, having been 'a London bus driver before he was called up for this show'.

The 4.2" mortars were hefty objects, each standing five feet tall. They fired from a platform or 'mobile base plate' that weighed over half a ton. The platform and mortar would be towed into action by a tractor. The wheels of the platform would then be jacked up for firing, allowing it, literally, to sink, or to be driven by the recoil, into the ground; it would often have to be winched out afterwards by the towing tractor. As a weapon it was pretty effective. Tony's troop could fire at least twelve rounds a minute from each of the four mortars, and the bomb itself was lethal over a two hundred-yard radius.

Being 'independent' of a regiment, 170 Mortar Battery (despite its number, the first and only one ever raised) was under the direct orders of the Brigadier, who was also 'independent', though currently 'under command for operation' to the 1st U.S. Corps. The Americans were very appreciative, having just awarded Brodie their Silver Star, but according to Tony were careful not to give his brigade all 'the dirty jobs', in case they got wiped out or, indeed, 'stole their thunder'. Tony had never been an admirer of 'Uncle Sam' but, disconcertingly, even the most junior ranks now held the American 'Brass Hats' in contempt. 'We all long for a British Commander who would at least have some idea of how to fight this sort of war,' he wrote wistfully.[9]

Happily, the dwindling morale of the poorly trained, pampered and bewildered American troops had been vigorously addressed by 8th Army's new commander, the inspirational, no-nonsense World War II veteran, General Matthew Ridgway. If they asked him why they were fighting in Korea, he told them it was 'because of the properly constituted authorities of our respective governments. Further comment is unnecessary.' Pressed as to what they were fighting for, he replied: 'The real answer lies in the resolve of the free world to fight communism, a regime in which men shot their prisoners, enslaved their citizens, and derided the dignity of man; a regime which sought to displace the rule of law and to do away with the concept of God'. Under Ridgway's command, the defeatism of the American troops was rapidly dispelled and their discipline was almost miraculously transformed. It was noticed that they even started to wash their vehicles.[10]

---

[9] Letters 214, 215, 216, 218, 220.

[10] Hastings, *The Korean War,* pp.226-9; Hickey, *The Korean War,* pp.167, 171, 174.

Imjin

Ridgway was determined to push past Suwon to the Han river, east of Seoul. At long last, his infantry were ordered to leave the comfort and convenience of their vehicles and take to the hills. 29 Brigade's role was to provide close support in this cautious advance; hence the attention to clearing the outlying villages of real, or imagined, insurgents. The large Chinese bridgehead to the immediate south of the Han was, however, no fiction.

Tony laconically relates that the Brigade 'simply took over a sector of the line where the Americans had been stuck', and 'advanced for eight miles until stopped by the now flooded Han river. The country was a tangled mass of snow clad mountains rising from 3,000 to 4,000 ft from the floor of the valleys below, their sides thick with pines and with great rock cliffs crowning their summit like forbidding white hats.'

A single, narrow track, barely negotiable even by a jeep, ran through this bleak wasteland; and on every peak, the Chinese were dug in 'like rabbits in a warren'. There was no option but to climb up each hill in turn and flush them out. Brodie had trained his men for such assaults and they were expected to travel as lightly as possible, the heavier loads being carried by doughty Korean porters on their traditional wooden 'A' frames.[11] It seems that the R.U.R. 'had the most difficult ascent; the battalion was sent 4,000 yards out on a limb to relieve the U.S. 5th Cavalry … [T]he position was occupied, and patrolling began.' Meanwhile, some sappers helped them construct 'a hair-raising jeep track from the valley … to keep the rifle companies supplied'. Tony's role was to rain mortar fire on the Chinese as they prowled below.

'For my own part,' he writes, 'I spent the full two weeks with the leading Company of the R.U.R. For three nights I slept without even a blanket, making a kind of nest of pine branches

---

[11] On the role of these 'unsung heroes', see Mackenzie, *The Imjin and Kapyong Battles,* p.27; Hickey, *The Korean War,* p.171.

with my Wireless Operator and I sleeping on top of each other for warmth.' He wrote later that they were sustained by Horlick's Tablets, a tin of which, sent from home, he had in his pocket. Casualties were light (a mere half dozen), but one man was shot and wounded within a foot of Tony. Pine-wood fires were cautiously lit during the day for the melting of snow, as there was no other drinking water. The Chinese would be sure to mark the position of any visible smoke or flame and attack it by night; three in the morning was their preferred hour for doing this.

In action for the first time, the Glosters took the neighbouring 'Hill 327' after a near-vertical climb; and on 20 February the R.U.R, who had tank and artillery support, including Tony's mortars, 'scaled the topmost ridge of the range alongside the U.S. 24th Infantry Regiment'. Naturally, Tony and his wireless operator went with them; the Larkhill method, unlike that of the Americans, was for the artillery commander physically to accompany the commander of the unit he was supporting, and thus be in a position to respond to his immediate needs.[12] 'The climb up,' he writes, 'was so steep that we even took off our Battledress Blouses and left behind everything we thought we could possibly do without. The R.U.R. riflemen took just their rifles and bayonets with fifty rounds slung in bandoliers around their necks. My wireless operator and I had to carry a large wireless set and its batteries, each weighing forty pounds, up the steep cliff. The plan was that our sleeping bags and food would be brought up by porters as soon as we had consolidated our position at the top.'

He continues: 'Unfortunately the Americans on our right were not where they had said they were.' The porters had therefore to be held back while the Ulsters cleared the intermediate ridge that over-looked their route, leaving no time for them to ascend before nightfall. 'The result was that nearly six hundred men had to spend the night sleeping, if they could, in the snow at the top of

[12] *Ibid.*, p.187.

the mountain without even a full Battledress, without fires or bedding and without food for nearly twenty-four hours. In spite of this there were only a dozen or so cases of exposure,' including the redoubtable C.O., Ikey May. The resilience of these men, including the grumbling reservists who at the start of the war had mischievously sung 'The Red Flag', is quite astonishing.

Using the wireless, Tony directed the fire of his mortars (which had a range of over two miles) from their positions on the lower ground, putting down over three tons of mortar bombs on the Chinese. At first light, having softened them up in this way, 'we rushed down the spur onto their main defences. The Irish blood was up; a night spent in the snow was not to their liking and a horde of yelling Riflemen charged down the mountain, up to their knees in soft snow, like a pack of devils from hell.'

The Chinese had suffered heavy casualties under Tony's bombardment; the shocked survivors sprang from their holes and fled in terror before the Irish banshees. As anticipated, they scuttled down the hill and onto a still-frozen section of the Han river. But Tony 'had thought of that one and had the guns from 45th Field Reg[imen]t waiting for the word to fire. The 25 p[oun]d[e]r shells smashed the ice, the result can be left to the imagination.'

Reunited with their porters and transport, the R.U.R 'enjoyed a short well-earned rest', and on 20 February were relieved by the same American regiment, the 24th Infantry, that had so badly let them down. 'As you can guess there were some very cutting remarks passed to them from the Irish.' If the men of the 24th seemed disorganised and poorly motivated, it was because they were one of the fourteen all-black units in the American Far East Command, racially segregated under mediocre white officers and denied any normal prospect of promotion. Their own divisional commander had already identified them as 'untrustworthy in the face of the enemy'.[13] They had in that case been an extraordinarily poor choice to serve alongside the R.U.R.

Thankfully, the weather was improving. The snow in the valleys had given way to a sea of mud. Now provided with splendid rubber boots, the weary soldiers were to spend a week in bombed-out Suwon (which had been recaptured on 9 February), where Tony found four habitable houses for his men. 'I believe I have been put up for an M.C.,' he wrote proudly. 'A B[riga]de Order gave the honour of taking the final mountain to the R.U.R., "who without the wonderful support given to them by 'B' Troop 170 Mortar Battery R.A. would never have captured their objective". That was my Troop.'[14]

At this point Tony peeled off to Seoul in support of the R.O.K. Army, occupying stylish quarters in an old Officers' Club. The city was not entirely ruinous, but it was eerily deserted, and far from secure. On the first day he spotted, through his field glasses, an entire company of P.L.A. descending into a railway cutting, and quickly trained his mortars on them.

Much to his satisfaction, he was left for a while to his own devices. Every morning, Tony and the wireless operator would range along the south bank of the Han, looking for targets on the other side. Though very close to the enemy and separated only by the gushing river, his O.P.s were well hidden and only thrice attracted attention (the Chinese shells always missed). He writes of observing the wildlife through a hole in the bank. 'B' Troop fired over twenty tons of ammunition in ten days, and by the time that fire was returned, they had usually 'slipped away down the ruined streets to spend the night at our firm base some seven miles to the rear'. In one incident, Tony watched as a single Chinese soldier emerged cautiously from his cramped foxhole, determined to dig a new one. Soon, some thirty unsuspecting

---

[13] Hickey, *The Korean War,* pp.184-5. The 24th was disbanded in 1952.

[14] Letter 219; Hickey, *The Korean War,* pp.180-1.

Chinese were milling around with shovels. That was the moment when Tony gave the order to fire.

By 3 March, however, a jealous Brigadier Brodie had recalled 'B' Troop to his base at Suwon, and had reunited it with the R.U.R., whose depleted ranks had been filled by 180 reinforcements,[15] both officers and men. Very conscious that his father had been the Padre to the Irish or 'Bloody Hand' Division, including the R.U.R.'s forerunner the Irish Rifles, during his own wartime service, Tony had to agree that they belonged together.[16]

By the time the Ulstermen celebrated St Patrick's Day on 17 March, they were still 'sitting in our school building doing nothing except holding ourselves ready to dash off anywhere at a moment's notice'. Tony took a photograph of the long, two-storey school building, which had an impressive portico, and another of the regiment's five pipers, practising in front of a line of lorries. He and Brigadier Brodie were the only non-regimental guests at the dinner, and a toast was drunk to Tony's father, their former padre.

In the fine spring weather, Tony had kept his men in shape with a route march, and they had practised carrying the mortars up to higher positions on their backs. On 22 March, the order at last came to pack up and move. They left at 9 a.m. the following day, travelled seventy miles over 'awful' roads, on which wrecked vehicles had regularly to be bulldozed out of the way, and spent the night in a bombed-out factory in Seoul. Tony composed a letter before going to bed, while four fellow officers, sitting at the end of the same table, were absorbed in a game of bridge.[17]

---

15 Tony has 'over 200', but the actual figures were 59 in February and a further 121 in March: information kindly provided by Gavin Glass, M.B.E., Curator of the Royal Ulster Rifles Museum in Belfast.

16 Letters 220, 221; uncredited newspaper cutting, 'Patience Rewarded - 30 Chinese Cop It', in Tony's collection; Hickey, *The Korean War,* pp.200 (on Seoul, which only fell on 14 March) and 206 (on the reinforcements).

17 Letters 221, 222.

A drive across the Han river, spearheaded by 29 Brigade, proved abortive. Notwithstanding the American intelligence reports, the Chinese had, in fact, melted away like the winter snow. In the course of this 'little jaunt', not a single shot was fired. But Ridgway had alternative plans for the British. He had decided to establish a protective line along the Imjin river, north of Seoul. It was currently held by members of the 3rd U.S. Infantry Division. However, the Chinese having evaporated here, too, 29 Brigade were ordered to take over. They were on the line by 31 March. Thankfully, the incessant rain of the past week had given way to pleasant spring weather.[18]

To Brodie, it was utterly absurd that a mere brigade should be expected to hold the huge sector that had previously been allotted to an entire division. The Glosters, Northumberlands and R.U.R. had been reinforced by a Belgian infantry battalion, but these units were to be spread very thinly indeed across a nine-mile front. A range of hills, rising to 2,000 feet, dominated the Imjin river which bowed before them. It was shallow here, and all too easy to cross, but it was at least plainly visible from the high ground. Brodie might have concentrated the four battalions so they could provide effective mutual support. Instead, he had spread the rifle companies among the various hills, where they were unable to cover, or in some cases even see each other, and were seldom less than a mile apart from their nearest neighbour. The R.U.R., now commanded by Major Gerald Rickord, had been placed on the far right, 'about two miles ahead of the main line and the other side of the Imjin river'.[19] They were supported, of course, by 'Battling Baker'. The Northumberlands took the right flank on the south side, with the Glosters on the left. The Belgian battalion were in reserve until 20 April, when they relieved the R.U.R. on the north bank. Tony's troop, however, remained in position to give them continued support.

---

[18] Letter 223; Hickey, *The Korean War,* p.203.

[19] Letter 224.

With time on their hands, 29 Brigade had dug and wired a fall-back line, but in the forward positions, the ground was too rocky for deep digging. They had to content themselves with shallow slit trenches, and such natural cover as they could find. An air of complacency prevailed. Whilst some men sunbathed on the slopes, others went off to Tokyo on leave, including the C.O. of the R.U.R. Not enough was done to clear fields of fire by removing the thick scrub. The positions were neither wired, nor mined. But there was still no sign of the Chinese, and it was expected that the Brigade would soon be moving on.[20]

Daily reconnaissance probes to the north found little more than observation posts, and morale suffered during three weeks of idleness. 'It is very bad from the soldiering point of view,' wrote Major Pat Angier of 'A' Company, the 1st Glosters, 'as it is impossible to prevent the men from getting complacent and this weakness will be repaid in lives should the enemy care to counter-attack … It is all very strange and quite unlike a normal war.'[21]

However, the Chinese had been carefully plotting the U.N. positions, had identified 29 Brigade as an obstacle to their rapid advance on Seoul and, by Sunday 22 April, had almost invisibly advanced in great numbers to the river. First contact that day was with the Belgian battalion. Commanded by Lieutenant-Colonel Albert Crahay, the Corps de Volontaires pour la Corée were, indeed, enthusiastic and extremely tough volunteers to a man. With their brown berets and proud *'Vive la Belgique'* banner, they are described as 'bearded, wild-looking men', and were highly esteemed by the British who served with them. The downside is that they were only about half the strength of a British battalion.[22] Yet they were now to face the terrifying 'human wave' formation

---

[20] Hickey, *The Korean War,* pp.205-9; Hastings, *The Korean War,* pp.249-53; Mackenzie, *The Imjin and Kapyong Battles,* pp.29, 31-6.

[21] Hickey, *The Korean War,* p.208.

[22] Mackenzie, *The Imjin and Kapyong Battles,* p.27; Hastings, *The Korean War,* p.258.

of the Chinese. 'At eight in the evening,' Tony writes, 'we were attacked by between ten to twelve thousand Chinese supported by artillery and mortar fire, that is more than ten to one against us.'

At about 10.30 p.m., Brodie ordered the battle-patrol of the R.U.R. to secure the pontoon bridges at 'Ulster Crossing' (vehicle and foot bridges that had been set up by engineers during their tenure there),[23] which was the Belgians' line of withdrawal, but they were beaten back. Meanwhile, hordes of Chinese had been charging across the river at the shallower 'Gloster Crossing' and attacking both the Northumberlands and the Glosters in their isolated positions, which could not possibly be held for long against such numbers. In the midst of a fierce moonlit battle, Major Angier of 'A' Company, the Glosters, who 'was constantly on his feet, touring the platoons in an inferno of fire', was killed in a hail of bullets. His last words to his C.O. were to reassure him: 'Don't worry about us; we'll be all right'. At first light, a final radio call was received: 'We've had it, Cheerio'. Then the line went dead.

At that same moment the Northumberlands, finding themselves overlooked by Chinese machine-guns, were compelled to fall back. The rifle companies were too far apart to support each other, but individual riflemen behaved magnificently, delaying the rout and exacting a heavy price on the enemy.[24] Their worthy brothers-in-arms, the Belgians, were also engaged in a fierce battle, with Tony's mortar troop in support: 'We held on all night and all the next day until it was quite beyond doubt that unless we pulled out as soon as possible all would be lost.'

The Belgians being completely surrounded, Brodie thought they should destroy their vehicles and heavy weapons, including Tony's mortars, and fight their way out on foot. The idea of

---

[23] Mackenzie, *The Imjin and Kapyong Battles,* pp.29-30, 33, 46-7.

[24] Hickey, *The Korean War,* pp.220-4; Hastings, *The Korean War,* pp.257, 262-3; Mackenzie, *The Imjin and Kapyong Battles,* pp.55-67.

leaving behind his mortars was anathema to Tony. That night, they 'made a dash for it across country. The infantry swam the river, got into the mountains and away. Clearly, we could not follow their example without leaving our guns and vehicles behind to fall into the hands of the enemy, so we charged across the single pontoon bridge which was already surrounded by Chinese.' The bridge was a mere fifteen feet wide; if any vehicle were to be immobilised, it would be disastrous for those that followed. Yet the enemy were only fifty feet away, commanding the heights on the south bank and the bridge egress points. Luckily, four U.S. Sherman tanks had arrived to distract them.

The wounded having been evacuated by helicopter, a column of eighty Belgian vehicles led the way, speeding across the narrow bridge with all guns blazing. The battalion doctor, who rode in one of the trucks, said it was like being in a rodeo. Four vehicles were hit but, thankfully, none was immobilised on the bridge, and no one was killed. 'There was a God for the Belgians,' the M.O. wrote; 'we passed [over the bridge] without suffering a death.' Tony, deprived of sleep and no doubt running on adrenaline, then led his column in a similar dash. It is very curious that Tony should have practised this precise manoeuvre - leading a column of vehicles and guns across a pontoon bridge by night - in the autumn of 1941, while stationed in Kent, and that the outcome should have been identical. 'All the guns, all the vehicles except one and every single man in the Troop got through untouched,' he wrote. 'We did a twelve mile drive across open fields in the dark and found our way back through our rather disorganised lines.' His commentary echoes that of the Belgian M.O. 'I still cannot believe how we managed to get away with it; we must certainly have been under God's special care.'[25]

The spirited Glosters were less fortunate. Whilst they continued to wreak havoc on the Chinese, the report of a patrol leader had been bleak: 'There's not just dozens of them down

---

[25] Letter 224 (and *cf.* letter 42); Mackenzie, *The Imjin and Kapyong Battles,* pp.67-70.

there - there's thousands'. In fact, the entire Chinese 63rd Army had been massing on the farther bank. The battle with these fresh troops raged all night; and at first light on 24 April, the 400 survivors rallied with their C.O. on 'Hill 235', thereafter known as 'Gloster Hill'. Unhelpfully, Brodie had informed the divisional commander that their situation had become 'pretty sticky', a form of British understatement that was entirely lost on the American. He should have been told explicitly of the imminent disaster. No reinforcements were forthcoming and the Glosters were ordered to hold their position. The *sang-froid* of their taciturn C.O., Lieutenant-Colonel James Power ('Fred') Carne, was extraordinary. Under his inspirational leadership, the morale of the battalion never faltered, despite the hopelessness of their position. As Brodie admitted later, ordering this brave man to stay put 'was probably one of the worst moments in my life'.[26]

Having made their dash from the river the previous night, the exhausted Belgians, along with 'Battling Baker', had been directed to a holding position near Brodie's headquarters, to rest and reorganise. Their fighting strength had been reduced to less than a hundred men. On the afternoon of 24 April, they were nevertheless required to take up a blocking position less than a mile to the west, and to hold it against continual waves of Chinese. For a third night, there was no sleep for the men, nor any respite from the fighting. Then, on 25 April, all remaining units were ordered to withdraw, in circumstances ominously similar to those at Happy Valley. The Northumberlands and the R.U.R. had to run the gauntlet through the narrow road, which had already been cut off by the enemy. The Belgians, supported by tanks and Tony's mortars, joined them in a fighting withdrawal, in which Colonel Crahay was wounded, the survivors eventually regrouping at Tokchong, four miles back, to form a new blocking position.[27]

---

[26] *Ibid.*, pp.75-93.

[27] *Ibid.*, pp.95-111.

The events are thus summarised by Tony: 'Three more days and nights of continual battle [had] followed; each morning we found ourselves surrounded and forced to fight our way out of a trap. The casualties we inflicted were unbelievable as the Chinese were in mass formation and made no attempt to take cover.' The Northumberlands, some of whom had been less than steadfast, had lost about a hundred men, including their brave C.O., Lieutenant-Colonel Kingsley Foster, who is said to have had a premonition of his own death. As for the R.U.R - only recently replenished after their mauling at Happy Valley - when they rallied on the far side of the line, only 14 officers and 260 men answered the roll call. The men had expended most of their ammunition as well as their lives; around 12,000 mortar rounds had been fired. They were in no condition to carry on. Towards midnight on 25 April, they were relieved by the 15th Regimental Combat Team of the U.S. Army and pulled from the line.[28]

As for the Glosters, when dawn broke on 26 April, the Chinese were within yards of their positions on Hill 235, and began to sound their bugles, signalling a further attack. At the suggestion of the tough, pipe-smoking adjutant, Captain Anthony Farrar-Hockley, Drum-Major Bass bravely stood up in his slit trench and rattled off every call of the day in turn, from 'Cookhouse' to 'Officers Dress for Dinner'; he omitted only one - 'Retreat'. Bass's spirited renditions so confused the Chinese that their own bugling ceased. For a while, the superb supporting gunnery of 45 Field and, eventually, the multiple runs of U.S. fighter-bombers helped to stave off the inevitable. Then the Glosters were alone again, with dwindling supplies of ammunition. As the batteries faded on his wireless, an emotional Brigadier Brodie sent Colonel Carne a final message: 'NO ONE BUT GLOSTERS COULD HAVE DONE IT'.

---

[28] Mackenzie, *The Imjin and Kapyong Battles,* pp.55-72 (and p.66 on Colonel Kingsley's premonition). The recent replenishment is unlikely to have made the Ulsters up to their ideal strength of around 600.

On Carne's orders, break-out parties began to make their way to the rear, which by then was over a dozen miles away. Only 170 of the original 850 men made it to safety. At 138, the casualties had been surprisingly light (the R.U.R. had suffered an almost identical toll, of six officers and 130 other ranks), and 1 Glosters was far from having been wiped out, as was initially supposed; the Chinese were keen, for propaganda purposes, to take as many prisoners as possible, and fired warning shots to round them up. 570 men, including Colonel Carne, Captain Farrar-Hockley and most of the gunners of 'C' Mortar Troop, commanded by Captain Frank Wisbey, were led away into a long, brutal and, for some, fatal captivity in Red China.[29]

There but for the grace of God went Tony. Behind the lines on 26 April, a Reuter's war correspondent avidly noted down the details of his 'little exploit'. He had now had four nights without sleep. He must have been befuddled by fatigue, yet he was grateful, astonished and jubilant. That same day, he wrote to his parents: 'My Troop had not one man wounded; we only lost the one truck ... May God be with us all.'[30]

---

[29] Hastings, *The Korean War,* pp.253-71; Hickey, *The Korean War,* pp.210-33; Anthony Farrar-Hockley, *The Edge of the Sword* (London, 1954), pp.15-67; Mackenzie, *The Imjin and Kapyong Battles,* pp.75-93, 95-102. The casualties were 58 Glosters and 5 gunners killed, with 75 wounded (Hickey, p.232). The figures for the R.U.R. are from the Roll Call that was taken after the battle, from a strength of 19 officers and 901 other ranks; happily, many of the missing men had been taken into captivity (*ex info.* Gavin Glass, M.B.E., Curator of the Royal Ulster Rifles Museum, Belfast). In letter 225 (dated 30 April), Tony inaccurately puts the R.U.R.'s losses at 194 men and 10 officers, with the Northumberlands losing 'about a hundred all ranks'.

[30] Letters 224, 225, 227; uncredited newspaper cutting, 'Korea Hero Coming Home for Course', in Tony's collection. Although the cutting is undated, Tony's first sleepless night must have been that of 22/23 April.

EPILOGUE

Tony sent home six more letters from Korea. Despite being thrown back into the action, his tone is consistently buoyant and optimistic, like someone who has stared into the face of death and come through.

Replenished from Japan, 29 Brigade was very quickly restored to fighting strength and, on 28 April 1951, was sent back to the front line, albeit to 'a very quiet and peaceful sector on the extreme west with the Royal Navy on our left, the Han estuary to our front and the city of Seoul, or what is left of it, to our right'. The Brigade's heroic stand on the Imjin had exhausted the Chinese, who are estimated to have lost 10,000 men, and had prevented them from re-taking Seoul. The participants in the battle, especially those 'Glorious Glosters', have passed into legend.

The expendability of Chinese lives is sobering. These were not all fanatics, but mostly uneducated peasants who, harangued daily by screeching commissars, had been broken into blind obedience. Many were overjoyed when taken prisoner and more than happy to talk. The more common fate, however, was to be thrown into battle in 'human waves' and mown down 'like bowling pins', as an American machine-gunner was to put it.[1]

On the night of 29 April, a cluster of the enemy, spotted on the farther bank of the Han in Tony's sector, received the full weight of U.N. firepower, including the naval guns. A tank recce group went out in the morning and counted no fewer than 1,100 dead. The slaughter seemed oddly out of place on such a lovely spring day. The skies were blue, and the larches and abundant willows a vivid green. The mountains were carpeted with flowers, the fields strewn with cherry trees in full blossom. The countryside seemed unreal in its beauty, 'like the backdrop for some play or opera'.[2]

---

[1] Hickey, *The Korean War,* p.173; Hastings, *The Korean War,* p.234.

[2] Letter 225.

The sector otherwise remained 'very quiet' and there were opportunities to drive off to the sea at Inchon for swims. The military convoys threw up clouds of very fine dust, which 'found its way into everything', and the men had to be issued with goggles and face masks to keep it out. One of the Belgian officers came for dinner in the mess and read Tony's palm. The Brigade was encamped on the exposed slope of a steep hill, about six miles from Kimpo. When a storm blew up on 13 May, Tony lay contentedly in his six-foot tent, which, as usual, was dug down to a depth of four feet, and listened to the beating rain.

On 23 May, the Brigade abandoned their carefully-prepared positions on the Han and advanced across the river, a good four hours' drive, 'to a place just north of Seoul'. It was close to the battleground of April, so burial parties went off in search of British dead. In their new front line, on the same, southern bank of the meandering Imjin, they dug deeper trenches than before, blasting them from the solid rock where necessary, and laid careful wire and mine defences. It was for the enemy to make the next move. 'We are waiting for another big push from the Chinese,' Tony wrote, 'but I doubt they will choose this sector as we gave them such a bloody nose last time they tried it.'[3]

He was right about that, and instead was sent off, rather unwillingly, on leave. 'Rest and Recreation' centres had been set up in various parts of Japan for the benefit of all ranks. Parties were flown directly from the airfield at Kimpo to Tachi, on the

---

[3] Letters 226, 227, 228, 231 (on blasting the dug-outs); Hickey, *The Korean War,* p.237; James Jacobs, *From the Imjin to the Hook* (Barnsley, 2013), pp.78-9. Among the often grisly detritus, Tony 'was surprised to discover in a sandy cove several damaged Chinese 75mm mountain guns, the old fashioned kind with wooden spoke wheels'. He had the least damaged of these towed away as a souvenir. Eventually brought back to England, where it was re-spoked and cleaned up by a R.E.M.E. armourer, it is known as the 'Imjin Gun', and has accompanied 170 Battery, itself known as the 'Imjin Battery', on every subsequent posting, all new recruits being apprised of its story. The author, Jim Jacobs, an eager National Serviceman who had volunteered for overseas duty, served with 'A' Troop at the Battle of Imjin (when it supported the Northumberlands) and beyond. For Tony's own account, which was published in *The Gunner* (Nov 1975), p.13, see Appendix.

outskirts of Tokyo. Tony and a fellow officer awaited an available flight with hordes of boisterous Americans, one of whom procured them a place on a Flying Boxcar. The nervous passengers strapped on parachutes and Mae Wests 'and the vast 30 ton machine at last climbed into the air like some overfed vulture'. 'The old kite will never make it,' said the pilot, as he headed off into the eye of a storm.

Five and a half hours later, the aircraft put down at a very wet Tachi. Tony had elected to stay in an Australian-run, five-star hotel in the centre of Tokyo. The drive into town was a revelation. The suburbs reminded him of Surrey. People in European clothes picked their way through the puddles under brightly-coloured umbrellas. There were crowded trams, a bustling railway station, neon signs and modern, high-rise buildings. When they arrived at the hotel, two white-coated porters unloaded the luggage from their car. Ten minutes later, the two gunners were both soaking in their first proper bath for eight months. The day was rounded off with a seven-course meal and the first of four nights between clean sheets. For a long time they had only been able to dream of such luxury.

Tony soon discovered that this was a thoroughly 'Americanised' city, a far cry from 'the Japan of the picture books'. A photograph in his album shows a pleasant, palm-fringed beach resort that he must also have visited, possibly the now heavily-urbanised Chiba. For an authentic Japanese experience, it would have been better if he had opted for one of the more out-of-the-way leave centres, such as Kure.[4] (This, ironically, was the object of the amphibious invasion for which, in early 1946, he been trained on Lake Beale.)

Tony flew back to Korea on 9 July, and it was confirmed that he would be starting his long-deferred course at Shrivenham in early October, having been nominated for it by Brigadier Brodie. Thankfully, the very tough entrance exam had been waived in his

---

[4] Letters 226, 229, 230; Hickey, *The Korean War,* p.207; Hastings, *The Korean War,* p.369.

case. He fully appreciated that, after years in India and Korea, his returning to 'school' was going to require a major readjustment.

Soon he was in action again, advancing over the Imjin on the back of a tank, towards the Chinese lines. 'After a day spent probing and searching for a weak spot we mounted a final attack. As the setting sun shot blood-red streaks through the black banks of clouds of the coming storm and as the first massive rain drops fell from the leaden sky, the artillery opened up and the air force swept in to drop their deadly cargoes on the targets marked by coloured smoke from my mortars. By the time the infantry moved in it was dark except for the light of the almost full moon shining through gaps in the racing clouds. The Chinese fled, only to be met by the bursting mortar bombs and the rattle of machine-gun fire. Those who did not come out left their Napalm blackened bodies in the fox-holes that had become their graves. Our work done, the force made its way back to the tanks, called the rolls and once more crossed the rising river, tired, wet and hungry. Such is war.'

When he wrote on 22 July he was 'alone in my O.P. on the savage mountain', apart from his small party of gunners, in the midst of the continuing storm. It had rained incessantly for four days. The dug-out was flooded, and everything and everyone was soaking wet. Visibility was much reduced by the swirling mists and by 'great sweeping curtains of rain'. The Imjin, four hundred feet below, was swollen to a 'raging muddy brown torrent'; at least it would be less easy to cross.

Tony had just been shown a note from Headquarters: 'It is highly recommended that, because of the shortage of trained Gunner Captains, Captain A.P.H.B. Fowle R.A. be retained in this theatre until the last possible moment and that a special air passage then be arranged. Signed, Brigadier Commanding 29 Independent Infantry Brigade.' It was gratifying to learn that he was so valued, but he also did his sums: 'that mystic body the

War Office says "at least one month's leave before the course".' Tony reckoned he would be home by late August.[5]

What Tony may not have been shown was the recommendation of his Battery Commander, Major T.V. Fisher-Hoch, that he be awarded a Military Cross. 'This officer has consistently shown the greatest energy, & gallantry in action,' wrote the Major on 17 June. 'He has performed outstanding work as an O.P. & has always been in the forefront of any action. His example to his men has been of the very highest order. I strongly recommend the award of an M.C.' The recommendation was received at Brigade Headquarters on 6 July; and on 23 July, when Tony was still holed up on the 'savage mountain', was approved by General Sir Horace Robertson, the Australian Commander-in-Chief of the British Commonwealth Forces in Korea.

The citation reads as follows:

> 'Captain Fowle has been consistently in action since joining the Battery and has as an O.P. taken part in three major actions and several patrol actions in which he has been in close contact and under heavy fire from the enemy. On 23rd April, when his Troop was cut off with the Belgian Battalion he was responsible for finding a route which ran over two major obstacles and was under direct fire from enemy small arms and mortar. Captain Fowles *[sic]* brought his Troop through this with the loss of only one vehicle.
>
> 'At all times his willingness to take part in any action, his cheerfulness, coolness and apparent lack of fatigue have been a constant example to his men. He has maintained the highest of standards and the excellent support given by his Troop has been due to his enthusiasm and unselfish work.'[6]

---

[5] Letters 230, 231.

[6] National Archives, WO/373/114.

Brodie was right about the shortage of trained gunner captains, and Tony was not relieved until early September, which was indeed the last possible moment. Instead of boarding a plane in the first week of August, he was supporting two companies of the R.U.R. in a 'recce in force'. It was planned to last eight hours and the objective was to capture a prisoner. The rain was torrential, and, by the time they got back to the swollen river with their prisoner, the rope ferry that carried them across had been washed away. A 'tight box' was formed round the bridgehead and the men were condemned to four very wet nights in the mud.

Initially without bedding, washing kit or shovels, they were extremely hungry by the evening of the second day, when they at last received an airdrop of supplies. More equipment was parachuted down on the third day, for the Chinese were aware of their predicament and preparing to attack. The Ulstermen secured their position on the top of a hill, and Tony got his mortars half way up, with 'thirty riflemen to look after my chaps during the night'.

It was on the third night that the Chinese attacked. There was some 'grim' close-quarter fighting, 'but no one got hurt - on our side'. The 'little yellow men' had retreated by dawn and the sun came out. The men were able to sleep in the bright sunshine and dry off. At the same time the river had finally calmed down, allowing for the party to be boated across. That operation took most of the day, and Tony, characteristically, was one of the last to leave. 'I got over with the rear-guard at 5.30 p.m.,' he writes, 'after all the men and the stores had been shipped over.'

Even during the battle of the Imjin, there had been no acceptable excuse to grow a beard. The R.U.R. had been particularly strict in that regard, and believed that officers should 'set an example'. Tony now had one for the first time and so did everyone else, as none of them had thought to bring their shaving kit. When Brigadier Brodie caught sight of Tony in this state, he was highly amused. 'You should go back for another week,' he said, 'then it would be long enough to curl.'[7]

Tony's award of a Military Cross was gazetted on 7 September, five days before his arrival in England. He reported to the Depot at Woolwich, took some leave, and started his course at Shrivenham in October. On the cold Wednesday of 27 February 1952, he took a day out of the classroom in order to attend an investiture at Buckingham Palace. It was the first presided over by Queen Elizabeth. Those lining up to be honoured were all men.

The ceremony began at 11 a.m. and the first award was of a Victoria Cross. The recipient, 'Big Bill' Speakman, was a private in the Black Watch, but had been attached in Korea to the King's Own Scottish Borderers. He stood six feet six inches tall and, in the defence of yet another anonymous ridge, 'Hill 217', had thrown everything he had at the enemy, including, eventually, empty beer bottles, the beer having being used to cool the overheated gun barrels. According to the citation, Speakman's 'gallantry and utter contempt of personal danger were beyond praise'.

Fifty-six men of lesser distinction, mostly civilians, stepped forward to receive knighthoods, each one kneeling before the young Queen and being dubbed with the tap of a sword on each shoulder. Then a file of military men marched forward, all faultlessly turned out in their dress uniforms. A variety of decorations and awards was distributed, most of them for gallantry, whether in Korea or on operations elsewhere. Twelfth on the list was Tony Fowle, his proud mother and sister looking on.

There were men there with whom Tony had served in Korea - Majors Butler, Huth and Hedley of the 8th King's Royal Irish Hussars, Major Brook of the Royal Northumberland Fusiliers, Captains Ormrod and Piper and Lieutenant Butler, also of the 8th

---

[7] Letter 232; Mackenzie, *The Imjin and Kapyong Battles,* p.87 (on battlefield shaving).

Hussars. Also present were the wife and daughter of the Northumberlands' brave C.O., Colonel Foster, who had been killed on Day 3 at Imjin. These ladies were handed Foster's posthumous D.S.O. in a private audience with the Queen.[8]

The person Tony took most pleasure in seeing was surely his old friend and mentor, Lieutenant-Colonel James Hepper. In command of the 1/7 Gurkhas in Malaya, Hepper had been 'chasing bandits in the jungle and thoroughly enjoying life'.[9] He was now collecting a D.S.O. for his trouble, to add to a previous award of an O.B.E. The pair had corresponded regularly, but they may not have met since December 1946, when Tony had relinquished his command of Zhob Battery at Landi Khotal.

From October 1942, Hepper had been Tony's companion in a series of adventures. Had they not been the joint guests of honour at the *burra-khana* in the desert, being escorted in both directions by a cavalcade of armed tribesmen? And was it not Hepper who had initiated Tony into serious mountaineering? Their first attempt had been thwarted when their jeep broke down; they had had to trudge home over 25 miles of rough hill country, encountering 'some fairly big rivers' along the way. Together they had hard-ridden to hounds with the Peshawar Vale and in steeplechases. No mountain peak within their reach had been left unscaled, no fast-flowing river unswum. On one of their final expeditions, descending from a summit of 12,000 feet, Tony appears to have saved Hepper's life, extricating him from a narrow ledge at great risk to himself.

Since his departure from England in February 1942, Tony had experienced a life of adventure such as would be unimaginable today. He had travelled extensively in the Middle and Far East and the Indian sub-continent, acquiring the most intimate knowledge of their climate and landscape, and of their varied

---

[8] *Investiture at Buckingham Palace on Wednesday, 27th February, 1952* (order of service). Tony was photographed outside in his 'British Warm', with his mother and sister.

[9] Letter 216.

peoples and languages. This was at a precious moment in history. With a King-Emperor still imposing a sort of unity and order on the world, there was nowhere that was inaccessible to a British officer, especially to one as inquisitive and determined as Tony. Himself the representative of a dying breed, he had been the privileged witness to the full romance of the ancient world, even as it was expelling its last gasp; but also to the ensuing disruption, to the displacement of peoples and the casual, often wilful destruction of age-old communities and cultures. Now the whole world is tarnished by mass tourism and by the 'Americanisation' of its speech, dress, food, music, architecture and much else - invariably crude substitutes for what they have replaced - or simply by the pursuit of wealth. But Tony had known the cradles of mankind in all their richness and diversity.

This had been, for him, a period of immense personal fulfilment, and the realisation, not least through Hepper's influence, of his dreams. At last he had taken his place in a column of Indian mountain gunners, that most romantic and picturesque of military formations. Aged 23, he had been presented with his first battery, and promoted to the rank of major. Finally, in 1951, he had achieved the command in battle for which he had long yearned. Such had been the evolution of Tony Fowle, M.C., the mountain gunner of the Khyber, Kashmir and Korea.

APPENDIX

GUN AND ROD IN THE IMJIN VALLEY

by Lieutenant-Colonel A.P.H.B. Fowle, M.C., R.A. (retd.)[1]

Both the July and August 1975 issues of the Gunner have stirred memories of 29 Bde and the battle of Solma-Ri.[2] The capture of the Imjin Gun in the 'Unforgettable Valley' has a lighter side which, though known to most members of B Troop 170 (Independent) Mortar Battery RA, for reasons which will become clear, could not be given wide publicity at the time.

The weeks before the battle of Solma-Ri were marked by a brooding quiet punctuated by occasional company or battalion sweeps by day and bursts of burp-gun fire at night. During these comparatively peaceful days 'B' Troop, which had been supporting the 1 RUR, moved north of the Imjin river to support the Belgium Battalion. Here it shared the occasional 'rough red', deepened its sun tan and generally enjoyed the glorious April weather which came as such a welcome change from the rigours of the arctic winter. The main river flowed cool and blue about a mile to our rear, immediately to our right a tributary formed the boundary between 29 Bde and the US 7 Cavalry Division. This smaller river was cold, fast flowing and though deep could be waded by anyone familiar with a salmon rod. Its most interesting feature was not its tactical significance but the fact that it held an abundance of Snow Trout, or Chush as we called them in India. These almost white fish ran up to about a pound in weight and, best of all, rose freely to a dry fly.

One Sunday afternoon some two weeks before the battle temptation became too great, there was nothing on so while most

---

[1] Tony's article, the original draft of which is transcribed here, was subsequently published in *The Gunner: The Magazine of the Royal Regiment of Artillery* (Nov 1975), p.13.

[2] Solma-Ri is an alternative name given to the Battle of the Imjin River.

gunners and infantry slept in the sun, taking trout rod and tackle I walked up the river for about a mile pretending I was back on the Itchen. After an hour or so my haversack was bulging with a dozen or more fighting trout. The shadows were starting to lengthen when, from my perch on a rock ledge in the middle of the river, I noticed out of the corner of my eye that I was no longer alone. While completely absorbed in casting my fly up stream a Chinese patrol had moved quietly up behind me and now stood on the bank watching this strange sight with obvious amazement.

It was no longer possible to pretend that I had not noticed them, it was equally impossible to run for it. So, with what was intended to be a cheerful wave, they were slowly shown the contents of my bag. The sight of the fish was greeted with loud and evidently approving Chinese noises. Equally slowly, each fish was carefully lifted out and thrown across the water to be scrambled for by the patrol. When the last trout was safely stowed in a Chinese pocket I gave a farewell wave and, with my heart in my mouth, turned away to carry on fishing. What could they do? No civilised man could shoot a fly fisherman in the middle of a river, especially after relieving him of his catch. Anyway I was obviously quite mad and therefore probably harmless. They went away as quietly as they had come, so did I but in the opposite direction and rather more quickly.

April drew to a close. The battle was over and we were again in support of the 1 RUR on the banks of the Imjin. 'B' Troop, together with the survivors of 'C' Troop, being clustered round a hoochie just south of Gloucester Hill. War has been correctly described as long periods of boredom punctuated by short periods of intense fright, boredom was again our chief enemy. Were the fish still rising? The question must be answered, so, taking my Jeep and Gunner Lawrie who acted as radio operator, batman,

OPA,[3] provider of US rations or gillie as the occasion demanded, set out on a recce of the main river bank upstream from the ford.

The water level had dropped considerably since my last visit leaving a broad band of gravel and rock between the river and its cliff-like banks. The banks themselves were indented with small coves washed out by the spring floods. In one of these coves was a gun. It stood fully deployed for action facing towards Gloucester Hill. The sights were in the carrier, a gun rule lay between the trails and open ammunition boxes waited on the ground to the rear. Carefully searching for mines or booby-traps we walked over to the gun position; the breech was open and the chamber empty, all that was missing was the detachment. Within the hour the gun was bouncing back to the troop position behind Sgt. Pennifold's 15 cwt.

Nearly ten years later I was DS[4] Guns at Shrivenham where more conventional trout can be caught in chalk streams without fear of armed action by other than a keeper with a shot gun. One afternoon my telephone rang; the BC[5] of 170 (Imjin) Bty was taking his battery overseas, could we please look after a Chinese mountain gun for them until they returned? Yes, it was the same equipment that I had last seen on the banks of the Imjin but its travels from Korea to Hong Kong and then on to England by way of Germany had taken their toll. It was in a sorry condition, the sights were missing and two spokes were broken. A hunt round the villages of Berkshire revealed a wheelwright who was only too pleased to exercise his old art, the rug in the back of my car still carries a circular grease mark from the wheel hub as a reminder of the journey. The REME fitters and AIGs[6] from the gun sheds, which used to be such a feature of the RMC of S,[7]

3 Observation Post Assistant.

4 Directing Staff.

5 Battery Commander.

6 Assistant Instructors in Gunnery.

7 Royal Military College of Science.

turned their attention to painting and repair so that soon the Imjin gun was back in its original condition. It is good to know that the trophy that I still think of as 'my' gun is now so well looked after and is given pride of place on the Imjin day parade.

It was all a long time ago. Certain details have become clouded during the 25 years since I fought by, and fished in, the Imjin but my sense of relief on seeing the departure of that Chinese patrol will always remain a most vivid memory.

KEY TO THE LETTERS

From Cranleigh School, Surrey
1. Sept 1939
2. Oct 1939

From Benmore Forestry School, Kilmun, Argyll
3. March 1940
4. April 1940
5. 4 May 1940
6. 5 May 1940
7. 16 May 1940
8. 'Monday Night', May 1940
9. 24 June 1940
10. 7 July 1940
11. 'Wednesday'

From Elizabeth Barracks, Strensall, Yorks
12. Undated
13. 25 Nov 1940
14. [Dec?] 1940
15. 5 Jan 1941
16. 19 Jan 1941
17. 30 Jan 1941

From 6th Field Training Regiment, Dairy, Ayrshire
18. 16 Feb 1941
19. 24 Feb 1941

From Bourlon Lines, Catterick, Yorks
20. 14 March 1941
21. 20 March 1941
22. March 1941
23. April 1941
24. 23 April 1941
25. 13 May 1941
26. 25 May 1941
27. 5 June 1941
28. 15 June 1941
29. 28 June 1941
30. 6 July 1941
31. 11 July 1941
32. 21 July 1941
33. 27 July 1941

From Christian Court, Eastry, Kent
34. 17 Aug 1941

From The Old Vicarage, Ash, Kent
35. 2 Sept 1941
36. 24 Sept 1941

From Christian Court, Eastry, Kent
37. 11 Oct 1941

From Broadstairs, Kent
38. Oct 1941
39. 4 Nov 1941
40. 8 Nov 1941
41. Undated
42. [Autumn 1941]
43. [Late Nov 1941]
44. Christmas 1941

From West Down, Tilshead, Salisbury Plain
45. [Dec 1941]
46. Jan 1942

From Ashfield House, Burton-on-Trent, Staffs
47. Feb 1942
48. 8 Feb 1942

On board the troopship Mooltan, *sailing from Liverpool to Durban,* via *Freetown*
49. 11 Feb 1942
50. Feb 1942

From the Base Depot R.A., Middle East, at Almaza, Egypt
51. Undated
52. Undated
53. 20 May 1942
54. 24 May 1942
55. 26 May 1942
56. 28 May 1942

From the Officers' Mess, 2 Royal Horse Artillery
57. 7 June 1942

From the School of Artillery, Egypt
58. 10 June 1942
59. 23 June 1942
60. 26 June 1942
61. 29 June 1942

From the Indian Army Depot at Mena, Egypt, a camp by the 'great pyramids'
62. 4 Aug 1942
63. 16 Aug 1942
64. 19 Aug 1942
65. 22 Aug 1942

From Damascus, in transit
66. 29 Aug 1942

From a camp beside the Tigris, near Baghdad
67. 4 Sept 1942

From a camp in the middle of nowhere, guarding Iraqi oilfields
68. 12 Sept 1942

From 'Hillside', an even remoter outpost in northern Iraq
69. 18 Sept 1942
70. 18 Sept 1942
71. 25 Sept 1942

From the camp in the middle of nowhere
72. 28 Sept 1942
73. 29 Sept 1942

From another desert camp near Mussayib on the Euphrates, south of Baghdad
74. 3 Oct 1942
75. 13 Oct 1942
76. 18 Oct 1942
77. 26 Oct 1942
78. 1 Nov 1942

From a new position about 25 miles away, on a desolate plain
79. 8 Nov 1942
80. 13 Nov 1942
81. 22 Nov 1942
82. 6 Dec 1942
83. 10 Dec 1942
84. 20 Jan 1943

From an encampment by the wild River Kifri, in Kurdistan
85. 13 Feb 1943
86. 20 March 1943
87. 16 April 1943
88. 2 May 1943
89. 13 May 1943
90. 26 May 1943
91. 19 June 1943

From a new encampment, closer to H.Q.R.A.
92. 23 June 1943
93. 11 July 1943
94. 18 July 1943

From Tony's brother Michael, serving with the Eighth Army in North Africa
95. 29 July 1943

From a camp near Kermanshah, Persia

96. 4 Aug 1943
97. 15 Aug 1943
98. 25 Aug 1943
99. 12 Sept 1943
100. 27 Sept 1943
101. 10 Oct 1943
102. 15 Oct 1943
103. 5 Nov 1943

From H.Q.R.A., at a superior encampment in the Iraqi desert

104. 23 Nov 1943
105. 30 Nov 1943
106. 10 Dec 1943
107. 2 Jan 1944
108. 31 Jan 1944
109. 10 Feb 1944
110. 26 Feb 1944
111. 29 Feb 1944
112. 20 March 1944
113. 7 April 1944

From Cairo, while attending a course

114. 1 May 1944

From the Officers' Club, Beirut, 'a few yards from the sea', where he is on leave

115. 16 May 1944
116. 22 May 1944

From a very secret location in coastal Syria, 'a Paradise'

117. 3 June 1944
118. 24 June 1944
119. 2 July 1944
120. 25 July 1944
121. 26 July 1944
122. 2 Aug 1944
123. 4 Aug 1944
124. 7 Aug 1944

From a temporary encampment in the mountains, en route *to the east*

125. 22 Aug 1944

From another mountain encampment, that of Divisional H.Q., at an unspecified location, probably between Mosul and Kirkuk

126. 3 Sept 1944
127. 8 Sept 1944
128. 15 Sept 1944
129. 19 Sept 1944
130. 27 Sept 1944
131. 17 Oct 1944

From R.A. Base Depot, inland from Karachi, India

132. 3 Dec 1944
133. 9 Dec 1944
134. 15 Dec 1944

From his bungalow at 11 Mall Road, or from the Officers' Mess, 29 Indian Light Mountain Regiment, Peshawar

135. 22 Dec 1944
136. 30 Dec 1944
137. 3 Jan 1945

From encampments in the field, 29 Indian Light Mountain Regiment being on exercise

138. 12 Jan 1945
139. 27 Jan 1945
140. 3 Feb 1945
141. 16 Feb 1945

From his bungalow at 11 Mall Road or from the Officers' Mess, 29 Indian Light Mountain Regiment, Peshawar, a return to 'luxury'

142. 20 Feb 1945

143. 22 Feb 1945
144. 10 March 1945
145. 23 March 1945
146. 27 March 1945
147. Easter Day 1945
148. 7 May 1945
149. 13 May 1945
150. 9 June 1945
151. 16 June 1945
152. 1 July 1945
153. 30 July 1945

From the fort at Landi Khotal
154. 23 Aug 1945
155. 4 Sept 1945

From the Officers' Mess, Peshawar
156. 26 Sept 1945

From the R.A. Officers' Mess, Woolwich, at the end of three months' leave in England
157. 28 Dec 1945

From an encampment beside Lake Beale, India
158. 7 Feb 1946
159. 23 Feb 1946
160. 5 March 1946

From Kohat, Waziristan
161. 20 March 1946
162. 8 April 1946
163. 29 April 1946
164. 13 May 1946

From Subedar *Raj Wali Khan in London*
165. June 1946

From Kohat, Waziristan
166. 3 July 1946
167. 28 July 1946

From Thal, in the volatile Kurram Agency, after a month's leave in the mountains
168. 2 Oct 1946
169. 1 Nov 1946
170. 7 Dec 1946

From the Homeward Bound Trooping Depot, Deolali, India
171. 31 Dec 1946

From the S.S. Cameronia *in a raging storm, somewhere due north of Crete*
172. 17 Jan 1947

From a P. & O. liner (one of the 'Strath' class?) off Cherbourg, after leave and a gunnery course in England
173. March 1948

From Colaba, near Bombay, 'the Gateway to India'
174. 2 April 1948

From a transit camp near Karachi
175. 13 April 1948

From the School of Artillery, Nowshera, Pakistan
176. 16 April 1948
177. 1 May 1948
178. 24 May 1948
179. 16 June 1948
180. 9 July 1948
181. 26 July 1948
182. 11 Aug 1948

From four locations in the Kaghan Valley, culminating at Babusar Top, the gateway to Gilgit, which is a contested region of Kashmir
183. 27 Aug 1948

From hospital in Abbottabad, Pakistan, near the southern end of the Kaghan Valley
184. 7 Oct 1948

From another hospital in Nowshera, Pakistan
185. 15 Oct 1948
186. 21 Oct 1948

From the School of Artillery, Nowshera, Pakistan, after service on the 'cease-fire line' in Kashmir
187. 7 Nov 1948
188. 17 Dec 1948
189. 4 March 1949
190. 11 March 1949
191. 3 May 1949
192. 25 May 1949
193. 11 June 1949
194. 12 Dec 1949
195. 29 Dec 1949
196. 14 Jan 1950
197. 11 Feb 1950
198. 6 March 1950
199. 1 April 1950
200. 12 April 1950
201. 19 May 1950

From Divisional Headquarters in Peshawar, Pakistan
202. 27 June 1950

From the School of Artillery, Nowshera, Pakistan
203. 20 July 1950

From the S.S. Caledonia *in the Red Sea, bound for England*
204. 18 Aug 1950

From the S.S. Lancashire, *a requisitioned troopship,* en route *to Korea*
205. 27 Oct 1950
206. 3 Nov 1950

From his squalid quarters at the Pong Sang Primary School, Taegu
207. 22 Nov 1950
208. 25 Nov 1950
209. 29 Nov 1950
210. 4 Dec 1950
211. 14 Dec 1950
212. Christmas Day 1950

From a hole in a snow-covered bank overlooking the Imjin River
213. 7 Jan 1951

From Chonan, a few miles behind the line, where he is quartered in a traditional Korean house
214. 17 Jan 1951
215. 21 Jan 1951
216. 23 Jan 1951

From a 'Rest Area' in a dried-up river bed at Osan, south of Suwan
217. 4 Feb 1951
218. 14 Feb 1951

From a house in Suwan, which Tony has requisitioned for his battery
219. 22 Feb 1951
220. 3 March 1951

From yet another abandoned school, elsewhere in Suwan
221. 18 March 1951

From a bombed-out factory in Seoul
222. 22 March 1951
223. 30 March 1951

From Seoul, in the aftermath of the Battle of Imjin
224. 26 April 1951

From an encampment on the Han Estuary near Kimpo, west of Seoul
225. 30 April 1951
226. 7 May 1951
227. 15 May 1951

From a new position on the farther side of the Han, just north of Seoul
228. 25 May 1951

From a five-star hotel in the centre of Tokyo, while on leave
229. 3 July 1951

From an unspecified location in Korea
230. 11 July 1951

From his dug-out on a mountainside, north of the Imjin
231. 22 July 1951

From Brigade Headquarters, somewhere in Korea
232. 14 Aug 1951

GLOSSARY AND ABBREVIATIONS

AA	Ack-Ack/Anti-Aircraft Gun
ABCA	Army Bureau of Current Affairs
ADC	Aide-de-Camp
atta	whole-wheat flour, mixed with water to make *chapatis*
ATS	Army Territorial Service
BDRA	Base Depot Royal Artillery
BOR	British Other Rank
Brig.	Brigadier
B.Sc.	Bachelor of Science
burra khana	great feast (Hind.)
chapati	unleavened flatbread (Hind.)
chittar	panther/leopard (Hind. 'variegated')
CCRA	Corps Commander Royal Artillery
CO	Commanding Officer
CPO	Command Post Officer
CPVA	Chinese People's Volunteer Army
CRA	Commander Royal Artillery
CRO	Commonwealth Relations Office
dhurri	blue rug issued to all Indian troops
DSO	(Companion of the) Distinguished Service Order
Dussehra	Hindu holiday marking the triumph of the god Rama
ENSA	Entertainments National Service Association
EPIP	European Private's Indian Pattern Military Tent
gee	clarified butter used for cooking (Hind.)
GHQ	General Headquarters
GOC-in-C	General Officer Commanding-in-Chief
gook	man (Korean), later pejorative
GPO	Gun Position Officer
GSO	General Staff Officer
havildar	sergeant (Hind.)
HMS	His Majesty's Ship
HQ	Headquarters
HQRA	Headquarters Royal Artillery
ICRC	International Committee of the Red Cross
ICS	Indian Civil Service
IG	Instructor of Gunnery
ITC	Infantry Training Course
KOYLI	King's Own Yorkshire Light Infantry
kukri	Gurkha short sword
lascar	Indian sailor (Hind.)
LDV	Local Defence Volunteers
MC	Military Cross
MO	Medical Officer
MP	Military Policeman
MT	Motor Transport
munshi	teacher (Hind.)

NAAFI	Navy, Army and Air Force Institute
naik	corporal (Hind.)
NCO	Non-Commissioned Officer
NKPA	North Korean People's Army
NWFP	North-West Frontier Province
OC	Officer Commanding (below CO)
OCTU	Officer Cadet Training Unit
OP	Observation Post (Officer)
OTC	Officer Training Corps
P&O	Peninsular and Orient
PAIF(orce)	Persia and Iraq Force
PLA	People's Liberation Army
PM	Punjabi Mohammedan
PO	Potential Officer
PT/PTI	Physical Training/Instructor
pugaree	a light, pleated head- or hat-band or turban
Q	Quartermaster
QA/QARANC	Queen Alexandra's Royal Army Nursing Corps
RA	Royal Artillery
Ramadan	Islamic month of fasting
RAOC	Royal Army Ordnance Corps
RE	Royal Engineers
REME	Royal Electrical and Mechanical Engineers
RHQ	Regimental Headquarters
RIAF	Royal Indian Air Force
RIASC	Royal Indian Army Service Corps
ROK	Republic of Korea
RSM	Regimental Sergeant-Major
RTO	Railway Transport Officer
RTR	Royal Tank Regiment
RUR	Royal Ulster Rifles
sahib	a respectful form of address, 'sir' (Arabic)
shikar	hunting, sport (Persian)
shikari	hunter or tracker (Hind.)
Shop, the	The Royal Military Academy, Woolwich
SOE	Special Operations Executive
SS	Steamship
subedar	VCO equivalent to Lieutenant
TA	Territorial Army
UN	United Nations
US	unserviceable
VCO	Viceroy's Commissioned Officer
WAAF	Women's Auxiliary Air Force
wallah	suffix denoting a person with a trade or occupation (Hind.)
YMCA/'Y.M.'	Young Men's Christian Association
2i/c	Second-in-Command

'The Mountain Gunner', by Snaffles (detail).
The artist, himself a former gunner, was steeped in the works of Kipling.
This water-colour was dated at Landi Khotal, 1928,
some 17 years before Tony served there.

* 9 7 8 1 9 1 7 8 3 7 1 2 5 *

ND - #0100 - 071025 - C9 - 229/152/15 - CC - 9781917837125 - Gloss Lamination